Top Careers
for
Business Graduates

Also available:
Top Careers for Communications Graduates
Top Careers for Liberal Arts Graduates

Business Graduates

Checkmark Books®
An imprint of Facts On File, Inc.

Checkmark Books
An imprint of Facts On File, Inc.
132 West 31st Street
New York NY 10001

Top careers for business graduates.
    p. cm.— (Top careers)
  Includes bibliographical references and index.
  ISBN 0-8160-5488-6 (pb. : alk. paper)
    1. Business—Vocational guidance—United States. 2. Business education—graduates—United States. 3. Occupations—United States. 4. Business education—United States. I. Series.

HF5382.5.U5T67 2003
650'023'73—dc21   2003055051

Checkmark Books are available at special discounts when purchased in bulk quantities for businesses, associations, institutions, or sales promotions. Please call our Special Sales Department in New York at (212) 967-8800 or (800) 322-8755.

You can find Facts On File on the World Wide Web at http://www.factsonfile.com

Text design by David Strelecky

Cover design by Cathy Rincon

Printed in the United States of America

MP FOF 10 9 8 7 6 5 4 3 2 1

This book is printed on acid-free paper.

CONTENTS

Why Do You Need a College Degree?

More people are receiving college degrees than ever before. In 2000, more than 1 million students earned bachelor's degrees. By 2001, 58 percent of all individuals between the ages of 25 and 29 had completed some amount of college education. The National Center for Education Statistics reports that 29 percent of this same age group held at least a bachelor's degree.

With a large number of college graduates entering the work force, many employers now require a college degree for jobs that previously had lower educational requirements. This "educational upgrading" has occurred primarily in occupations that are considered desirable and that pay well. Employers want workers with good communication, teamwork, and problem-solving skills. They want workers who learn quickly, who adapt and adjust to workplace challenges, and who have the desire to excel and achieve. Above all, they want college graduates.

In this book you will read about more than the importance of a college degree. You will also find information on how to define and evaluate your skills and interests, how to choose a major, how to make the most of your college program, and how to turn your college degree into a satisfying job. In particular, this book focuses on students interested in studying business. Whether your interests include math, sports, travel, or any number of things, the business world can offer you a wide range of exciting and potentially lucrative career opportunities. Choosing your major and obtaining a college degree are the first steps toward landing your first job in business, but it will be up to you to turn that job into a rewarding lifelong career. This book aims to help you do just that by tackling the first steps knowledgeably. The following is a brief description of the contents:

Section I

Introduction: Meet the Business Major provides an overview of college coursework most often associated with a business education. This section also provides basic information on the personal and professional skills that you will develop as a business major, potential employers, starting salaries, and sources to find more information.

Chapter 1: Your High School Years will help you select a major and prepare for college study while you are still in high school. You will read about suggested courses, self-assessment tests, methods of exploring your major of interest, and tips on choosing a college.

Chapter 2: Making the Most of Your Experience as a Business Major will help you make the best use out of your college years, even if you are not sure of a major. Topics include typical business curricula, the benefits of choosing a minor, methods of career exploration, and preparing for the work force.

Chapter 3: Taking Your Business Degree to Work offers tips on the following: finding your life direction after graduation, job searching, improving your resume, applying for jobs online, tips for successful interviewing, and the benefits of a graduate degree.

Section I also includes informative interviews with college professors, administrators, and workers in the field who provide further insight on the business major and its career options. You will also find helpful sidebars about real business issues, salary statistics, top undergraduate and graduate programs in business, top cities and employers for the field, and a glossary of terms most often associated with business.

Section II

The second half of the book features profiles of 35 careers in the business field. Each article discusses an occupation in detail.

The **Quick Facts** section provides a brief summary of the career, including recommended school subjects, personal skills, work environment, minimum educational requirements, salary ranges, certification or licensing requirements, and employment outlook. This section also provides acronyms and identification numbers for the following government classification indexes: the Dictionary of Occupational Titles (DOT), the Guide to Occupational Exploration (GOE), the National Occupational Classification (NOC) Index, and the Occupational Information Network (O*NET)-Standard Occupational Classification System (SOC) index. The DOT, GOE, and O*NET-SOC indexes have been created by the U.S. government; the NOC index is Canada's career-classification system. Readers can use the identification numbers listed in the Quick Facts section to access further information on a career. Print editions of the DOT (*Dictionary of Occupational Titles*. Indianapolis, Ind.: JIST Works, 1991) and GOE

(*The Complete Guide for Occupational Exploration*. Indianapolis, Ind.: JIST Works, 1993) are available from libraries, and electronic versions of the NOC (http://www23.hrdc-drhc.gc.ca/2001/e/generic/welcome.shtml) and O*NET-SOC (http://online.onetcenter.org) are available on the World Wide Web. When no DOT, GOE, NOC, or O*NET-SOC numbers are present, this means that the U.S. Department of Labor or the Human Resources Development Canada have not created a numerical designation for this career. In this instance, you will see the acronym "N/A," or not available.

The **Overview** section is a brief introductory description of the duties and responsibilities involved in this career. A career may have a variety of job titles. When this is the case, you will find alternative career titles, as well.

The **History** section describes the history of the particular job as it relates to the overall development of its industry or field.

The Job describes in detail the primary and secondary duties of the job.

Requirements discusses high school and postsecondary education and training requirements, certification or licensing, if necessary, and any other personal requirements for success in the job. The majority of the careers in *Top Careers for Business Graduates* require a minimum of a bachelor's degree, but a few careers have a minimum educational requirement of a graduate degree. For example, the career of college business professor requires a master's or doctorate degree, but individuals with a bachelor's degree may be able to find work at a community college. Conversely, the book includes a few careers that do not require a college degree; however, some college-level business courses are highly recommended for these positions. Examples include customer sales representatives, retail business owners, and supermarket managers.

Exploring offers suggestions on gaining experience in or knowledge of the particular job before making a firm educational and financial commitment to pursuing it as a career. While in high school or the early years of college, you can explore clubs and other activities, for example, that will give you a better understanding of the job.

The **Employers** section gives an overview of typical places of employment for the job and may also include specific employment numbers from the U.S. Department of Labor.

Starting Out discusses the best ways to land your first job, be it through college placement offices, newspaper ads, or personal contacts.

The **Advancement** section describes what kind of career path to expect from the job and how to move along that path.

Earnings lists salary ranges and describes the typical fringe benefits.

The **Work Environment** section describes the typical surroundings and conditions of employment—whether indoors or outdoors, noisy or quiet, social or independent, and so on. This section also provides typical work hours, any seasonal fluctuations, and the stresses and strains of the job.

The **Outlook** section summarizes the job in terms of the general economy and industry projections. For the most part, Outlook information is obtained from the Bureau of Labor Statistics and is supplemented by information taken from professional associations. Job growth terms follow those used in the *Occupational Outlook Handbook* to describe growth for a career through 2010.

- Growth described as "much faster than the average" means an increase of 36 percent or more.
- Growth described as "faster than the average" means an increase of 21 to 35 percent.
- Growth described as "about as fast as the average" means an increase of 10 to 20 percent.
- Growth described as "little change or more slowly than the average" means an increase of 0 to 9 percent.
- "Decline" means a decrease of 1 percent or more.

Each career article concludes with **For More Information,** which lists organizations that can provide career information on training, education, internships, scholarships, and job placement.

Whether you are a high school student unsure of a college major, a college student interested in learning more about careers, or an adult thinking of returning to school, this book will help you learn more about the business major and the career options available to those who pursue it.

MEET THE BUSINESS MAJOR

WHAT IS BUSINESS?

The field of business encompasses the organization, planning, directing, and promoting of individuals, organizations, and businesses. Effective business management makes up the backbone of economic, political, and social systems at all levels. There are three main types of businesses: manufacturing firms, merchandisers, and service enterprisers. Businesses can also be classified as for-profit and not-for-profit organizations. The majority of businesses seek to earn a profit. The goal of nonprofit and not-for-profit companies is to provide an educational, social, or charitable service rather than to make a profit. Any profit these businesses might make is fed back into the organization to enhance its mission.

According to the U.S. Department of Education, approximately 253,162 students graduated with an undergraduate degree in business in 2000. Another 111,664 graduated with a master's degree, and 1,193 graduated with a doctorate.

WHAT COURSES WILL I TAKE?

Undergraduate business students study a variety of courses that vary depending on their chosen major. Typical classes include basic management, accounting, statistics, methods of operation, macro- and microeconomics, sales and marketing, finance, personnel management, property and equipment maintenance, and security. Many business programs now also require at least one course in ethics. Business is expanding globally, so students who plan to become involved in international business should study a foreign language.

WHAT WILL I LEARN?

The major skills developed through business-major classes are requirements for any business career. These include organizational skills, leadership ability, oral and written communication skills, time-management skills, attentiveness to details, brainstorming ability, and policy-making and implementation skills.

INTERVIEW: Pamela Park-Curry and Daniel Jenson

Pamela Park-Curry is the Director of Undergraduate Career Development at Ohio State University's Fisher College of Business. Daniel Jensen is the Undergraduate Program Chair at Fisher. Fisher was recently named one of the top 15 undergraduate programs in the nation by U.S. News & World Report. *The college offers both undergraduate and graduate degrees in business. Park-Curry and Jensen spoke with the editors of* Top Careers for Business Graduates *about their program and the business major in general.*

Q. What types of jobs can students pursue with a bachelor's degree in business?

A. (Pamela Park-Curry) A bachelor's degree in business opens doors to career-track positions in just about any business sector, as well as not-for-profit organizations and the government. Of course, this all depends on what the student did while in school. While coursework is important, students also are wise to take advantage of opportunities to build leadership skills through student organizations, and to gain practical experience through internships and research projects. Service projects also provide valuable experience and may open the door to a career with a nonprofit agency.

Fisher College graduates are working as brand managers with product manufacturers, such as Procter & Gamble; as consultants with major consulting houses, such as Accenture and McKinsey & Company; and as accountants with the major accounting firms or with corporations. Graduates are also working in various positions in the financial services industry, including banks, brokerages, and insurance; in manufacturing and distribution; and in human resources departments. Fisher B.S.B.A.'s (Bachelor of Science in Business Administration) also take jobs in computer and management information systems operations.

A business degree will also provide the basic skills needed if you want to start your own business or go on to graduate school. While many students pursue an M.B.A., typically after working for several years, students also attend law school or specialized masters programs in accounting or human resources, for example.

In terms of current opportunities, the recent Congressional expansion of accounting and auditing regulations is expected to have a substantial impact on the demand for entry-level accounting students, both in the federal government and in the corporate world. Transportation and logistics, supply chain management, and human resources are additional fields with high demand in the federal government as well as business. Opportunities also exist for civilian careers within the U.S. military forces.

In the nonprofit sector, a marketing major might publicize fundraising campaigns, while a real estate major might work in urban development

Q. What are the most important personal and professional qualities for business majors?

A. **(Pamela Park-Curry)** Good communications skills, analytical and problem-solving skills, leadership experience, ability to work in teams and to value team member diversity, and a good sense of ethics. Regardless of the professional field, all are essential for success.

Q. Are new students prepared or unprepared for the curriculum?

A. **(Daniel Jensen)** As freshmen, most undergraduate students are not focused on a particular specialization in business because their knowledge of the complexities of business is limited at that point. Students typically select their specialization at the end of their sophomore year or early in the junior year, after they have completed some foundation coursework in business and have a stronger sense of what business is about. By that time they are usually pretty well focused on what they want to do or at least what they want to study during their last two years. Also, admission to Fisher College and the business major is competitive, so preparation is usually very solid.

Q. What is the most important piece of advice that you have to offer business majors as they graduate and look for jobs?

A. **(Pamela Park-Curry)** The best time to offer advice is when a student is entering college, not at graduation. Students need to begin their academic programs with the end in mind. While they may not know exactly what they want to do after graduation, knowing that the end goal is a career will encourage them to ask questions and seek out resources throughout their academic program. They should be asking what employers are seeking, how to get involved in student organizations, how to get an internship, what study abroad options are available, and how can they get practical business experience from international opportunities. Counselors, professors, and networking opportunities through student organizations are valuable resources to tap for answers to such questions. Active participation in student business organizations will also help them clarify that they are on the right track. Fisher College, for example, has 22 student organizations, business fraternities, and honorary societies, most with a specific career emphasis, such as accounting, finance, marketing, logistics, and real estate.

Q. Are there any misconceptions about the business major that you'd like to clear up? What advice would you give students who major in business?

A. **(Pamela Park-Curry)** Don't major in business or a particular area of business because you've heard there's a strong job market for that area—job markets shift quickly. Instead, choose a major that peaks your interest and learn how many ways the skills learned under that academic umbrella can be applied in the job market. Your undergraduate studies will help you launch a career that could last decades. Ask more questions than simply "Can I get a job with this major?"

If you like international business, take a double major, combining international studies with another business field. International business is more a perspective and an appreciation for the global nature of business. Employers often want someone with a particular skill set, such as finance, accounting, or operations management, who can contribute in the long run to their international endeavors. Companies typically don't recruit international business majors the way they recruit marketing, human resources, or transportation and logistics majors.

Q. Are there any changes in this job market that students should expect? What are the hot areas in this field?

A. **(Pamela Park-Curry)** Expect change—constant change. Be adaptable and flexible and continue to learn through training opportunities, professional associations, and reading widely. If you continue to learn, you will be aware of changes that are on the horizon and be better prepared to handle them.

Consulting was hot-hot-hot up to 2000, and then it just went cold. Information systems was hot, but has cooled off now. Accounting has been solid and remains strong. Transportation and logistics and supply chain management are promising. Undergraduates may also want to look at health care and the food and beverage industries, which are promising. These industries have jobs for just about any business major.

Q. Is anything new in store for business programs at the Fisher College of Business?

A. (Daniel Jensen) We are contemplating adding courses in entrepreneurship, in response to growing interest in starting businesses among students at both the graduate and undergraduate levels. Students are finding entrepreneurship courses an attractive addition to studies in various majors, both in the business college and in other colleges. We have a very active entrepreneurship student organization that draws students from across the university, both graduate and undergraduate. And our annual business plan competition offers opportunities for students to write a business plan and have it critiqued by successful entrepreneurs. Students with winning plans get valuable assistance to start their business ventures. Details about the competition and the proposed Center for Entrepreneurship are available online at: http://www.centerforentrepreneurship.com.

WHERE WILL I WORK AND HOW MUCH WILL I EARN?

Business majors are employed all over the country. Urban areas offer many opportunities, with many corporate headquarters located in cities such as New York, Chicago, and Washington, D.C. However, business graduates work not only in the corporate world, but also in hospitals, nonprofit organizations, and schools—practically any entity that requires management of staff or activities. Possible careers range from advertising account executive to supermarket manager to college professor. Because of the wide variety of jobs available to business majors, a "typical" salary is hard to measure; however, the National Association of Colleges and Employers reports that the average starting salary offered to business administration and management majors was $36,634 in 2003.

FOR MORE INFORMATION

You can research the many facets of business on the Web. The following are just a sample of the good sites available:

Business Week Online
http://www.businessweek.com

Teaching Kids Business
http://www.teachingkidsbusiness.com

Teenpreneur
http://www.blackenterprise.com/teenpreneur.asp

CHAPTER 1

YOUR HIGH SCHOOL YEARS

If you think you're too young to consider a career in business, think again. It's never too early to think about your life's direction. Sure, you're in high school now, but college is on the horizon. Before you know it you'll be throwing your graduation cap in the air, ready to enter the competitive business work force. Starting your career planning now will help you realize your goals for the coming years; it will also give you a solid advantage over some of your fellow graduates who did not plan as thoroughly and carefully as you did.

SUGGESTED COURSES

While in high school, take a wide range of classes to establish a solid background in the basic areas of mathematics, English, history, and science. Though you may not know the extent of your business interest, take a sampling of the business classes available at your high school. Good choices include economics, business management, finance, and basic accounting. These courses will not only be educational and provide a good foundation for more advanced college classes, but studying a variety of business topics can help you better gauge your interest in different careers.

Ask your advisor or college counselor for suggestions of other classes that will prepare you for a business major. Classes such as computer science, foreign languages, and statistics are good examples of nonbusiness classes that build valuable skills for a future business career.

ASSESSMENT TESTS

Test taking doesn't always have to be a stressful trial to get good grades. Certain tests are available to help you decide if a business major is right for you. Many of these tests, called self-assessment tests, are best done while you're in high school so you can choose a college and plan your courses accordingly. Typical test questions help you evaluate your college and career options by focusing on your values, interests, academic strengths, and personality. The following are some of the more popular tests available. While some of these, like the SAT, are mandatory for college admissions, others are simply valuable tools that will help you envision your goals. (Note that most of the following require prior registration and a fee.)

- Scholastic Aptitude Test (SAT): The SAT is a three-hour test measuring verbal and mathematical reasoning skills. Many colleges and universities use the SAT as an indicator of academic performance in addition to grades, class rank, extracurricular activities, the personal essay, and teacher recommendations. Visit http://www.collegeboard.com for more information.

- American College Testing Program (ACT): Similar to the SAT, the ACT is designed to assess high school students' academic abilities and estimate their college performance. The test covers four basic areas: English, math, reading comprehension, and scientific reasoning. For details, visit http://www.act.org.

- Kuder Career Planning System: The Kuder test helps individuals evaluate their interests, skills, and values. Suggested college majors and careers are ranked based on survey responses. For sample tests and more information, visit http://www.kuder.com.

- Myers-Briggs Type Indicator: This assessment test identifies an individual's personality type using four general, but opposite, dispositions: extraversion/introversion, sensate/intuitive, thinking/feeling, and judging/perceiving. Based on responses to test questions, the individual is characterized as one of 16 personality types. Although most organizations charge a fee for this test, you can visit http://www.humanmetrics.com/cgi-win/JTypes1.htm for a free test based on the Myers-Briggs Type Indicator.

- Armed Services Vocational Aptitude Battery (ASVAB): The ASVAB, administered by the U.S. Department of Defense, is a multi-aptitude test available at over 14,000 high schools nationwide. The tests evaluate students' vocabulary skills, reading comprehension, math skills, math reasoning, general science knowledge, shop and technical skills, mechanical knowledge, and knowledge of electronics. Scores are combined to reveal three general scores for verbal, math, and academic ability. See http://asvabprogram.com for more information.

OTHER WAYS TO EXPLORE

Although assessment tests are useful, there are many other ways to explore your potential interest and skill in business.

- If your high school has a business club, be sure to join it. Consider running for a club office. Many of these clubs sponsor guest speakers who have valuable stories to tell about their business experiences. These events also present you with the opportunity to ask questions and join in on discussions.

- If your school doesn't offer a business club, check out the Junior Achievement (JA) organization (http://www.ja.org) and see if there is a chapter near you. JA encourages business leaders in the community to talk to groups of students about how they started their careers and how to be successful in business in the future.

- Business careers require leadership skills. Think about running for a position in student government or another student organization. Any sort of leadership position will build your communication and organizational skills and certainly will look good on your college applications.

- Take part in other events that show you are active in your business community, such as fund-raising activities or part-time jobs with local establishments. Work experience at a part-time or summer job, whether it's a retail position at the mall or a job as a filing assistant in an office, will expose you to working with others, reporting to a manager, and being responsible for certain tasks. Maintaining a job while going to school will also show potential colleges and employers that you can manage multiple responsibilities.

- Read about the latest developments in the business world, from stock prices to companies on the rise. Helpful publications include *Business Week* (http://www.businessweek.com), which provides a list of the Top 100 Hot Growth Companies, and *U.S. News & World Report* (http://www.usnews.com).

- Business doesn't always have to be about work. You can use the Internet to play games that will use business strategies and tactics. One such game is *Gazillionaire,* developed by online educational developer Lavamind. *Gazillionaire* is described on its website as "a cross between *Monopoly* set in outer space and *Wall Street* in wonderland." Sound like fun? Check it out at http://www.gazillionaire.com. Another business-oriented online game is *Rags to Riches* (http://www. headbone.com/wtvrags), developed by Headbone Interactive. In this game, you play the role of band manager as you set ticket prices, choose concert venues, and budget for advertising, all in the hopes of raking in money.

- There is also a wealth of information on business news available on the Internet. Listed below are a few good sites to explore.

About: Business Majors
http://www.businessmajors.about.com

Business Wire
http://www.businesswire.com

Careers in Business
http://www.careers-in-business.com

INTERVIEW: Kevin Piskadlo

Kevin Piskadlo is an Academic Advisor/Concurrent Instructor at University of Notre Dame's Mendoza College of Business in Notre Dame, Indiana. The University offers undergraduate business degrees in the following concentrations: Accountancy, Finance and Business Economics, Management, Marketing, and Management of Information Systems. Graduate degree programs offered include: Master in Business Administration, Master of Science in Accountancy, and Master of Science in Administration. Piskadlo spoke with the editors of Top Careers for Business Graduates *about his program and the business major.*

Q. What types of jobs can students pursue with a business degree?

A. Students graduating with a business degree find themselves well prepared to enter almost any career of their choosing, and they are not limited to pursuing only the most obvious business careers. Similar to most business programs, we demand that our students experience a solid foundation of liberal arts courses to both expand their knowledge as well as provide them with critical thinking and writing skills. This exposes them to a wide variety of opportunities both inside and outside of the business world and hones skills that are imperative for any career.

With Notre Dame's emphasis on community service and experiential learning, many of our students pursue a variety of social service positions. These include teaching in programs like the Alliance For Catholic Education, Teach for America, and Teaching English in Japan, or applying for other service-related projects such as Holy Cross Associates or the Peace Corps. Students also pursue careers in government at the local, state, and national level. Many of our students are also interested in entrepreneurial projects and/or plan on returning to a family business. Business students are also well prepared to pursue advanced degrees in business, law, or the humanities.

Q. What are the most important personal and professional qualities for business majors?

A. We all use our skills and creativity in different ways. Those who are often the most successful in business have strength and creativity in identifying problems, create solutions to these problems, and develop ways for systems to work more efficiently. In addition, corporations have a major impact on our society. Perhaps because I am a business ethics instructor, I tend to believe that all businesses and corporations have a social responsibility to our society and community. I believe that successful business majors should know and understand that their actions will affect not only shareholders but the greater society as well. Current events (Enron, WorldCom, etc.) have validated this, and we can see the far-reaching impacts that these careless organizations have had on countless numbers of people.

As technology improves and the world gets smaller, an appreciation of diversity and the ability to work with people of all backgrounds and all cultures has also become extremely important.

Q. What are the typical expectations of a student who enters your program? Are new students prepared or unprepared for the curriculum?

A. Students are well prepared for the curriculum. The university's admissions department selects a very qualified class. Many business students see a business education as a safe (or "practical") major that will guarantee employment when they graduate. However, it is important for students to pick their major, because it is something that they enjoy studying—not because they believe that they are more likely to graduate with a job.

Q. What can students do in college to prepare for landing their first job?

A. During your first year [in college], you should start to develop a relationship with the professionals in the career center and slowly start the career-decision process. Take advantage of all the services they offer (cover letter writing, resume critiques, job search strategies, etc.) and start to use breaks and vacations to intern, job shadow, informational interview, and network. This affords students the opportunity to apply their classroom education with "real world" experiences as well as begin to make connections with business professionals. It is important to realize that the most successful job searchers are those who are well prepared and multifaceted. On-campus recruiting is not the only means for finding employment.

Q. Do a large number of your students pursue an M.B.A. after completing requirements for the undergraduate degree in business? What advice do you have for students pondering a continuation of their studies?

A. Many of our students are interested in earning an M.B.A., but it is rare that this is done right after they complete undergraduate training. We do stress that students pursue work experience before [pursuing an M.B.A.]. There are several reasons for doing this:

- Though many students know that they want to pursue a business career, few know exactly what it is that they want to do, or know enough about a particular career to know what they should concentrate on in business school.

- The average M.B.A. student has several years of experience, which is crucial in contributing to classroom discussions, preparing case studies, etc.

- Some companies will pay for students to return for their advanced degree.

CHOOSING A COLLEGE

Deciding on a college can be as daunting as choosing a major or career. You have a lot to consider before making a decision, such as size, location, cost, and curriculum, among other factors. Students who decide on their major early often choose a college that has a good reputation for their field. However, not all students are sure of their future career path. For this reason, they may choose a college with a broad range of academic options. Many resources can help you narrow your college choices.

Guidance Counselors

Your high school's guidance counselor should be one of the first people you consult when weighing your college options. He or she will have information on programs, application deadlines, campus environments, and financial aid opportunities. Some guidance counselors keep track of recent high school graduates and may be able to give you names and contact information of students at colleges that interest you.

Before you meet with your counselor, make a list of the things you are looking for in a school. Would you like to attend a small or large campus? Do you want to commute to school or live on campus? Do you want to be in rural or urban surroundings? What is your tuition range? Keep this list and all other college information organized in a folder or binder so that you can find the appropriate information when you need it.

College Recruiters

Most high schools host several different recruiters from colleges and universities across the country. Acting as school representatives, these recruiters talk with groups of students about their schools' educational programs, faculty, campus life, tuition and other expenses, and scholarship and loan opportunities. In addition to making a presentation, recruiters field questions from students.

Recruiters are there for your benefit. Take full advantage of the opportunity to meet with them, learn more about their school, and ask your own questions. If there is a college that you are interested in that will not be represented at your high school, ask your guidance counselor for assistance in scheduling a meeting with a representative.

College Fairs

College fairs provide another good place to meet college recruiters. These gatherings of college and university admissions representatives take place throughout the United States. At these fairs you can gather brochures about schools and talk to representatives one-on-one. They can answer your questions about educational programs, courses, admissions and financial aid requirements, campus activities, and any other information that will help you narrow your college options. Just like you did before visiting your guidance counselor, make a list of the things you are looking for in a school (size, programs, locations, etc.) and focus your attention on schools that seem to fit these preliminary guidelines. Be sure to bring a pen, paper, and a large folder or binder to hold your college information and notes. Visit http://www.nacac.com/fairs_ncf.html for helpful tips and a list of college fairs, organized by date.

Contact Colleges Yourself

To learn more about colleges, you can also take matters into your own hands. Contact college admissions offices directly to obtain their catalogs. You can also view catalogs and other information on colleges at their websites. Visit CollegeSource Online (http://www.collegesource.org) to view over 22,000 complete college catalogs.

Campus Visits:
Giving Schools a Test Drive

Talking to counselors, students, and recruiters is a great way to gather information, but the best way to gauge your interest in a college is by visiting a school in person. Campus visits enable you to go beyond a school's neatly crafted brochure and walk the streets, meet the students and faculty, sample a few classes, and even taste "Spaghetti Surprise" in the campus dining hall.

However, don't just show up on campus; be sure to schedule your visit with an admissions counselor to make the most of your visit. Most likely, a college admissions representative will match you with a student of similar interests to help show you around campus.

Before you leave home, make a list of the facilities and school features that you'd like to see. Share this list with your student guide or college representative so you'll be sure to check out all these sites and experiences during your stay. Campus visits can be fun: you can see, and often spend the night in, a dorm, take in the campus social atmosphere, and most importantly, attend classes.

Scheduling a formal campus tour also lets the admissions department know that you are interested in the school. If time allows, you might be asked for a short interview with an admissions counselor during your visit. Again, come to this interview with plenty of thoughtful questions for the counselor.

If you are unable to visit colleges, check out the website CampusTours (http://www.campustours.com), which offers virtual campus tours of over 850 colleges and universities.

Last, but Not Least

Your family, friends, and teachers are great sources for help and guidance when picking out a school. But ultimately you should decide on a school that is right for *you*, not your parents or friends.

For more information on choosing the right college, visit:

Adventures in Education
http://www.adventuresineducation.org

College Board
http://www.collegeboard.com

College Is Possible
http://www.collegeispossible.org

CollegeLink
http://www.collegelink.com

CollegeNet
http://www.collegenet.com

CollegeNews
http://www.collegenews.org

Colleges.com
http://www.colleges.com

Princeton Review
http://www.princetonreview.com

CHAPTER 2

MAKING THE MOST OF YOUR EXPERIENCE AS A BUSINESS MAJOR

So you've made it to college. Your bags are unpacked, the pictures of your hometown friends are on display, and the Yaffa blocks are set up and holding every piece of clothing you own. You have your shower shoes, your blacklight, and your minifridge, and you're prepared to tackle the challenges of campus life. But what about your academic goals? How are you going to decide on a major, let alone your direction in life, in just a year?

Well, relax; you'll be in good company. Most college freshmen (and some unfortunate seniors) don't yet know their major or life's direction. Most schools have general educational requirements that must be fulfilled by all students, no matter what their chosen major. Freshman year is a great time not only to complete these required classes, but also to learn the basics on a lot of different subject areas. Introductory-level classes such as Biology, Calculus, and English Composition may help you identify fields you excel in and enjoy before you start a business curriculum. For this reason, your freshman year is a good time to re-evaluate the goals you started making back in high school, now that the stressful college-entrance process is behind you. You may find that your interests are progressing along a different path, and now is a perfect time to alter those goals if you so desire after careful consideration.

However, if you're reading this book, you are probably considering a major in business. Congratulations: you're joining a group that annually welcomes more than 250,000 young, talented individuals hoping to become tomorrow's business leaders. Your college courses will prepare you for the challenges that lie ahead in the working world: finding a job, earning money, pleasing your managers, and advancing in your career. If you plan carefully and choose your courses wisely, your college background will help you conquer these challenges.

SUGGESTED COURSES

All colleges offer different curricula. Your required courses will depend on your chosen business concentration, such as management, finance, marketing, sales, or accounting. Examples of business classes include financial accounting, business statistics, international business, macro- and microeconomics, business law, marketing, organizational behavior, and human resources management.

In the wake of recent accounting scandals in the business world, colleges have begun emphasizing a new facet of business: ethics. Ethics courses cover the corporate responsibilities that are often not mentioned in other business classes and that, as a result, are often taken for granted in daily business operations. These may include honesty and fairness, community awareness, respect for

Business Students Learn About More Than the Bottom Line

For decades colleges and universities have taught students of the "triple bottom line." This is the concept that corporations should not only be concerned with their profit margin, but should also be aware of their effect on society and the environment. After the recent exposure and collapse of corrupt firms such as WorldCom and Enron, business classrooms are again placing emphasis on ethics in business practices.

The *Christian Science Monitor* reports that being good is not only the right thing to do, but the profitable thing, as well. Businesses that practice what is called *corporate social responsibility* (CSR) oftentimes outperform businesses that do not. Different from the principles of business ethics, which focus on avoiding corporate wrongdoing, CSR is concerned with the impact of businesses on the world around them. For example, opening a new discount store in a lower income neighborhood may benefit the company with a potential increase in sales revenue and helpthe community by providing low-cost goods and job openings.

While one course on CSR and business ethics will not be enough to eliminate corruption in the business world, increased education on these issues is a good start. Classes can help students start to talk and think about issues of corporate responsibility, and in turn, can influence them to act conscientiously when they become business leaders.

the environment, and other principles and ideas. However, teaching ethics can be difficult, and most colleges are handling the organization of the courses in their own way.

At the University of Michigan business students are asked to write a case study about the most challenging ethical dilemma they have faced in their lifetime. They must describe how they handled the situation and then apply the same type of dilemma to a business environment. Would they resolve it the same way? How would the ethical ramifications differ? The *Chicago Tribune* reports that, despite differing approaches to the topic, experts and educators are most concerned with keeping business ethics within schools' curricula, even in times of economic stability and less corporate scandal.

Computer science is another often overlooked but important area of study for business majors. More and more companies rely on computers to run their business, so you can count on using one in your future job. Most employers require their employees to be familiar with basic office programs, and some may be looking for more specialized computer skills. You should make sure that you become comfortable using staple software of the business world such as word processing programs like Microsoft Word or Corel WordPerfect and spreadsheet programs like Microsoft Excel. For more advanced work you may be called on to make Microsoft PowerPoint presentations or lay out a brochure using QuarkXpress or Adobe PageMaker. Another skill useful in any field is the ability to write or alter a website using Web programming languages such as HTML or XML. Such skills can be an attractive asset to employers.

INTERVIEW: Pamela S. Schindler

Pamela S. Schindler is a Professor of Management at Wittenberg University in Springfield, Ohio. She is also the director of the Management Department's Center for Applied Management. Wittenberg offers business management as an undergraduate major or a minor. Students who choose the major concentrate in one of the following disciplines: accounting, finance, human resources, international business, marketing, operations, or pre-law. Professor Schindler spoke with the editors of Top Careers for Business Graduates *about her program and the major.*

Q. **What types of jobs does a business major prepare students for?**

A. The list is too numerous to detail, but management/business majors end up managing in profit, nonprofit, and government environments. One of our majors has been the personal assistant to David Copperfield, the illusionist; others are working for the four accounting firms, or as consultants, currency traders, retail store managers, branch bank managers, district sales reps and managers, financial planners, etc. We have several majors serving in the Peace Corps in its new business development initiative, while others are in marketing research or investment analysis.

Q. **What do you think are the most important personal and professional qualities for business majors?**

A. Recruiters worldwide tell us the ability to quickly and concisely write and verbally articulate information is crucial, along with the ability to work in teams and encourage the best work of others, and to be able to generate top-quality output for a sustained period of time, sometimes under pressure.

   Recruiters rank second the desire and ability to grow and learn on the job. We often hear that too many students think that their business degree is the only credential [they need], while to employers it represents only the entry ticket. Every candidate has to be able to demonstrate their ability to use the knowledge they have gained in their business program, while sharing their understanding that the desire to learn and grow is more valuable to an employer than what they have learned thus far.

Q. **When the average student enters your program, what are their expectations? Are these expectations realistic or unrealistic? Are new students prepared or unprepared for the curriculum?**

A. This is a tough question. Many students carry into college the unrealistic expectation that the degree is all they need (as noted above). We dispel that preconception as quickly and frequently as possible. The managers we bring to campus help reinforce how important application of knowledge really is.

   Some, even in the face of overwhelming evidence that entry-level jobs are limited, seek only those careers that are difficult to enter directly from college. Examples are advertising, sports marketing, arts management, and anything in the music or recording industries.

Students also believe they can start far higher in the chain of command than is realistic. They seem to forget that all those in higher positions have paid their dues by working in the trenches and that they will need to do this as well.

Teachers are prone to inflate the abilities of former students by clearly remembering only the standouts in prior classes. That said, what students often aren't prepared for is the level of work that is expected in college—not only the quantity but also the quality. College faculty expectations are far different than those of high school teachers. And employer expectations are far higher than ours.

Also, many students are not prepared for the wide variety of writing styles that are needed in the typical business curriculum. The term paper is rarely seen in actual business writing, so it is usually limited to lower level courses. Students—especially business students—need to be flexible and aggressive in acquiring the skill to write in other styles: reports, proposals, statistical presentations, public relations, annual reports, briefs, competitive analyses, etc.

Q. What advice can you offer to business majors as they graduate and look for jobs?

A.

- Find a mentor early. This is someone who will help you find opportunities and grasp them before they slip away, or help create opportunities where none seem to exist.

- Take every opportunity to follow your passion—whatever that passion is.

- Take every opportunity to learn. Grasp every opportunity to increase your value as an employee, a spouse, a parent, or a community contributor.

- Embrace change, don't fight it. Those who embrace change more easily see opportunities and modify their behavior to adapt to change.

- Maintain contact with your favorite professor. This might have been the one who challenged you the most, or someone whose opinion you valued. This person can serve as an impartial observer as the graduate sets career goals or contemplates career moves.

Q. Are there any changes in the business job market that students should expect?

A. Technology guarantees that business students face numerous changes in their careers. Many of the careers that exist today, especially those in the technology arena, didn't exist 10 years ago. Data shows that today's graduates will work for far more companies than their parents did, and experience more major career shifts. Continuing to learn and keeping abreast of the changes in technology are the only strategies the business student has to ensure a successful work life.

Q. **What areas of the business world have been especially promising in recent years?**

A. Changing demographics, especially the aging of the population, guarantee the growth of jobs dealing with insurance, financial planning, recreation, senior housing, and health care. Shifts in the technology sector guarantee speed of change and continuing need for businesses and organizations to keep abreast of these changes to remain competitive.

Q. **What is the future of the management program at Wittenberg?**

A. Business, as a program on college campuses, is strong and growing. Our challenge is to keep the curriculum relevant given the changes I've noted above. An influx of talented new teachers, as baby-boom generation professors retire, will keep business programs nationwide more timely and relevant. Partnerships with industry and with practitioner-managers are the other link to relevancy. We've done this at Wittenberg with our Executive-in-Residence programs, advisory boards, and our Center for Applied Management. These same models, while on a larger scale than ours, are being effectively employed in many business programs. Thus the role of our business program alumni—in keeping the business curriculum focused on the skills, knowledge, and aptitudes businesses and managers need—will only increase in importance.

DON'T FORGET A MINOR

How can you enhance your business major? How about adding a specialty minor? If you know exactly what you'd like to do after you graduate, consider choosing a specific minor to complement your business degree. For example, if you have chosen to go into international business, obtaining a minor in a foreign language would be wise. Potential employers might also look upon minors in English or communications as valuable assets, as they round out your skill set and reflect good language and analytical skills. Two things to keep in mind when selecting a minor are the following: how will the minor affect your existing business workload (be careful not to over-load your schedule), and how can the minor be viewed as an asset to future employers?

EXPLORE AND GET YOUR FOOT IN THE DOOR

Courses alone won't teach you everything you need to know about business. There are many other ways to make the most of your college experience as a business major:

- Try to get an on-campus job. Whether you work in the library or in the admissions office, you'll gain valuable business experience simply by working with others and helping fellow students. You'll also get accustomed to working on a schedule, recording your hours, and, the best part, receiving a paycheck.

- Look for opportunities to work in the local business community. Some college business programs offer work-study arrangements that combine classroom time with work in a local establishment. You may be able to work as an office assistant, answer phones at a local law firm, help out at a bar or restaurant, or shadow a bank teller. Regardless of where you work, the experience will serve you well.

- Get involved in the advertising department of your school's newspaper. Many campus papers depend on ad revenue from local businesses to cover the cost of production. You may not be interested in reporting, but working in the advertising or business department will give you great sales experience in seeking and securing clients, organizing ads, and satisfying the needs of both the advertiser and the paper.

- Take a leadership role in a campus organization or club in which you are interested or already involved, including fraternities or sororities, sports clubs, or yearbook committees. Holding an office will give you good experience in planning events, organizing other students, and speaking in public—not to mention that it will look great on your resume.

- Speaking of clubs, join a campus organization that encourages business or leadership skills. Colleges may give these clubs different names, such as Young Entrepreneurs or Young Leaders.
- The Internet offers some good resources for basic information on business. Visit the following sites the next time you're online:

Business Schools.com
http://www.businessschools.com

New York Times Business Section
http://www.nytimes.com/pages/business

U.S. Small Business Administration
http://www.sba.gov

PREPARING FOR THE WORKFORCE

As you enter the second half of your undergraduate years, you need to be concerned with more than just your grades. Securing a job is going to take much more than scoring an "A" on your next business test. Start thinking about and developing your employment prospects now. You'll be that much further ahead of your competition after graduation.

There are many things you can do to prepare for the working world. First, keep up your grades and work hard all the way through the end of your senior year. This may be difficult as you worry about getting a job, moving out on your own, and plans for your spring break vacation. But it is imperative that you finish your college major as strongly as you started.

INTERVIEW: Smita Narayen

Smita Narayen is a worker in General Electric's financial management program. It is a two-year rotational program that consists of four six-month rotations. She rotates between different finance functions, while concurrently taking classes. Narayen spoke with the editors of Top Careers for Business Graduates *about her experience and the business major in general.*

Q. Please briefly describe your primary and secondary job duties.

A. I work in the controller's group this rotation, working on account reconciliation and developing detailed reports, based on our ledger, to communicate what we are reporting. The ledger is where we record all of our transactions, such as payments that we receive from clients or supplies that we order (basically any exchange that involves money). We use the information from the ledger to build balance sheets and income statements. I also perform internal audits on how activity is posting to our general ledger. In addition, I'm taking finance classes taught by our company's professionals.

Q. How did you train for this job? What was your college major?

A. My college major was finance, which is within the College of Business Administration at the University of Illinois at Urbana-Champaign. In the financial management program, my training is constant. As I'm working, I'm going to classes. Since our group rotates every six months, we're constantly put in different environments with different expectations. However, there was no initial, formalized training period. The type of work that we do is too broad and varies too much by rotation and person to have an actual formal training program.

Q. Did this major prepare you for your career or, in retrospect, would you pursue another major? If so, what major?

A. The major prepared me for my career. I believe that in school, however, I learned a lot of high-level concepts (strategy, etc.) that I won't really use in everyday business work—especially in an entry-level position.

Q. Did you participate in any internships while you were in college?

A. Yes, I participated in one internship the summer after my junior year at General Electric Appliances in Louisville, Kentucky. It was a great learning experience. However, when working for a big company like GE, it's easy to get lost in the crowd. So, if you want to get recognized, you really have to work hard. I also volunteered at Merrill Lynch during my Christmas break sophomore year in order to gain more experience in the finance field. It was unpaid, but it was a pretty good experience.

Q. What are the most important personal and professional qualities for people in your career?

A. The ability to work hard is very important. Sometimes the work you do isn't the most exciting, and in business, at least in my position, the work doesn't finish when you go home. You also need to be willing to put yourself in uncomfortable situations—for example, working on a project where you don't understand everything. You have to be willing to be outside of your comfort zone and put yourself in situations that will allow you to learn. Business, and even finance, is so diverse and broad that you'll never understand all of it. Also, you have to be very professional. Make sure you know what you're talking about when you're assigned to a project. Do your homework and make sure you can speak intelligently about your project or your client. Also, you have to be very personable. Since you deal with so many different types of people, you have to be able to adapt and talk to everyone intelligently and socially.

Q. What is the most important piece of advice that you have to offer college students as they graduate and look for jobs in this field?

A. Do your homework on where you would like to work. I've worked for both a small company (less than 120 employees) and a huge, global company (a few hundred thousand employees). Consider whether a big company or a small company is a better fit for you. Consider the type of work you're going to be doing and whether you will enjoy it or not. Another big factor to consider is how a company treats its entry-level employees; it says a lot about the company. If they treat their entry-level employees well, then they probably want them to stick around for a long time, which shows real growth potential. You also should know how much you're going to learn in the job. Is it going to be a position where you're constantly growing, or will it be repetitive and boring?

Q. What are your future employment plans?

A. I'll probably stay within my company for quite awhile. Since GE is a huge company, you can make your entire career here, and a lot of people do. I'll probably stay in finance, although I really want to experience different areas of it. GE is a stable company and offers a stable program.

The Internship

Internships are monitored work arrangements in which you have the chance to apply your business study to actual business surroundings. Internships may involve specific learning goals or they may aim for some basic experience. Interns are usually hired for much more than filing. Student interns may sit in on departmental meetings, assist with projects, and support the staff in any given business function. Whether paid or unpaid, full- or part-time, business internships will give you the chance to learn more about a business, gain working experience, and make connections in an industry.

According to the National Association of Colleges and Employers, internships often give students the competitive edge needed to find a job. During times of sluggish economic growth, more highly qualified students are applying for a limited number of jobs. Having an internship on your resume will signal to employers that you have achieved more than just good grades. The following websites offer information about internships:

InternshipPrograms.com
http://internships.wetfeet.com

Internships.com
http://www.internships.com

InternWeb.com
http://www.internweb.com

Using Your Connections

Take advantage of the sources of business knowledge that have been surrounding you for the past few years. Your professors and advisors are great resources for job advice and may be able to provide you with contacts or job leads to explore. Besides advice, your college's faculty can provide you with another job necessity: a letter of recommendation. Ask the teachers who know you well and have witnessed your hard work. An advisor who has worked with you for several years is a good choice, as is a professor who might have coached your struggle to overcome a tough subject.

Job Fairs and Corporate Recruiters

So you've signed up for the right classes, scored an internship, and obtained glowing recommendations. Now how do you meet employers? Besides the work contacts you've made through your internship, another good way to explore employers is at a job fair. These may be held at your college campus, a local hotel, or a large exhibition hall. Your college's career center should know of any corporate recruiters that are visiting the college or the nearby area. According to CollegeGrad.com, a job site that focuses on entry-level workers, you should bring the following items to your next career fair:

- **Resume.** Bring several copies of your resume (spotless and printed on quality paper) to hand out to each employer you meet.
- **Letters of recommendation.** Those letters from your professors serve as a personal testament to your abilities.
- **Portfolio.** A 9 x 12 inch leather-bound folder will come in handy to store your resumes and letters of recommendation. It will also be useful for holding any notes taken during your interviews with employers and any information you pick up at the fair.
- **Briefcase.** Your portfolio may not be big enough to handle the number of pamphlets, booklets, and brochures you will collect at a good career fair.
- **Attire.** Even if the career fair takes place on your college campus, don't dress in typical college fashion. Leave the jeans and sweatshirts at home and put on a conservative business suit. Because the time spent with employers will be shorter than even a typical office interview, you have to make a good impression. Dressing neatly and conservatively will ensure that the employers' attention is spent on *you*, not what you are wearing.

After checking with your college's career counselor, visit the following websites to learn more and search for fairs by employer and state:

American Job Fairs
http://www.americanjobfairs.com

CareerFairs.com
http://careerfairs.com

CollegeGrad.com
http://www.collegegrad.com

JobWeb Online Career Fair
http://www.jobweb.com/employ/fairs

The Job Fair, Inc.
http://www.thejobfair.com

Information Interviewing

Another way to gain contacts in the field and learn more about the different facets of a business is through information interviews. These are different from traditional interviews, where you are vying for an actual position. Information interviews are informal conversations with working professionals for the sole benefit of the student. By talking with working bankers, managers, and accountants, for example, you can ask questions you may have about their line of work, how they got into their job, what skills are required, and tips on how you can best prepare to enter a similar job.

Like a traditional interview, dress and act appropriately and have written questions ready. Have a notepad and pen to write down their answers for future reference. Here are some recommended questions:

- I have done some research on this position, and _____ is what I've found. Can you tell me more about what sort of work is done here?
- What is a typical day like at this job?
- What sort of advancement potential does this career have?
- What do you think is most rewarding about your position? Most challenging?
- Why did you decide to work for this company?
- Who are your major clients? Major competitors?
- How do you suggest that students find jobs in this field?
- If you are in charge of hiring, what do you look for in candidates?
- What additional training or education should I pursue to enhance my potential for finding a position within this field?
- How have you been able to balance the demands of the office with your personal life? Do you often find yourself bringing home additional work that you didn't finish at the office?
- How stressful is your job?

- What do you like least about this career?
- At the end of your interview, thank your interviewer for his or her time and then follow up with a written note. These interviewees are not only great sources of information, but they may come in handy as a source for future job leads.

For more details on information interviews, visit the following websites:

About.com: Informational Interviewing
http://jobsearch.about.com/cs/infointerviews

Career Key: Information Interviewing
http://www.careerkey.org/english/you/
    information_interviewing.html

Quintessential Careers: Informational Interviewing Tutorial
http://www.quintcareers.com/informational_interviewing.html

CHAPTER 3

TAKING YOUR BUSINESS DEGREE TO WORK

YOU'VE GRADUATED . . . NOW WHAT?

If you are one of the millions of college graduates who, diploma in hand, looks at the working world like it's the jaws of doom, don't fret. Many new graduates lack direction once the cap and gown are off. You probably have many questions, such as what jobs should you seek out, and which companies should you target?

Before you can answer these questions, you need to do a self-assessment test. You may have taken this type of test before in high school or college, whether it was the Myers-Briggs or another formal test, to decide which classes to take or major to choose (see Chapter 1). With this assessment test, focus on your future career. Keeping in mind all that you've learned about the business world from your major, write down specific interests and skills you have developed in your schoolwork and work experience. Then think about jobs that will best utilize your strengths and preferences. Are math and computers your strengths, or are you more confident writing and communicating with others? Perhaps it's a combination of both.

After writing down and evaluating your skills and interests, consider some of the following questions:

- Do you enjoy working independently or as part of a group?
- Are you good at motivating yourself to get work done, or do you need more interaction and supervision to stay motivated and focused?
- Are financial rewards (such as a higher salary) important to you, either out of necessity or desire? Or are you more concerned with finding a job that fulfills you, regardless of the size of your paycheck?
- Does location of a job matter to you? Do you want to stay close to family and/or friends? Do you prefer a city, suburban, or rural environment?

- Do you need or want a flexible work schedule? Would you be willing to work occasional long or irregular hours or on weekends?

Now consider more narrowly focused questions, such as how your career goals relate to your plans for family, travel, or personal growth. The answers you come up with will help you resolve the biggest question of them all: What do I want to do with my life? The key is to keep in mind your strengths and skills and to find a job and work environment that fit your personality.

INTERVIEW: Frank D. Postula

Frank D. Postula is a cost estimator and senior principal systems engineer working on advanced systems economic analysis for Raytheon Missile Systems. Postula spoke to the editors of Top Careers for Business Graduates *about his job and training.*

Q. Please briefly describe your primary and secondary job duties.

A. Primary: Support advanced system development with estimates of costs throughout an asset's life cycle, which involves development, production, operations and support, and disposal. Development consists of the engineering effort needed to design and test a new product. The approach during this phase of an asset's life is to do "concurrent engineering," that is, to consider not only the technical performance of the asset but also the producability, maintainability, affordability, etc. Production is the phase where the asset is manufactured for delivery to the user. Cost considerations are the material and labor content as well as the facility, equipment, tooling, overheads, etc. Operations and support deals with the maintenance and repair of the asset as well as training the user regarding the asset's operation. The user's cost of operation may also be included in this analysis. Finally, disposal is the phase in which the asset is decommissioned. It is disassembled, and components are recycled, scrapped, or (with regard to hazardous materials) disposed of in an environmentally acceptable manner.

Secondary: Support advanced system development with Cost as an Independent Variable analyses to ensure that satisfactory performance is attained within an affordable cost.

Q. How did you train for this job? What was your college major?

A. My training was mainly on-the-job. My college degrees were Bachelor of Science in Aeronautical Engineering, a Master of Science in Mechanical Engineering, and Master of Science in Acquisition and Contract Management. This latter degree involved courses in contract management, business management, negotiations, business law, government law and regulations, proposal preparation, and accounting.

Q. Did these majors prepare you for your career or, in retrospect, would you have pursued a different educational path?

A. Yes, these majors directly support my career path. They provide the insight into both the technical and business aspects of developing systems.

Q. What was your career path out of college?

A. I began my career as an areothermodynamic engineer working on ICBMs and reentry vehicles. Later, I became a program manager for a radioisotopic thermoelectric generator for the first GPS-type satellite. Then I managed a cost-forecasting group for a company making nuclear power plants. Then I managed a cost-estimating group for a company making tactical missiles. Everything I've done has been at the "cutting-edge" of technology.

Q. What are the most important personal and professional qualities for people in your career?

A. You need good communication skills, both written and verbal. You also need to be a self-starter to seek out any information that is needed.

Q. What is the most important piece of advice that you have to offer college students as they graduate and look for jobs in this field?

A. Get work experience in engineering, project management, and/or business development to gain the background that is important to being an effective cost engineer.

Q. What is the future employment outlook for your career?

A. Since money, along with time, is an enabler of all enterprise activity, managers are always going to ask "how much does it cost and how long will it take?" Cost engineers assist in defining the answers to these questions. As a result, I believe there will always be a demand for this profession.

JUMP-START YOUR JOB SEARCH

Once you've narrowed your job interests using questions such as those above, you need to find employers that are hiring for positions that appeal to you. This can be a tricky task, especially during a slower economy. Most employers hire fewer workers during periods of slow economic growth and sagging profits than during more prosperous times. As a result, more graduates compete for fewer positions, which is all the more reason for you to focus your energy and fine tune your job search as much as possible.

NETWORKING

One way to jump-start your job search is talking to the people you know. Although this might sound too easy, you probably have more contacts for potential job leads than you might realize. Your former professors, academic advisors, family, and friends can give you helpful advice, if not direct leads to employers.

Another source of contacts is your college or university. Most schools have alumni departments that track the locations and jobs of recent graduates. Contact your college's alumni relations department for names of people in your area. Alumni sometimes organize groups for social and professional reasons, especially in larger cities. Check your college's website or consult your alumni relations department to see if there is a group in your area. If you live near a chapter, get involved in the next meeting or social gathering: Not only will you have fun and meet new people, but your fellow alumni may work in industries or companies you hope to break into.

Previous summer or part-time jobs can also provide you with employment contacts. Even if the job was in a different industry from the one that now interests you, try contacting old managers and co-workers for advice and possible leads. If you completed an internship during your college years, now is the time to follow up with an email, resume, and/or letter. If your previous employer is not hiring at the time, be sure to keep in contact in case there are future openings.

CREATING A RESUME THAT GETS NOTICED

Before you follow up with your contacts, you need to create and fine-tune your resume. Along with your cover letter, the resume serves as your one chance to grab an employer's attention, so be sure that it shines.

The Content

A resume is a one-page document that lists your contact information, educational and work experiences, and skills and activities that will make you an attractive candidate in the eyes of a prospective employer. Recording your contact information, educational background, and extracurricular activities is the easy part. The challenge is summing up your work experience and job skills to make yourself stand out from the other candidates. The following list offers tips for tackling this crucial part of your resume.

- Write down a list of all the jobs or positions you've held (paid or unpaid) that have fostered your current career goals. Unless you were a manager, leave out your freshman year job at McDonald's.

- Record your job responsibilities. Don't worry about using fancy language to describe your jobs just yet; just be sure to list all the tasks that you handled.

- List the skills that you learned from handling these job duties, such as specific computer programs or particular organizational skills. For example, if you worked at the box office of your college theater, you probably acquired accounting, customer-relations, and some publicity skills. Be sure to examine each experience from every possible angle.

- Take a trip to the library or bookstore and pick up a resume guide. These resources should have examples of quality resumes. Look over the job descriptions that are used, and see if any could be applied to your own experience.

- Return to your list of job duties, and write short sentences using some of the active-language examples found in the resume guide's job descriptions. "Action" words include short, definitive sentence starters like "managed," "organized," and "coordinated." The point here is to be as succinct and effective as possible. Just don't copy verbatim from your resume guide.

The Format

Resumes are usually organized in one of two ways: chronologically or functionally. Look at your resume books, and choose the format that you think would work best for you, but note that most employers favor a chronological format. Don't worry about making your resume look stylish or ornate; this will only distract employers from what is really important: your skills.

Keep the layout as clean and uncluttered as possible, and be sure that the type is easy to read (12pt is a standard). Employers sometimes have hundreds of resumes to review for one position, so they won't waste their time trying to decipher a page of small text and long paragraphs. Short bulleted lists offer a concise and easy-to-read format for your work and educational experiences.

Last but not least, feel free to increase the type size on the element you want the employer to remember most: your name!

Share It with Others

Once you're through with this first draft (notice the word "draft"; this should not be your final version), show it to family members, friends, and other connections and ask for suggestions. Write and rewrite until it is the best representation of what you have to offer a company.

Create Several Versions

Before sending out your winning resume, take note: The most successful resumes are the ones that are tailor-made to fit a particular position. That means that every time you apply for a job, you should review your resume and adjust skills and experiences that can apply directly to the position. You are much more likely to be considered for a job if you highlight specific ways in which your past education and experiences can be an asset to the hiring employer. Thus it's a good idea to keep several drafts of your resume on hand, each of which is tailored for a certain type of position.

For example, say you are applying for an entry-level marketing position in both non-profit and for-profit organizations. A non-profit community outreach program may take a greater interest in your off-campus volunteer activities, whereas a software manufacturer may want to read more about your minor in computer programming. In this job-seeking example, having two separate resumes highlighting your different skills and experiences would serve you well.

The Cover Letter

Always include a cover letter with your resume. As with your resume, the letter must be polished and tailored to the job for which you are applying. Address the cover letter to the individual in charge of hiring. If a name is not included in a job listing, call the company to inquire, or visit the company's website and check the staff listings. If you still can't find what you're looking for, addressing the letter to "Human Resources" should get it into the hands of the right person. The heading of the letter should include your name, address, and phone number, as well as the same for the person to whom you're sending it.

As with your resume, your cover letter should be concise. The body of the letter should contain three short paragraphs, as follows:

- The first paragraph should mention the position for which you are applying and where you saw the job listing. Employers like to keep track of how and where their applicants learn about positions. For example, a good first paragraph might simply state, "I am applying for the position of Advertising Assistant, which I saw advertised in *The Daily Bugle* on 22 March 2003." If a friend or associate recommended you for the job, you can mention that here, as well, but only if that person gives you permission to do so.

- In the second paragraph, state briefly why the job interests you and why you will be a valuable addition to the company. Do not restate the contents of your resume here: simply touch on one or two of your strongest skills and what you can bring to the position. Most importantly, write with confidence. Avoid phrases like "I think I would be . . ." or "I feel that I . . . ." Rather, state simply, "I will be . . ." and "I am . . . ." Clear and definitive language, as opposed to cluttered equivocation, is more likely to grab the attention of the person reading your cover letter and resume.

- In the third paragraph, encourage the employer to review your resume and provide any additional information that may have been requested in the job listing, such as salary requirements, ability to travel or relocate, etc. Here you can also state that you will follow up on your resume submission, but do this only if you honestly plan to do so by phone or letter. Do not include such a statement if the job listing states that only suitable candidates will be contacted. This is the employer's way of saying, "Don't call us, we'll call you."

Resume Advice from Those Who Trash Them

Companies receive resumes by the handful, by the pile, and occasionally by the ton. The number of resumes that come across a typical hiring manager's desk can be overwhelming, especially during times of slow economic growth. Fortunately for them (but not for the job seekers), many applicants commit glaring errors that send their resume right into the trash bin. The following is the monster.com top-10 list of resume mistakes, reported by the recruiters and hiring managers who see them every workday.

1. Spelling errors, typos, and bad writing

   Fix: Read your resume carefully, use spell check, and have friends and family members look it over for mistakes you might have missed.

2. Too many duties, not enough explanation

   Fix: Instead of simply listing your previous job descriptions, describe your accomplishments. Employers don't need to know exactly what you did at your last job, but instead, they want to hear about the direct results of your efforts. For example, list any improvements you brought to your previous job or department.

3. Employment dates are wrong or missing completely

   Fix: Include time ranges in months or years for all work positions. Explain any gaps in your work history in your cover letter. Employers need dates to verify your experience and gain a sense of your overall work history.

4. You don't seem to know your name and address

   Fix: Double-check your contact information each and every time you update your resume. The whole point of the resume is to get a phone call asking for an interview. Employers will not look you up to contact you.

5. Converted or scanned resume shows formatting errors

   Fix: If you are emailing your resume, save and send it in plain-text (ASCII) format. Even if you send your resume by fax or mail, use plain text because some employers scan resumes for easy browsing. Fancy fonts, boxes, or colors are unnecessary on a professional resume and will only cause problems.

(continues)

Resume Advice from Those Who Trash Them
(continued)

6. Resume organized by function

   Fix: Most employers prefer a chronological resume, where work and school experience is listed by date, over a functional one, where experience is listed by skills or functions performed. Month- or even year-long gaps in employment (which become obvious in chronological resumes) are more common now than in previous years and can be filled with volunteer work or continued education.

7. Too long

   Fix: Highlight only the work and educational experience relevant to the job at hand. Recruiters don't have the time to read long resumes.

8. Too wordy

   Fix: Similar to #7, pare down your work, school, and other descriptions to include just the most important highlights.

9. Unqualified

   Fix: Apply only to jobs for which you are qualified. You're not only wasting the employer's time, you're wasting your own when you apply for positions that require higher degrees or more work experience than you have.

10. Too personal

    Fix: Include your fondness for stamp collecting if you are applying to work in a hobby shop. Otherwise, leave it off your resume. In other words, list only information that is pertinent to the employer and the open position. Listed activities and interests should be included only if they are related to the job.

FOR MORE INFORMATION

Hundreds of books and other resources are available for resume assistance, many of which include examples of resumes that work. The following are a few web sites to explore for more information:

Career-Resumes
http://www.career-resumes.com

CollegeGrad.com
http://www.collegegrad.com/resumes

JobStar: Resumes
http://jobstar.org/tools/resume

JobWeb Guide to Resumes and Interviews
http://www.jobweb.com/Resumes_Interviews

Resume.com
http://www.resume.com

The Resume Place, Inc.
http://www.resume-place.com

APPLYING FOR JOBS ONLINE: SERIOUS INTERNET SURFING

The Internet has revolutionized the way employers and employees find their right match. Not only can you browse jobs online, but you can also apply for them through email. In fact, many employers prefer, if not require, that applicants submit resumes by email. According to a survey by the National Association of Colleges and Employers, 90 percent of employers prefer applicants to respond to job listings online. While it seems resume advice is available in nearly endless quantities, many career-seekers have questions about how to prepare their resumes for email responses to online job postings. Here's a quick list of the things to consider before you hit the Send button:

- If submitting your resume online, save it as "Text Only" to convert it into ASCII format. This is the only way to guarantee that the recipient of your resume will read it in the manner and format in which you intended. Fonts and automatic formatting that you may have used in a word processing program may not be correctly converted when the resume reaches the desk of an employer. Sending your resume in text-only format also ensures that employers receive your information free from possible attachment viruses. Only send your resume as another type of attachment, such as Microsoft Word, if the ad explicitly states that you should do so.
- Once you save your resume as text, clean up the body of the email, watching out for new line and section breaks. If you used bullets, use asterisks (*) instead. If you used formatted section breaks, use dashes (—) to separate sections.
- When you prepare your email to send to the employer, write your cover letter in the body of the email, then attach the

text-only version of your resume. When the employer reads your email, your resume will actually be viewed in the body of the email instead of as a separate attachment.

■ Make sure this text-only resume is as clean and error-free as your original. As one recruiter on the Monster.com website puts it, "Do you know what we call people who submit electronic resumes with typos? We call them unemployed."

■ Be sure to mention the name of the position, any job codes that may have been mentioned in the ad, and the words resume and cover letter in the Subject line of the email. The latter is just in case the employer automatically looks for an attachment and overlooks your cover letter in the body of your email.

Some employers enable you to apply for jobs directly from their company websites. If this is the case, follow the directions on the site very closely, and have your cover letter and resume in plain-text format at the ready.

THE PRESCRIPTION
FOR A PERFECT INTERVIEW

If all goes well, your well-crafted resume and cover letter will score you a few interviews. These one-on-one encounters with employers can be intimidating, but there is much you can do to prepare before stepping into an employer's office and shaking the hand that may one day feed you. Follow these tips for a successful interview:

1. **Do your homework.** Research the company before your interview so you can better understand the job for which you are applying. With the growth and popularity of the Internet, almost all companies have an online presence. Check out the company's website and explore its departments, services, locations, and other open positions. This research will not only help you to understand the job, but it will enable you to ask more intelligent questions. Be sure to take notes.

2. **Listen hard . . . then speak up.** When asked a question, carefully consider what the interviewer asked, think a moment, then answer. This sounds simple, but it is often hard to do when under pressure.

3. **Ask away.** Certainly you will want to be attentive to all the interviewer has to say about the company's corporate

structure, work environment, and the specifics of the job. But when the tables are turned and it's your time to ask questions, be sure to do so. Have a list of questions made up beforehand covering issues that might not be touched on by the employer. For example: What sort of training will I receive on the job? Who will I be reporting to? How many people will I be working with? This will show that you are truly interested in the job and in getting to know more about the employer.

4. **Dress conservatively.** A dark blue or black suit is recommended for most business interviews. While what you wear shouldn't score you points with an employer, poor, sloppy dress and overdressing can definitely work against you.

5. **Be punctual.** If you can't make it to an interview on time, how is the interviewer going to think you'll be able to make it in to the office on time every morning?

6. **Say thanks.** Your mother was right: Be polite. Always thank the interviewer for his or her time, and follow up with a handwritten or emailed note that reiterates your gratitude and (when appropriate) your continued interest in the job.

INTERVIEW: Hitesh Bhakta

Hitesh Bhakta is a franchise owner, owning and operating several economy hotels. Bhakta spoke with the editors of Top Careers for Business Graduates *about his work and educational experience.*

Q. Please briefly describe your primary and secondary job duties.

A. I'm not sure if I can organize it into primary and secondary job duties, but there are certain major responsibilities that have to be done to ensure the success of a business. I'm responsible for making sure that my hotels hold their market presence. I also have to make sure that my payroll and operating expenses are within the budget that I set up. One of the most important tasks is making sure that certain larger hotels that are revenue generators are still profitable.

Before, much of this work was done by the hotel's individual franchisor, and I handled more of the managing and marketing of the larger business. Today, with the constant pressures to keep costs down, I have more operating responsibilities with my hotel properties. The costs are changing. For example, insuring my hotels has become much more costly. Insurance used to rank number 13 or 14 on my list of expenses; now it might be in my top five. It is becoming harder and harder to insure hotels these days.

Q. What was your college major?

A. Even though the hotel business actually was my family's own business, I studied pre-law. But regardless of whether students study business, law, or a liberal arts field, a college education is imperative.

One thing about the immigrant experience, as a whole, is that many parents insist their children attain formal education. Then, after years of study, if you want to join the family business, then you can do so. The skills and lessons taught in higher learning institutions are invaluable. To a small business owner, higher education is crucial not only for the knowledge gained, but the networking opportunities that are available among faculty, staff, and other students.

My hotel-related training started when I was in high school, helping out in the family business. Before I went away to school, I knew exactly how to make a bed.

One thing to remember is that business involves risk. You cannot learn this in books. I don't think any institution can or will ever be able to teach this to students—it must be learned on the job. Successful business owners and other entrepreneurs must be applauded for their ability to take risks and come out on top. These are the true heroes.

Q. Did you participate in an internship while you were in college?

A. All through college, I helped my family in the hotel. Any spare time that I had was spent in the family business. That's how it usually works out. It can be the most underpaid, overworked job, but it is also highly rewarding. You have to work the long hours to get the respect from customers and establish your name in the industry.

Q. What are the most important personal and professional qualities for people in your career?

A. The two most important personal qualities that come to mind are trust and credibility—not only in dealing with the hotel customers, but also with employees. One thing to note is that the hotel business is a very personal one. We have, on average, 80–100 master bedroom suites in our hotels, and each of them are rented out to people who may stay there three nights, five nights, or even longer. You can get to know people during the course of their stay.

On the professional side, I think it's important to have a diverse range of skills. The hotel industry requires a lot of different talents and knowledge, and those with a varied background are better prepared. Most hotels have training periods of two to four weeks, for new employees. I think this is crucial to create a competent, helpful staff. Hotel work can be simple, but still needs to be taught through a training period or another method of formal education.

Q. What is the most important piece of advice that you have to offer college students as they graduate and look for jobs in this field?

A. The hotel industry is truly becoming a global market. Here's one interesting fact: There are more Hilton hotels being built outside of the United States that there are Hiltons being built inside the country. Don't limit yourself by looking locally for a job in the hospitality industry. You will miss out on a wealth of job opportunities.

Tips for the Dining Interview

Many business interviews, especially for higher level jobs, may occur out of an office setting. If you find yourself in a lunch or dinner interview, take note:

1. Remember you are there for the interview, not a free meal.

2. Don't arrive famished—or full.

3. Order something at a reasonable price. If the interviewer orders first, order something similar in size and price.

4. Never drink at an interview, even if the interviewer orders a cocktail or beer. You're the one in the hot seat—make sure you have your full faculties intact.

5. Order something safe. Avoid options that are overly spicy, messy, or stinky. (No spaghetti, hot wings, or garlic bread!)

6. Always thank the interviewer for the meal and the interview, regardless of whether or not you liked your meal, the service, or the location. Follow up with a thank-you note in the next week.

A New Breed: The Situational Interview

When most people think of a job interview, a question-and-answer session between a job seeker and a hiring manager usually comes to mind. However, a new trend in applicant evaluation has emerged. Some employers now look at an individual's ethical makeup as much as his or her education and job experience. In light of recent developments in the business world, with many of the industry's most powerful workers being scrutinized for unethical business practices, employers want to hire good people as much as they want to hire skilled people.

In these situational, or behavioral, interviews, applicants are put through real-life job situations (such as being verbally harassed by an upset customer) and then are analyzed based on their gut instincts, actions, words, and even body language. According to the *Handbook of Industrial and Organizational Psychology*, while the traditional sit-down interview is reported to be approximately 7 percent effective in predicting job performance, the situational interview is approximately 54 percent accurate.

Unlike standard interviews, these character evaluations are tough to prepare for. The only thing to do is be yourself, think before you speak and act, and ensure that your responses reflect your years of education and training.

For More Information

Here are some online resources for more interview advice:

Ask the Interview Coach
http://www.asktheinterviewcoach.com

Collegegrad.com: Interviewing Information
http://www.collegegrad.com/intv

Monster: Interview Center
http://interview.monster.com

Salary.com: Job.interview.net
http://www.job-interview.net

YOU HAVE THE JOB . . . NOW WHAT?

Once you've landed a job, you will need time to settle into the company and the position. Depending on the individual and the position, this could take some time or happen very quickly. In that time, workers learn about their company's corporate structure, other jobs in the company, and how things falls into place in that organization.

After some time, however, most workers desire new duties, responsibilities, and challenges in their work. A bigger paycheck may also be a motivating factor. In general, workers can advance in one of two ways. Some choose to move laterally, switching to a similar position or level in another department or with another company for more pay. Other workers choose to move vertically, moving to a position of higher authority within a company or with another employer.

The Graduate Factor

Although maintaining excellent job performance and a solid professional reputation are the best ways to advance in your career, furthering your education is also invaluable in increasing your chances for promotion. The business world offers many advancement opportunities to those with a bachelor's degree. However, now more than ever, a graduate degree (or higher) is becoming commonplace among managers and executives. If you hope to advance to high-level management, you will need to consider graduate school.

Graduate school applications can be lengthy and time-consuming. But before you even get to those, you will need to settle down for some more test taking. Having been a business major as an undergraduate, you may be interested in pursuing the Master of Business Administration (M.B.A.) degree. Most schools that award the M.B.A. degree require that you take the Graduate Management Admissions Test (GMAT) before you apply for admission. The GMAT evaluates verbal, mathematical, and analytical writing skills, not business or management skills. For more information on this test and on pursuing the M.B.A. degree, visit http://www.mba.com.

Most other graduate schools and programs require students to take the Graduate Record Examination (GRE) before applying. Similar to how the SATs and ACTs help evaluate incoming college students, the GRE is used to evaluate graduate school students. This achievement test is composed of verbal, quantitative, and analytical writing sections on various subjects. Visit http://www.gre.org to learn more.

For More Information

Business.GradSchools.com
http://business.gradschools.com

Graduate School Guide
http://www.graduateguide.com

Peterson's Graduate Schools and Programs
http://www.petersons.com/GradChannel

SECTION II

CAREERS

ACCOUNTANTS AND AUDITORS

QUICK FACTS

School Subjects Business Economics	**Certification or Licensing** Recommended
Personal Skills Following instructions Leadership/management	**Outlook** About as fast as the average
	DOT 160
Work Environment Primarily indoors One location with some travel	**GOE** 11.06.01
	NOC 1111
Minimum Education Level Bachelor's degree	**O*NET-SOC** 13-2011.00, 13-2011.01, 13-2011.02
Salary Range $21,947 to $59,500 to $100,000+	

OVERVIEW

Accountants compile, analyze, verify, and prepare financial records including profit and loss statements, balance sheets, cost studies, and tax reports. Accountants may specialize in areas such as auditing, tax work, cost accounting, budgeting and control, or systems and procedures. Accountants also may specialize in a particular business or field; for example, agricultural accountants specialize in drawing up and analyzing financial statements for farmers and for farm equipment companies. There are approximately 976,000 accountants and auditors employed in the United States.

HISTORY

Accounting records and bookkeeping methods have been used from early history to the present. Records discovered in Babylonia (modern-day Iraq) date back to 3600 B.C., and accounts were kept by the Greeks and the Romans.

Modern accounting began with the technique of double-entry bookkeeping, which was developed in the 15th and 16th centuries by Luca Pacioli (ca. 1450–ca. 1520), an Italian mathematician. After the Industrial Revolution, business grew more complex. As government and industrial institutions developed in the 19th and 20th centuries, accurate records and information were needed to assist in making decisions on economic and management policies.

The accounting profession in the United States dates back only to 1880, when English and Scottish investors began buying stock in American companies. To keep an eye on their investments, they sent over accountants who realized the great potential that existed in the accounting field and stayed on to establish their own businesses. Federal legislation, such as the income tax in 1913 and the excess profits tax in 1917, helped cause an accounting boom that has made the profession instrumental to all business.

Accountants have long been considered "bean counters," and their work has been written off by outsiders as routine and boring. However, an image that was once associated with death, taxes, and bad news has been making a turnaround. Accountants now do much more than prepare financial statements and record business transactions. Technology now counts the "beans," allowing accountants to analyze and interpret the results. Their work has expanded to encompass challenging and creative tasks such as computing costs and efficiency gains of new technologies, participating in strategies for mergers and acquisitions, supervising quality management, and designing and using information systems to track financial performance.

THE JOB

Accountants' duties depend on the size and nature of the company in which they are employed. The major fields of employment are public, private, and government accounting.

- *Public accountants* work independently on a fee basis or as members of an accounting firm, and they perform a variety of tasks for businesses or individuals. These may include auditing accounts and records, preparing and certifying financial statements, conducting financial investigations and furnishing testimony in legal matters, and assisting in formulating budget policies and procedures.

- *Private accountants,* sometimes called *industrial* or *management accountants,* handle financial records of the firms at which they are employed.

- *Government accountants* work on the financial records of government agencies or, when necessary, they audit the records of private companies. In the federal government, many accountants are employed as *bank examiners, Internal Revenue Service agents,* and *investigators,* as well as in regular accounting positions. Within these fields, accountants can specialize in a variety of areas.

- *General accountants* supervise, install, and devise general accounting, budget, and cost systems. They maintain records, balance books, and prepare and analyze statements on all financial aspects of business. Administrative officers use this information to make sound business decisions.

- *Budget accountants* review expenditures of departments within a firm to make sure expenses allotted are not exceeded. They also aid in drafting budgets and may devise and install budget control systems.

- *Cost accountants* determine unit costs of products or services by analyzing records and depreciation data. They classify and record all operating costs so that management can control expenditures.

- *Property accountants* keep records of equipment, buildings, and other property owned or leased by a company. They prepare mortgage schedules and payments as well as appreciation or depreciation statements, which are used for income tax purposes.

- *Systems accountants* design and set up special accounting systems for organizations whose needs cannot be handled by standardized procedures. This may involve installing automated or computerized accounting processes and includes instructing personnel in the new methods.

- *Forensic accountants and auditors* use accounting principles and theories to support or oppose claims being made in litigation.

- *Tax accountants* prepare federal, state, or local tax returns of an individual, business, or corporation according to prescribed rates, laws, and regulations. They also may conduct

research on the effects of taxes on firm operations and recommend changes to reduce taxes. This is one of the most
intricate fields of accounting, and many accountants therefore specialize in one particular phase such as corporate,
individual income, or property tax.

- *Auditors* examine and verify financial records to ensure that
  they are accurate, complete, and in compliance with federal
  laws. To do so they review items in original entry books,
  including purchase orders, tax returns, billing statements,
  and other important documents. Auditors may also prepare
  financial statements for clients and suggest ways to improve
  productivity and profits. *Internal auditors* conduct the same
  kind of examination and evaluation for one particular company. Because they are salaried employees of that company,
  their financial audits then must be certified by a qualified
  independent auditor. Internal auditors also review procedures and controls, appraise the efficiency and effectiveness
  of operations, and make sure their companies comply with
  corporate policies and government regulations.

- *Tax auditors* review financial records and other information
  provided by taxpayers to determine the appropriate tax liability. State and federal tax auditors usually work in government offices, but they may perform a field audit in a
  taxpayer's home or office.

- *Revenue agents* are employed by the federal government to
  examine selected income tax returns and, when necessary,
  conduct field audits and investigations to verify the information reported and adjust the tax liability accordingly.

- *Chief bank examiners* enforce good banking practices throughout a state. They schedule bank examinations to ensure that
  financial institutions comply with state laws and, in certain
  cases, they take steps to protect a bank's solvency and the
  interests of its depositors and shareholders.

REQUIREMENTS
High School

High school students preparing for an accounting career should be
proficient in arithmetic and basic algebra. Familiarity with computers and their applications is equally important. Course work in
English and communications will also be beneficial.

Postsecondary Training

Postsecondary training in accounting may be obtained in a wide variety of institutions such as private business schools, junior colleges, universities, and correspondence schools. A bachelor's degree with a major in accounting is highly recommended by professional associations for those entering the field and is required by all states before taking the licensing exam. It is possible, however, to become a successful accountant by completing a program at any of the above-mentioned institutions. A four-year college curriculum usually includes about two years of liberal arts courses, a year of general business subjects, and a year of specific accounting work. Better positions, particularly in public accounting, require a bachelor's degree with a major in accounting. Large public accounting firms often prefer people with a master's degree in accounting. For beginning positions in accounting, the federal government requires four years of college (including twenty-four semester hours in accounting or auditing) or an equivalent combination of education and experience.

Certification or Licensing

Certified public accountants (*CPAs*) must pass a qualifying examination and hold a certificate issued by the state in which they wish to practice. In most states, a college degree is required for admission to the CPA examinations; a few states allow candidates to substitute years of public accounting experience for the college degree requirement. Currently 38 states and jurisdictions require CPA candidates to have 150 hours of education, which is an additional 30 hours beyond the standard bachelor's degree. Nine additional states and jurisdictions plan to enact the 150-hour requirement in the future. This requirement can be met by combining an undergraduate accounting program with graduate study or participating in an integrated five-year professional accounting program. You can obtain information from a state board of accountancy or check out the website of the American Institute of Certified Public Accountants (AICPA) to read about new regulations and review last year's exam. The Uniform CPA Examination administered by the AICPA is used by all states. Nearly all states require at least two years of public accounting experience or its equivalent before a CPA certificate can be earned.

Some accountants seek out other credentials. Those who have earned a bachelor's degree, pass a four-part examination, agree to meet continuing education requirements, and have at least two years of experience in management accounting may become a Certified Management Accountant (CMA) through the Institute of Management Accounting.

The Accreditation Council for Accountancy and Taxation confers the following three designations: Accredited Business Accountant or Accredited Business Advisor (ABA), Accredited Tax Preparer (ATP), and Accredited Tax Advisor (ATA).

To become a Certified Internal Auditor (CIA), college graduates with two years of experience in internal auditing must pass a four-part examination given by the Institute of Internal Auditors.

The Information Systems Audit and Control Association confers the Certified Information Systems Auditor (CISA) designation to candidates who pass an examination and who have five years of experience auditing electronic data processing systems. Other organizations, such as the Bank Administration Institute, confer specialized auditing designations.

Other Requirements

To be a successful accountant you will need strong mathematical, analytical, and problem-solving skills. You need to be able to think logically and to interpret facts and figures accurately. Effective oral and written communication skills are also essential in working with both clients and management.

Other important skills are attentiveness to detail, patience, and industriousness. Business acumen and the ability to generate clientele are crucial to service-oriented business, as are honesty, dedication, and a respect for the work of others.

EXPLORING

If you think a career as an accountant or auditor might be for you, try working in retail, either part time or during the summer. Working at the cash register or even pricing products as a stockperson is good introductory experience. You should also consider working as a treasurer for a student organization requiring financial planning and money management. It may be possible to gain some experience by volunteering with local groups such as churches and small businesses. You should also stay abreast of news in the field by reading trade magazines and checking out the industry websites of the AICPA and other accounting associations. The AICPA has numerous free educational publications available.

EMPLOYERS

Nearly 1 million people are employed as accountants and auditors. Accountants and auditors work throughout private industry and government. About one-quarter of these people work for accounting, auditing, and bookkeeping firms. Approximately 10 percent are self-employed. Nearly 40 percent of all accountants and auditors are certified.

STARTING OUT

Junior public accountants usually start in jobs with routine duties such as counting cash, verifying calculations, and other detailed numerical work. In private accounting, beginners are likely to start as cost accountants and junior internal auditors. They may also enter in clerical positions as cost clerks, ledger clerks, and timekeepers or as trainees in technical or junior executive positions. In the federal government, most beginners are hired as trainees at the GS-5 level after passing the civil service exam.

Some state CPA societies arrange internships for accounting majors, and some offer scholarships and loan programs.

ADVANCEMENT

Talented accountants and auditors can advance quickly. Junior public accountants usually advance to senior positions within several years and to managerial positions soon after. Those successful in dealing with top-level management may eventually become supervisors, managers, and partners in larger firms or go into independent practice. However, only 2 to 3 percent of new hires advance to audit manager, tax manager, or partner.

Private accountants in firms may become audit managers, tax managers, cost accounting managers, or controllers, depending on their specialty. Some become controllers, treasurers, or corporation presidents. Others on the finance side may rise to become managers of financial planning and analysis or treasurers.

Federal government trainees are usually promoted within a year or two. Advancement to controller and to higher administrative positions is ultimately possible.

Although advancement may be rapid for skilled accountants, especially in public accounting, those with inadequate academic or professional training are often assigned to routine jobs and find it difficult to obtain promotions. All accountants find it necessary to continue their study of accounting and related areas in their spare time. Even those who have already obtained college degrees, gained experience, and earned a CPA certificate may spend many hours studying to keep up with new industry developments. Thousands of practicing accountants enroll in formal courses offered by universities and professional associations to specialize in certain areas of accounting, broaden or update their professional skills, and become eligible for advancement and promotion.

EARNINGS

Beginning salaries for accountants with a bachelor's degree averaged $39,397 a year in 2001; those with a master's degree averaged $43,272 a year, according to the National Association of Colleges and Employers. Auditors with up to one year of experience earned between $29,250 and $40,250, according to a 2001 survey by Robert Half International. Some experienced auditors may earn between $59,500 and $106,500, depending on such factors as their education level, the size of the firm, and the firm's location.

Public and private accountants follow similar salary increases, and generally the larger the firm or corporation, the higher the salary. In public accounting, low mid-level salaries range from $28,200 to $32,000, according to the U.S. Department of Labor, and upper mid-level salaries range from $30,000 in small towns to $75,000 in the largest cities with higher rates from the Big Five firms. Partners earn upwards of $100,000. Mid-level corporate accountants earn from $30,000 to $65,000, and managers bring in $40,000 to $80,000. Controllers earn an average of $85,100, and chief financial officers' salaries can exceed $142,900.

Government accountants and auditors make substantially less, though they do receive more benefits. According to the U.S. Department of Labor, in 2001 beginning salaries for accountants and auditors were approximately $21,947. A few exceptional candidates with outstanding academic records may start at $27,185. Employees with master's degrees or two years of professional experience may begin at $33,254. In 2000, the average annual salary for accountants and auditors employed by the federal government in nonsupervisory, supervisory, and managerial positions was $44,380. Accountants in large firms and with large corporations receive typical benefits including paid vacation and sick days, insurance, and savings and pension plans. Employees in smaller companies generally receive fewer fringe benefits.

WORK ENVIRONMENT

Accounting is known as a desk job, and a 40-hour workweek can be expected in public and private accounting. Although computer work is replacing paperwork, the job can be routine and monotonous, and concentration and attention to detail are critical. Public accountants experience considerable pressure during the tax period, which runs from November to April, and they may have to work long hours. There is potential for stress aside from tax season, as accountants can be responsible for managing multimillion-dollar finances with no margin for error. Self-employed accountants and those working for a small firm can expect to work longer hours; 40 percent work more than 50 hours per week, compared to 20 percent of public and private accountants.

In smaller firms, most of the public accountant's work is performed in the client's office. A considerable amount of travel is often necessary to service a wide variety of businesses. In a larger firm, however, an accountant may have very little client contact, spending more time interacting with the accounting team.

OUTLOOK

In the wake of the massive changes that swept through the industry in the last decade, the job outlook for accountants and auditors is good, with employment expected to grow about as fast as the average through 2010, according to the U.S. Department of Labor.

Several factors will contribute to the expansion of the accounting industry: increasingly complex taxation, growth in both the size and number of business corporations required to release financial reports to stockholders, a more general use of accounting in business management, and outsourcing of accounting services by small business firms.

As firms specialize their services, accountants will need to follow suit. Firms will seek out accountants with experience in marketing and proficiency in computer systems to build management consulting practices. As trade increases, so will the demand for CPAs with international specialties and language skills. And CPAs with an engineering degree would be well equipped to specialize in environmental accounting. Demand for recent college grads is falling as firms seek out seasoned professionals with marketing savvy, proven sales ability, and international experience.

While the majority of jobs will be found in large cities with large businesses, smaller firms will start up, and smaller business will continue to seek outside accountants. Accountants without college degrees will find more paraprofessional accounting positions, similar to the work of paralegals, as the number of lower and mid-level workers expands. Demand will also be high for specialized accounting temps; CPA firms have started to hire temps to smooth out their staffing through seasonal business cycles.

The role of public accountants will change as they perform less auditing and tax work and assume greater management and consulting responsibilities. Likewise, private accountants will focus more on analyzing operations rather than simply providing data and will develop sophisticated accounting systems.

Accounting jobs are more secure than most during economic downswings. Despite fluctuations in the national economy, there will always be a need to manage financial information, especially as the number, size, and complexity of business transactions increases. However, competition for jobs will remain, certification requirements will become more rigorous, and accountants and auditors with the highest degrees will be much sought after.

FOR MORE INFORMATION

For information on accreditation and testing, contact:
Accreditation Council for Accountancy and Taxation
1010 North Fairfax Street
Alexandria, VA 22314-1574
Tel: 888-289-7763
Email: info@acatcredentials.org
http://www.acatcredentials.org

For information about the Uniform CPA Examination and about becoming a student member, contact:
American Institute of Certified Public Accountants
1211 Avenue of the Americas
New York, NY 10036
Tel: 888-777-7077
http://www.aicpa.org

For information on accredited programs in accounting, contact:
Association to Advance Collegiate Schools of Business
600 Emerson Road, Suite 300
St. Louis, MO 63141-6762
Tel: 314-872-8481
http://www.aacsb.edu

For more information on women in accounting, contact:
Educational Foundation for Women in Accounting
PO Box 1925
Southeastern, PA 19399-1925
Tel: 610-407-9229
Email: info@efwa.org
http://www.efwa.org

For information on certification, contact:
**Information Systems Audit and Control Association and
    Foundation**
3701 Algonquin Road, Suite 1010
Rolling Meadows, IL 60008
Tel: 847-253-1545
http://www.isaca.org

For information on internal auditing and the CIA designation, contact:
Institute of Internal Auditors
247 Maitland Avenue
Altamonte Springs, FL 32701-4201
Tel: 407-937-1100
Email: iia@theiia.org
http://www.theiia.org

*For information about management accounting and the CMA designa-
tion, as well as student membership, contact:*
Institute of Management Accountants
10 Paragon Drive
Montvale, NJ 07645-1718
Tel: 800-638-4427
Email: ima@imanet.org
http://www.imanet.org

ADVERTISING ACCOUNT EXECUTIVES

QUICK FACTS

School Subjects Business English Speech	**Certification or Licensing** None available
	Outlook Faster than the average
Personal Skills Communication/ideas Helping/teaching	**DOT** 164
Work Environment Primarily indoors Primarily one location	**GOE** 08.01.02
Minimum Education Level Bachelor's degree	**NOC** 1122
Salary Range $20,000 to $55,940 to $150,000+	**O*NET-SOC** 11-2011.00

OVERVIEW

The *advertising account executive* coordinates and oversees everything related to a client's advertising account and acts as the primary liaison between the agency and the client. Account executives are also responsible for building and maintaining professional relationships among clients and coworkers to ensure the successful completion of major ad campaigns and the assurance of continued business with clients. Advertising account executives and related workers hold 707,000 jobs in the United States.

HISTORY

When the advertising industry formally developed in the late 1800s, advertisers themselves were usually the ones who handled the promotion of their products and services, placing ads in newspapers and magazines in order to reach their customers. As the number of newspapers increased and print advertising became more widespread, however, these advertisers called on specialists who knew how to create and coordinate effective advertisements. One such specialist, the advertising account executive, emerged to produce and handle the ad campaigns for businesses.

Advertising agencies were commonly used by companies by the 1920s, and account executives worked for such agencies. Together with a staff of creative professionals, the account executive was able to develop an advertising "package," including slogans, jingles, and images, as well as a general campaign strategy. In addition, account executives did basic market research, oversaw the elements that went into a campaign, and worked hand-in-hand with writers and artists to develop effective ads for their client companies.

Today, account executives handle all aspects of their clients' ad campaigns. As a result, they bring to the job a broad base of knowledge, including account management, marketing, sales promotion, merchandising, client accounting, print production, public relations, and the creative arts.

THE JOB

Account executives track the day-to-day progress of the overall advertising campaigns of their clients. Together with a staff commonly consisting of a creative director, an art director, a copywriter, researchers, and production specialists, the account executive monitors all client accounts from beginning to end.

Before an advertising campaign is actually launched, a lot of preparatory work is needed. Account executives must familiarize themselves with their clients' products and services, target markets, goals, competitors, and preferred media. Together with the agency team, the account executive conducts research and holds initial meetings with clients. Then the team, coordinated by the account executive, uses this information to analyze market potential and presents recommendations to the client.

After an advertising strategy has been determined and all terms have been agreed upon, the agency's creative staff goes to work, developing ideas and producing various ads to present to the client. During this time, the account executive works with *media buyers* (who purchase radio and television time and publication space for advertising) in order to develop a schedule for the project and make sure that the costs involved are within the client's budget.

When the ad campaign has been approved by the client, production can begin. In addition to supervising and coordinating the work of copywriters, editors, graphic artists, production specialists, and other employees on the agency team, the account executive must also write reports and draft business correspondence, follow up on all client meetings, interact with outside vendors, and ensure that all pieces of the advertising campaign clearly communicate the desired message. In sum, the account executive is responsible for making sure that the client is satisfied. This may require making modifications to the campaign, revising cost estimates and events schedules, and redirecting the efforts of the creative staff.

In addition to their daily responsibilities of tracking and handling clients' advertising campaigns, account executives must also develop and bring in new business, keep up to date on current advertising trends, evaluate the effectiveness of advertising programs, and track sales figures.

REQUIREMENTS
High School
You can prepare for a career as an advertising account executive by taking a variety of courses at the high school level. Basic courses in English, journalism, communication, economics, psychology, business, social science, and mathematics are important for aspiring advertising account executives.

Postsecondary Training
Most advertising agencies hire college graduates whose degrees can vary widely, from English, journalism, or marketing to business administration, speech communications, or fine arts. Courses in psychology, sociology, business, economics, and any art medium are helpful. Some positions require a graduate degree in advertising, art, or marketing. Others may call for experience in a particular field, such as health care, insurance, or retail.

While most employers prefer a broad liberal arts background with courses in marketing, market research, sales, consumer behavior, communication, and technology, many also seek employees who already have some work experience. Those candidates who have completed on-the-job internships at agencies or have developed portfolios will have a competitive edge.

Other Requirements
While account executives do not need to have the same degree of artistic skill or knowledge as art directors or graphic designers, they must be imaginative and understand the communication of art and photography in order to direct the overall progress of an ad cam-

paign. They should also be able to work under pressure, motivate employees, solve problems, and demonstrate flexibility, good judgment, decisiveness, and patience.

Account executives must be aware of trends and be interested in the business climate and the psychology of making purchases. In addition, they should be able to write clearly, make effective presentations, and communicate persuasively. It is also helpful to stay abreast of the various computer programs used in advertising design and management.

EXPLORING

Read publications like *Advertising Age* (http://www.adage.com), *Adweek* (http://www.adweek.com), and *Brandweek* (http://www. brandweek.com) to become familiar with advertising issues, trends, successes, and failures. Visit the Clio Awards website (http:// www.clioawards.com). Clios are awards for advertising excellence and given each year in the categories of TV, print, outdoor, radio, integrated media, design, Internet, and student work. The site also has information about advertising and art schools, trade associations, and links to some of the trade magazines of the industry.

To gain practical business experience, become involved with advertising or promotion activities at your school for social events, sports events, political issues, or fund-raising events. If your school newspaper or yearbook has paid advertising, offer to work in ad sales.

EMPLOYERS

More than 700,000 advertising, marketing, promotions, public relations, and sales managers work in the United States. Advertising agencies all across the country and abroad employ advertising account executives. Of the 22,000 agencies in the United States, the large firms located in New York, Chicago, and Los Angeles tend to dominate the advertising industry. However, four out of five organizations employ fewer than 10 people. These "small shops" offer employment opportunities for account executives with experience, talent, and flexibility.

STARTING OUT

Many people aspiring to the job of account executive participate in internships or begin as assistant executives, allowing them to work with clients, study the market, and follow up on client service. This work gives students a good sense of the rhythm of the job and the type of work required of account executives.

College graduates with or without experience can start their job searches in their schools' career placement offices. Staff there can set up interviews and help polish resumes.

The advertising arena is rich with opportunities. When looking for employment, you don't have to target agencies. Instead, search for jobs with large businesses that may employ advertising staff. If you want to work at an agency, you'll find the competition for jobs intense. Once hired, account executives often participate in special training programs that both initiate them and help them to succeed.

ADVANCEMENT

Since practical experience and a broad base of knowledge are often required of advertising account executives, many employees work their way up through the company, from assistant to account executive to account manager and finally to department head. In smaller agencies, where promotions depend on experience and leadership, advancement may occur slowly. In larger firms, management-training programs are often required for advancement. Continuing education is occasionally offered to account executives in these firms, often through local colleges or special seminars provided by professional societies.

EARNINGS

According to the U.S. Department of Labor, advertising account executives earned between $29,210 to $125,880 annually in 2001, with median annual earnings of approximately $55,940. In smaller agencies, the salary may be much lower ($20,000 or less), and in larger firms, it is often much higher (over $150,000). Salary bonuses are common for account executives. Benefits typically include vacation and sick leave, health and life insurance, and a retirement plan.

WORK ENVIRONMENT

It is not uncommon for advertising account executives to work long hours, including evenings and weekends. Informal meetings with clients, for example, frequently take place after normal business hours. In addition, some travel may be required when clients are based in other cities or states or when account executives must attend industry conferences.

Advertising agencies are usually highly charged with energy and are both physically and psychologically exciting places to work. The account executive works with others as a team in a creative environment where a lot of ideas are exchanged among colleagues.

As deadlines are critical in advertising, it is important that account executives possess the ability to handle pressure and stress effectively. Patience and flexibility are also essential, as are organization and time-management skills.

OUTLOOK

The growth of the advertising industry depends on the health of the economy. In a thriving economy in which many new products and services are developed and consumer spending is up, advertising budgets are large. Although the economy has been weaker as of late, the U.S. Department of Labor still predicts that employment for advertising account executives will grow faster than the average for all occupations through the next decade.

Most opportunities for advertising account executives will be in larger cities such as Chicago, New York, and Los Angeles, which enjoy a high concentration of business. Competition for these jobs, however, will be intense. The successful candidate will be a college graduate with a lot of creativity, strong communications skills, and extensive experience in the advertising industry. Those able to speak another language will have an edge because of the increasing supply of products and services offered in foreign markets.

FOR MORE INFORMATION

The AAF combines the mutual interests of corporate advertisers, agencies, media companies, suppliers, and academia. Visit its website to learn more about internships, scholarships, and awards.

American Advertising Federation (AAF)
1101 Vermont Avenue, NW, Suite 500
Washington, DC 20005-6306
Tel: 202-898-0089
Email: aaf@aaf.org
http://www.aaf.org

For industry information, contact:
American Association of Advertising Agencies
405 Lexington Avenue, 18th Floor
New York, NY 10174-1801
Tel: 212-682-2500
http://www.aaaa.org

For information on the practice, study, and teaching of marketing, contact:
American Marketing Association
311 South Wacker Drive, Suite 5800
Chicago, IL 60606
Tel: 800-AMA-1150
http://www.marketingpower.com

BUSINESS MANAGERS

QUICK FACTS

School Subjects Business Computer science	**Certification or Licensing** None available
Personal Skills Helping/teaching Leadership/management	**Outlook** About as fast as the average
Work Environment Primarily indoors One location with some travel	**DOT** 189 **GOE** 11.05.01
Minimum Education Level Bachelor's degree	**NOC** 0611
Salary Range $38,710 to $61,160 to $136,760+	**O*NET-SOC** 11-1011.00, 11-1011.02, 11-1021.00, 11-3031.01

OVERVIEW

Business managers plan, organize, direct, and coordinate the operations of firms in business and industry. They may oversee an entire company, a geographical territory of a company's operations, or a specific department within a company. Of the approximately three million managerial jobs in the United States, about 60 percent are found in retail, services, and manufacturing industries.

HISTORY

Everyone has some experience in management. For example, if you schedule your day so that you can get up, get to school on time, go to soccer practice after school, have time to do your homework, and get to bed at a reasonable hour, you are practicing management skills. Running a household, paying bills, balancing a checkbook, and keeping track of appointments, meetings, and social activities are also examples of managerial activities. Essentially, the term "manage" means to handle, direct, or control.

Management is a necessary part of any enterprise in which a person or group of people are trying to accomplish a specific goal. In fact, civilization could not have grown to its present level of complexity without the planning and organizing involved in effective management. Some of the earliest examples of written documents had to do with the management of business and commerce. As societies and individuals accumulated property and wealth, they needed effective record-keeping of taxes, trade agreements, laws, and rights of ownership.

The technological advances of the Industrial Revolution brought about the need for a distinct class of managers. As complex factory systems developed, skilled and trained managers were required to organize and operate them. Workers specialized in a limited number of tasks that required managers to coordinate and oversee production.

As businesses began to diversify their production, industries became so complex that management tasks had to be divided among several different managers, as opposed to one central, authoritarian figure. With the expanded scope of managers and the trend toward decentralized management, the transition to the professional manager took place. In the 1920s, large corporations began to organize with decentralized administration and centralized policy control.

Managers provided a forum for the exchange and evaluation of creative ideas and technical innovations. Eventually these management concepts spread from manufacturing and production to office, personnel, marketing, and financial functions. Today, management is more concerned with results than activities, taking into account individual differences in work styles.

THE JOB

Management is found in every industry, including food, clothing, banking, education, health care, and business services. All types of businesses have managers to formulate policies and administer the firm's operations. Managers may oversee the operations of an entire company, a geographical territory of a company's operations, or a specific department, such as sales and marketing.

Business managers direct a company's or a department's daily activities within the context of the organization's overall plan. They implement organizational policies and goals. This may involve developing sales or promotional materials, analyzing the department's budgetary requirements, and hiring, training, and supervising staff. Business managers are often responsible for long-range planning for their company or department. This involves setting goals for the organization and developing a workable plan for meeting those goals.

A manager responsible for a single department might work to coordinate his or her department's activities with other departments. A manager responsible for an entire company or organization might work with the managers of various departments or locations to oversee and coordinate the activities of all departments. If the business is privately owned, the owner may be the manager. In a large corporation, however, there will be a management structure above the business manager.

Jeff Bowe is the Midwest General Manager for Disc Graphics, a large printing company headquartered in New York. Bowe oversees all aspects of the company's Indianapolis plant, which employs about 50 people. When asked what he is responsible for, Bowe answers, "Everything that happens in this facility." Specifically, that includes sales, production, customer service, capital expenditure planning, hiring and training employees, firing or downsizing, and personnel management.

The hierarchy of managers includes top executives such as the *president*, who establishes an organization's goals and policies along with others, such as the chief executive officer, chief financial officer, chief information officer, executive vice president, and the board of directors. Top executives plan business objectives and develop policies to coordinate operations between divisions and departments and establish procedures for attaining objectives. Activity reports and financial statements are reviewed to determine progress and revise operations as needed. The president also directs and formulates funding for new and existing programs within the organization. Public relations plays a big part in the lives of executives as they deal with executives and leaders from other countries or organizations and with customers, employees, and various special interest groups.

The top-level managers for Bowe's company are located in the company's New York headquarters. Bowe is responsible for reporting certain information about the Indianapolis facility to them. He may also have to work collaboratively with them on certain projects or plans. "I have a conversation with people at headquarters about every two to three days," he says. "I get corporate input on very large projects. I would also work closely with them if we had some type of corporate-wide program we were working on—something where I would be the contact person for this facility."

Although the president or chief executive officer retains ultimate authority and responsibility, Bowe is responsible for overseeing the day-to-day operations of the Indianapolis location. A manager in this position is sometimes called a *chief operating officer* or *COO*. Other duties of a COO may include serving as chairman of committees, such as management, executive, engineering, or sales.

Some companies have an *executive vice president*, who directs and coordinates the activities of one or more departments, depending on the size of the organization. In very large organizations, the duties of executive vice presidents may be highly specialized. For example, they may oversee the activities of business managers of marketing, sales promotion, purchasing, finance, personnel training, industrial relations, administrative services, data processing, property management, transportation, or legal services. In smaller organizations, an executive vice president might be responsible for a number of these departments. Executive vice presidents also assist the chief executive officer in formulating and administering the organization's policies and developing its long-range goals. Executive vice presidents may serve as members of management committees on special studies.

Companies may also have a *chief financial officer* or *CFO*. In small firms, the CFO is usually responsible for all financial management tasks, such as budgeting, capital expenditure planning, cash flow, and various financial reviews and reports. In larger companies, the CFO may oversee financial management departments, to help other managers develop financial and economic policy and oversee the implementation of these policies.

Chief information officers, or *CIOs*, are responsible for all aspects of their company's information technology. They use their knowledge of technology and business to determine how information technology can best be used to meet company goals. This may include researching, purchasing, and overseeing the setup and use of technology systems, such as Intranet, Internet, and computer networks. These managers sometimes take a role in implementing a company's website. For more information on this career, see the article "Chief Information Officers."

In companies that have several different locations, managers may be assigned to oversee specific geographic areas. For example, a large retailer with facilities all across the nation is likely to have a number of managers in charge of various territories. There might be a Midwest manager, a Southwest manager, a Southeast manager, a Northeast manager, and a Northwest manager. These managers are often called *regional* or *area managers*. Some companies break their management territories up into even smaller sections, such as a single state or a part of a state. Managers overseeing these smaller segments are often called *district managers,* and typically report directly to an area or regional manager.

REQUIREMENTS
High School

The educational background of business managers varies as widely as the nature of their diverse responsibilities. Many have a bachelor's degree in liberal arts or business administration. If you are interested in a business managerial career, you should start preparing in high school by taking college preparatory classes. According to Jeff Bowe, your best bet academically is to get a well-rounded education. Because communication is important, take as many English classes as possible. Speech classes are another way to improve your communication skills. Courses in mathematics, business, and computer science are also excellent choices to help you prepare for this career. Finally, Bowe recommends taking a foreign language. "Today speaking a foreign language is more and more important," he says. "Which language is not so important. Any of the global languages are something you could very well use, depending upon where you end up."

Postsecondary Training

Business managers often have a college degree in a subject that pertains to the department they direct or the organization they administer, for example, accounting for a business manager of finance, computer science for a business manager of data processing, engineering or science for a director of research and development. As computer usage grows, many managers are expected to have experience with the information technology that applies to their field.

Graduate and professional degrees are common. Bowe, along with many managers in administrative, marketing, financial, and manufacturing activities, has a master's degree in business administration. Managers in highly technical manufacturing and research activities often have a master's degree or doctorate in a technical or scientific discipline. A law degree is mandatory for business managers of corporate legal departments, and hospital managers generally have a master's degree in health services administration or business administration. In some industries, such as retail trade or the food and beverage industry, competent individuals without a college degree may become business managers.

Other Requirements

There are a number of personal characteristics that can help one be a successful business manager, depending upon the specific responsibilities of the position. A manager who oversees other employees should have good communication and interpersonal skills. The ability to delegate work is another important personality trait of a good manager. The ability to think on your feet is often key in business management, according to Bowe. "You have to be able to think extremely quickly and not in a reactionary manner," he says. Bowe also says that a certain degree of organization is important, since managers are often managing several different things simultaneously. Other traits considered important for top executives are intelligence, decisiveness, intuition, creativity, honesty, loyalty, a sense of responsibility, and planning abilities. Finally, the successful manager should be flexible and interested in staying abreast of new developments in his or her industry. "In general, you need to be open to change because your customers change, your market changes, your technology changes," he says. "If you won't try something new, you really have no business being in management."

EXPLORING

To get experience as a manager, start with your own interests. Whether you're involved in drama, sports, school publications, or a part-time job, there are managerial duties associated with any organized activity. These can involve planning, scheduling, managing other workers or volunteers, fund-raising, or budgeting. Local businesses also have job opportunities through which you can get first-hand knowledge and experience of management structure. If you can't get an actual job, at least try to schedule a meeting with a business manager to talk with him or her about the career. Some schools or community organizations arrange job-shadowing, where you can spend part of a day observing a selected employee to see what his or her job is like. Joining Junior Achievement (http://www.ja.org) is another excellent way to get involved with local businesses and learn about how they work. Finally, take every opportunity to work with computers, since computer skills are vital to today's business world.

EMPLOYERS

There are approximately 3 million general managers and executives employed in the United States. These jobs exist in every industry. However, approximately 60 percent are in the manufacturing, retail, and service industries. In a 1998 survey of members of the American Management Association, 42.6 percent of the 4,585 participants worked in manufacturing. Approximately 32 percent worked in the for-profit services industry.

Virtually every business in the United States has some form of managerial positions. Obviously, the larger the company is, the more managerial positions it is likely to have. Another factor is the geographical territory covered by the business. Companies doing business in larger geographical territories are likely to have more managerial positions than those with smaller territories.

STARTING OUT

Generally you will need a college degree, although many retail stores, grocery stores, and restaurants hire promising applicants who have only a high school diploma. Job seekers usually apply directly to the manager of such places. Your college placement office is often the best place to start looking for these positions. A number of listings can also be found in newspaper help wanted ads.

Many organizations have management-trainee programs that college graduates can enter. Such programs are advertised at college career fairs or through college job placement services. However, these management-trainee positions in business and government are often filled by employees who already work for the organization and who have demonstrated management potential. Jeff Bowe suggests researching the industry you are interested in to find out what might be the best point of entry for that field. "I came into the printing company through customer service, which is a good point of entry because it's one of the easiest things to learn," he says. "Although it requires more technical know-how now than it did then, customer service is still not a bad entry point for this industry."

ADVANCEMENT

Most business management and top executive positions are filled by experienced lower level managers and executives who display valuable managerial traits, such as leadership, self-confidence, creativity, motivation, decisiveness, and flexibility. In small firms advancement to a higher management position may come slowly, while promotions may occur more quickly in larger firms.

An employee can accelerate his or her advancement by participating in different kinds of educational programs available for managers. These are often paid for by the organization. Company training programs broaden knowledge of company policy and operations. Training programs sponsored by industry and trade associations and continuing education courses in colleges and universities can familiarize managers with the latest developments in management techniques. In recent years, large numbers of middle managers were laid off as companies streamlined operations. Competition for jobs is keen, and business managers committed to improving their knowledge of the field and of related disciplines—especially computer information systems—will have the best opportunities for advancement.

Business managers may advance to executive or administrative vice president. Vice presidents may advance to peak corporate positions such as president or chief executive officer. Presidents and chief executive officers, upon retirement, may become members of the board of directors of one or more firms. Sometimes business managers establish their own firms.

EARNINGS

Salary levels for business managers vary substantially, depending upon the level of responsibility, length of service, and type, size, and location of the organization. Top-level managers in large firms can earn much more than their counterparts in small firms. Also, salaries in large metropolitan areas, such as New York City, are higher than those in smaller cities.

According to the U.S. Department of Labor, general managers had a median yearly income of $61,160 in 2000. To show the range of earnings for general managers, however, the Department notes that those in the computer and data processing industry had an annual median of $101,340; those in public relations, $84,610; and those at eating and drinking establishments, $38,710.

Chief executives earned a median of $113,810 annually in 2000. And again, salaries varied by industry. For example, the median yearly salary for those in management and public relations was $136,760, while those at commercial banks earned a median of $120,840. A survey by Abbott, Langer, & Associates found that chief executives working for nonprofits had a median yearly salary of $75,000 in 2000. Some executives, however, earn hundreds of thousands of dollars more than this annually.

Benefit and compensation packages for business managers are usually excellent, and may even include such things as bonuses, stock awards, company-paid insurance premiums, use of company cars, paid country club memberships, expense accounts, and gener-ous retirement benefits.

WORK ENVIRONMENT
Business managers are provided with comfortable offices near the departments they direct. Top executives may have spacious, lavish offices and may enjoy such privileges as executive dining rooms, com-pany cars, country club memberships, and liberal expense accounts.

Managers often travel between national, regional, and local offices. Top executives may travel to meet with executives in other corporations, both within the United States and abroad. Meetings and conferences sponsored by industries and associations occur reg-ularly and provide invaluable opportunities to meet with peers and keep up with the latest developments. In large corporations, job transfers between the parent company and its local offices or sub-sidiaries are common.

Business managers often work long hours under intense pres-sure to meet, for example, production and marketing goals. Jeff Bowe's average workweek consists of 55 to 60 hours at the office. This is not uncommon—in fact, some executive spend up to 80 hours working each week. These long hours limit time available for fam-ily and leisure activities.

OUTLOOK
Overall, employment of business managers and executives is expected to grow about as fast as the average, according to the U.S. Bureau of Labor Statistics. Many job openings will be the result of managers being promoted to better positions, retiring, or leaving their positions to start their own businesses. Even so, the compen-sation and prestige of these positions make them highly sought-after, and competition to fill openings will be intense.

Projected employment growth varies by industry. For example, employment in the service industry, particularly business services, should increase faster than the average, while employment in some manufacturing industries is expected to decline.

The outlook for business managers is closely tied to the overall economy. When the economy is good, businesses expand both in terms of their output and the number of people they employ, which creates a need for more managers. In economic downturns, busi-nesses often lay off employees and cut back on production, which lessens the need for managers.

FOR MORE INFORMATION

For news about management trends, resources on career information and finding a job, and an online job bank, contact:
American Management Association
1601 Broadway
New York, NY 10019-7420
Tel: 800-262-9699
http://www.amanet.org

For brochures on careers in management for women, contact:
Association for Women in Management
927 15th Street, NW, Suite 1000
Washington, DC 20005
Tel: 202-659-6364
Email: awm@benefits.net
http://www.womens.org

For information about programs for students in kindergarten through high school, and information on local chapters, contact:
Junior Achievement
One Education Way
Colorado Springs, CO 80906
Tel: 719-540-8000
Email: newmedia@ja.org
http://www.ja.org

For a brochure on management as a career, contact:
National Management Association
2210 Arbor Boulevard
Dayton, OH 45439
Tel: 937-294-0421
Email: nma@nma1.org
http://nma1.org

BUSINESS TEACHERS

QUICK FACTS

School Subjects
Business
English
Speech

Personal Skills
Communication/ideas
Helping/teaching

Work Environment
Primarily indoors
Primarily one location

Minimum Education Level
Bachelor's degree (middle
and secondary teachers)
Master's degree (college
professors)

Salary Range
$26,610 to $54,280 to
$100,000+

Certification or Licensing
Required by all states
(middle and secondary
teachers)
None available (college
professors)

Outlook
Faster than the average

DOT
090, 091

GOE
11.02.01

NOC
4121, 4141

O*NET-SOC
25-1063.00, 25-1011.00,
25-2022.0

OVERVIEW

Business teachers instruct students about business principles and theories. They may teach specialties such as business management, accounting, economics, business communications, business mathematics, international business, finance, labor relations and personnel management, marketing, and human resources. They develop teaching outlines and lesson plans, give lectures, facilitate discussions and activities, keep class attendance records, assign homework, and evaluate student progress. Business teachers employed in secondary schools and colleges usually teach classes that focus strictly on business or a business specialty. Middle school teachers may offer instruction on business-related issues as just one of many classes they teach during their school days.

HISTORY

Basic business skills were first taught to children in the New World in the Plymouth Colony in 1635. But until almost two hundred years later, the typical educational path for those interested in business was through an apprenticeship. Young boys who were interested in business education left their traditional schools to enter into apprenticeships in offices and stores. The business owners taught their apprentices basic math, shorthand, and bookkeeping skills, with the apprentices working an allotted time for the business owner in exchange for their training. In 1749, Franklin's Academy was established in Philadelphia. It is considered the forerunner of the modern high school. The Academy was divided into three departments: the Latin School, the English School, and the Mathematical School, which taught business subjects to young students. The first private business schools were created in the early 1830s. These schools offered instruction in bookkeeping and penmanship. It wasn't until 1862 that business education (bookkeeping and shorthand skills) became an accepted part of public high school curriculum. The Wharton School of Finance and Commerce, the oldest college-level school of business, was established at the University of Pennsylvania in 1881. This and other early business colleges focused on preparing students for managerial and executive training. Business teacher education programs began in the late 1890s. Today, the University of Wisconsin-Whitewater offers the oldest, continuously operating business teacher education program in the United States.

THE JOB

Middle and high school business teachers begin their day early in the morning. Before class, they respond to mail, email, or telephone messages; organize their teaching material; and meet with students who have questions about material taught in recent classes. They might also meet with fellow faculty or department heads to discuss coursework, testing, or other issues.

Once in class, business teachers use a variety of teaching methods to convey information to their students. They spend a great deal of time lecturing, but they also facilitate student discussion and develop projects and activities to interest the students in the subject. They show films and videos, use computers and the Internet, and bring in guest speakers. They assign essays, presentations, and other projects. Each individual subject calls upon particular approaches, and may involve computer labs, role-playing exercises, and field trips.

Outside of the classroom, middle and high school business teachers prepare lectures, lesson plans, and exams. They evaluate student work and calculate grades. In the process of planning their class, business teachers read textbooks and workbooks to determine reading assignments; photocopy notes, articles, and other handouts; and develop grading policies. They also continue to study alternative and traditional teaching methods to hone their skills. They prepare students for special events and conferences and submit student work to competitions. Some business teachers also have the opportunity for extracurricular work as athletic coaches or business club advisers.

College business professors teach at junior colleges or at four-year colleges and universities. At four-year institutions, most faculty members are *assistant professors, associate professors*, or *full professors.* These three types of professorships differ in regards to status, job responsibilities, and salary.

College business professors' most important responsibility is to teach students. Their role within a college department will determine the level of courses they teach and the number of courses per semester. Most professors work with students at all levels, from college freshmen to graduate students. They may head several classes a semester or only a few a year. Some of their classes will have large enrollment, while graduate seminars may consist of only 12 or fewer students.

Though college business professors may spend fewer than 10 hours a week in the actual classroom, they spend many hours preparing lectures and lesson plans, grading papers and exams, and preparing grade reports. They also schedule office hours during the week to be available to students outside of the lecture hall, and they meet with students individually throughout the semester. In the classroom, professors lecture, lead discussions, administer exams, and assign textbook reading and other research.

In addition to teaching, most business professors conduct research and write publications. Professors publish their research findings in various scholarly journals. They also write books based on their research or on their own knowledge and experience in the field. Publishing a significant amount of work has been the traditional standard by which assistant professors prove themselves worthy of becoming permanent, tenured faculty.

REQUIREMENTS
High School

To prepare for a career in business education, follow your school's college preparatory program and take advanced courses in business, mathematics, English, science, history, and government. Composition, journalism, and communications classes are also important for developing your writing and speaking skills.

Postsecondary Training

Your college training will depend on the level at which you plan to teach. All 50 states and the District of Columbia require public elementary education teachers to have a bachelor's degree in either education or in the subject they teach. Prospective teachers must also complete an approved training program, which combine subject and educational classes with work experience in the classroom, called student teaching.

If you want to teach at the high school level, you should major in business or business education. Similar to prospective elementary teachers, you will need to student teach in an actual classroom environment. A typical bachelor's degree program in business education will include classes on marketing, business law, business accounting, consumer education and personal finance, business communication, and computer technology.

To become a professor you will need at least one advanced degree in business. The master's degree is considered the minimum standard, and graduate work beyond the master's is usually desirable. If you hope to advance in academic rank above instructor, most institutions require a doctorate. Your graduate school program will be similar to a life of teaching—in addition to attending seminars, you'll research, prepare articles for publication, and teach some undergraduate courses.

Certification or Licensing

Elementary and secondary business teachers who work in public schools must be licensed under regulations established by the state in which they are teaching. If moving, teachers have to comply with any other regulations in their new state to be able to teach, though many states have reciprocity agreements that make it easier for teachers to change locations.

Licensure examinations test prospective teachers for competency in basic subjects such as mathematics, reading, writing, teaching, and other subject matter proficiency. In addition, many states are moving towards a performance-based evaluation for licensing. In this case, after passing the teaching examination, prospective teachers are given provisional licenses. Only after proving themselves capable in the classroom are they eligible for a full license.

Another growing trend spurred by recent teacher shortages in elementary and high schools is alternative licensure arrangements. For those who have a bachelor's degree but lack formal education courses and training in the classroom, states can issue a provisional license. These workers immediately begin teaching under the supervision of a licensed educator for one to two years and take education classes outside of their working hours. Once they have completed the required coursework and gained experience in the classroom, they are granted a full license.

Other Requirements

To be a successful business teacher (or any other kind of teacher), you must be patient, self-disciplined, and self-confident. You will also need to have excellent communication skills in order to convey your thoughts and ideas to your students. Strong people skills will be paramount, since you will need to deal with students, administrators, and other faculty members on a daily basis.

EXPLORING

To learn more about business skills, consider joining Business Professionals of America (BPA), a student membership organization that prepares students for the workforce. BPA offers competitions for middle, high school, and college students interested in developing and demonstrating their knowledge of workplace skills. For more information, visit http://www.bpa.org.

To explore a teaching career, look for leadership opportunities that involve working with children. You might find summer work as a counselor in a summer camp, as a leader of a scout troop, or as an assistant in a public park or community center. To get some firsthand teaching experience, volunteer for a peer tutoring program. Many other teaching opportunities may exist in your community. If you plan to teach younger children, look for opportunities to coach youth athletic teams or help out in day care centers.

If you are interested in becoming a college professor, spend some time on a college campus to get a sense of the environment. Write to colleges for their admissions brochures and course catalogs (or check them out online); read about the faculty members and the courses they teach. Before visiting college campuses, make arrangements to speak to business professors who teach courses that interest you. These professors may allow you to sit in on their classes and observe.

EMPLOYERS

Business teachers are employed at middle schools, high schools, community colleges, and colleges and universities. They may work at public and private institutions, vocational schools, and charter schools. Although rural areas maintain schools, more teaching positions are available in urban or suburban areas.

There are approximately 65,050 college business teachers employed in the United States, according to the U.S. Department of Labor. Employment opportunities vary based on area of study and education. With a doctorate, a number of publications, and a record of good teaching, college business professors should find opportunities in universities all across the country.

STARTING OUT

Middle and high school teachers can use their college placement offices and state departments of education to find job openings. Many local schools advertise teaching positions in newspapers. Another option is to directly contact the administration in the schools in which you'd like to work. While looking for a full-time position, you can work as a substitute teacher. In more urban areas with many schools, you may be able to find full-time substitute work.

Prospective college professors should start the process of finding a teaching position while in graduate school. You will need to develop a curriculum vitae (a detailed, academic resume), work on your academic writing, assist with research, attend conferences, and gain teaching experience and recommendations. Because of the competition for tenure-track positions, you may have to work for a few years in temporary positions. Some professional associations maintain lists of teaching opportunities in their areas. They may also make lists of applicants available to college administrators looking to fill an available position. You might also consider subscribing to *The Chronicle of Higher Education* (http://chronicle.com). This publication features job listings for college faculty, including business teachers.

ADVANCEMENT

As middle and high school teachers acquire experience or additional education, they can expect higher wages and more responsibilities.

Teachers with leadership skills and an interest in administrative work may advance to serve as principals or supervisors, though the number of these positions is limited and competition is fierce. Another move may be into higher education, teaching business classes at a college or university. For most of these positions, additional education is required.

At the college level, the normal pattern of advancement is from instructor to assistant professor, to associate professor, to full professor. All four academic ranks are concerned primarily with teaching and research. College business faculty who have an interest in and a talent for administration may be advanced to chair the business department or become a dean of their college. A few become college or university presidents or other types of administrators.

Other common career transitions are into related fields. With additional preparation, teachers can become librarians, reading specialists, or counselors. Business teachers may also decide to advance by moving out of the education arena to work in the business sector. They might get involved in corporate training, marketing, entrepreneurship, or management.

EARNINGS

There are no specific salary statistics available for middle and secondary school business teachers. The median salaries for middle and secondary school teachers were $43,570 and $43,280, respectively, in 2001, according to the Bureau of Labor Statistics.

Earnings for college business professors vary depending on their academic department, the size of the school, the type of school (public, private, women's only), and by the level of position the professor holds. The median salary for college business professors was $54,280 in 2001, according to the *2001 National Occupational Employment and Wage Estimates,* published by the U.S. Department of Labor. The lowest 10 percent earned less than $26,610, while the highest 10 percent earned $100,000 or more annually.

WORK ENVIRONMENT

Most teachers are contracted to work 10 months out of the year, with a two-month vacation during the summer. During their summer break, many continue their education to renew or upgrade their teaching licenses and earn higher salaries. Teachers in schools that operate year-round work eight-week sessions with one-week breaks in between and a five-week vacation in the winter.

Business teachers work in generally pleasant conditions, although some older schools may have poor heating or electrical systems. The work can seem confining, requiring them to remain in the classroom throughout most of the day.

Middle and high school hours are generally 8 A.M. to 3 P.M., but business teachers work more than 40 hours a week teaching, preparing for classes, grading papers, and directing extracurricular activities. Similarly, most college business teachers work more than 40 hours each week. Although they may teach only two or three classes a semester, they spend many hours preparing for lectures, examining student work, and conducting research.

OUTLOOK

According to the *Occupational Outlook Handbook (OOH)*, employment opportunities for teachers (grades K–12) are expected to grow as fast as the average for all occupations. The need to replace retiring teachers will provide many opportunities nationwide. The *OOH* predicts faster-than-average employment growth for college and university professors. College enrollment is projected to grow due to an increased number of 18- to 24-year-olds, an increased number of adults returning to college, and an increased number of foreign-born students. Job opportunities for college business professors will be even better. Retirement of current faculty members will also provide job openings. However, competition for full-time, tenure-track positions at four-year schools will be very strong.

FOR MORE INFORMATION

For information about careers, education, and union membership, contact the following organizations:

American Association of University Professors
1012 14th Street, NW, Suite 500
Washington, DC 20005
Tel: 202-737-5900
http://www.aaup.org

American Federation of Teachers
555 New Jersey Avenue, NW
Washington, DC 20001
Tel: 202-879-4400
Email: online@aft.org
http://www.aft.org

**National Council for Accreditation
   of Teacher Education**
2010 Massachusetts Avenue, NW, Suite 500
Washington, DC 20036
Tel: 202-466-7496
Email: ncate@ncate.org
http://www.ncate.org

National Education Association
1201 16th Street, NW
Washington, DC 20036
Tel: 202-833-4000
Web: http://www.nea.org

The following student membership organization offers business-related skills competitions. For more information, contact:
Business Professionals of America
5454 Cleveland Avenue
Columbus, OH 43231-4021
Tel: 800-334-2007
http://www.bpa.org

For information on professional development, contact:
National Business Education Association
1914 Association Drive
Reston, VA 20191-1596
Tel: 703-860-8300
Email: nbea@nbea.org
http://www.nbea.org

BUYERS

QUICK FACTS

School Subjects
Business
Mathematics

Personal Skills
Helping/teaching
Leadership/management

Work Environment
Primarily indoors
One location with
some travel

Minimum Education Level
High school diploma

Salary Range
$21,570 to $37,200 to
$70,750+

Certification or Licensing
Voluntary

Outlook
Decline

DOT
162

GOE
08.01.03

NOC
6233

O*NET-SOC
11-3061.00,
13-1022.00

OVERVIEW

There are two main types of *buyers*. *Wholesale buyers* purchase merchandise directly from manufacturers and resell it to retail firms, commercial establishments, and other institutions. *Retail buyers* purchase goods from wholesalers (and occasionally from manufacturers) for resale to the general public. In either case, buyers must understand their customers' needs and be able to purchase goods at an appropriate price and in sufficient quantity. Sometimes a buyer purchases a specific kind of merchandise, for example, jewelry buyers or toy buyers. *Government buyers* have similar responsibilities but need to be especially sensitive to concerns of fairness and ethics since they use public money to make their purchases. There are approximately 536,000 buyers and related workers currently working in the United States.

HISTORY

The job of the buyer has been influenced by a variety of historical changes, including the growth of large retail stores in the 20th century. In the past, store owners typically performed almost all of the business activities, including the purchase of merchandise. Large stores, in contrast, had immensely more complicated operations, requiring large numbers of specialized workers, such as sales clerks, receiving and shipping clerks, advertising managers, personnel officers, and buyers. The introduction of mass production systems at factories required more complicated planning, ordering, and scheduling of purchases. A wider range of available merchandise also called for more astute selection and purchasing techniques.

THE JOB

Wholesale and retail buyers are part of a complex system of production, distribution, and merchandising. Both are concerned with recognizing and satisfying the huge variety of consumer needs and desires. Most specialize in acquiring one or two lines of merchandise.

Retail buyers work for retail stores. They generally can be divided into two types. The first, working directly under a merchandise manager, not only purchases goods but directly supervises salespeople. When a new product appears on the shelves, for example, buyers may work with salespeople to point out its distinctive features. This type of retail buyer thus takes responsibility for the products' marketing. The second type of retail buyer is concerned only with purchasing and has no supervisory responsibilities. These buyers cooperate with the sales staff to promote maximum sales.

All retail buyers must understand the basic merchandising policies of their stores. Purchases are affected by the size of the buyer's annual budget, the kind of merchandise needed in each buying season, and trends in the market. Success in buying is directly related to the profit or loss shown by particular departments. Buyers often work with *assistant buyers,* who spend much of their time maintaining sales and inventory records.

All buyers must be experts in the merchandise that they purchase. They order goods months ahead of the expected sale date, and they must be able to predetermine marketability based upon cost, style, and competitive items. Buyers must also be well acquainted with the best sources of supply for each product they purchase.

Depending upon the location, size, and type of store, a retail buyer may deal directly with traveling salespeople (ordering from samples or catalogs), order by mail or by telephone directly from the manufacturer or wholesaler, or travel to key cities to visit merchandise showrooms and manufacturing establishments. Most use a combination of these approaches.

Buying trips to such cities as New York, Chicago, and San Francisco are an important part of the work for buyers at a larger store. For specialized products, such as glassware, china, liquors, and gloves, some buyers make yearly trips to major European production centers. Sometimes manufacturers of similar items organize trade shows to attract a number of buyers. Buying trips are difficult: A buyer may visit six to eight suppliers in a single day. The buyer must make decisions on the spot about the opportunity for profitable sale of merchandise. The important element is not how much the buyer personally likes the merchandise but about customers' taste. Most buyers operate under an annual purchasing budget for the departments they represent.

Mergers between stores and expansion of individual department stores into chains of stores have created central buying positions. *Central buyers* order in unusually large quantities. As a result, they

You Might Think It's a Waste of Time . . .

"I know I want to work in business, so why do I have to study English?" If you find yourself muttering this while studying vocabulary terms or picking the pronouns out of a sentence, take heart: Polishing your grammar and doing other homework while in high school provides you with crucial business skills.

Whether you want to sound competent in business meetings, edge out the competition in an interview, or balance a budget, good grades in English, math, science, and history will translate to good grades in your college major, and eventually to a good job in the field of business. In a time when available jobs are more scarce than they were a few years ago, the best educated candidates get the best positions. Although doing well in your major is important, prospective employers will be even more impressed by your competence in a wide variety of subjects.

have the power to develop their own set of specifications for a particular item and ask manufacturers to bid on the right to provide it. Goods purchased by central buyers may be marketed under the manufacturer's label (as is normally done) or ordered with the store's label or a chain brand name.

To meet this competition, independent stores often work with *resident buyers,* who purchase merchandise for a large number of stores. By purchasing large quantities of the same product, resident buyers can obtain the same types of discounts enjoyed by large chain stores, thereby creating savings for their customers.

Because they work with public funds and must avoid any appearance of favoritism or corruption, *government buyers* sometimes purchase merchandise through open bids. The buyer may establish a set of specifications for a product and invite private firms to bid on the job. Some government buyers are required to accept the lowest bid. Each purchase must be well documented for public scrutiny. Like other types of buyers, government buyers must be well acquainted with the products they purchase, and they must try to find the best quality products for the lowest price.

REQUIREMENTS
High School
A high school degree generally is required for entering the field of buying. Useful high school courses include mathematics, business, English, and economics.

Postsecondary Training
A college degree may not be a requirement for becoming a buyer, but it is becoming increasingly important, especially for advancement. A majority of buyers have attended college, many majoring in business. Some colleges and universities also offer majors in purchasing or materials management. Regardless of the major, useful courses in preparation for a career in buying include accounting, economics, commercial law, finance, marketing, and various business classes, such as business communications, business organization and management, and computer applications in business.

Retailing experience is helpful to gain a sense of customer tastes and witness the supply and demand process. Additional training is available through trade associations, such as the National Association of Purchasing Management, which sponsors conferences, seminars, and workshops.

Certification or Licensing

Certification, although not required, is becoming increasingly important. Various levels of certification are available through the American Purchasing Society and the National Association of Purchasing Management. To earn most certifications you must have work experience, meet education requirements, and pass written and oral exams.

Other Requirements

If you are interested in becoming a buyer, you should be organized and have excellent decision-making skills. Predicting consumer tastes and keeping stores and wholesalers appropriately stocked requires resourcefulness, good judgment, and confidence. You should also have skills in marketing to identify and promote products that will sell. Finally, leadership skills are needed to supervise assistant buyers and deal with manufacturers' representatives and store executives.

EXPLORING

One way to explore the retailing field is through part-time or summer employment in a store. A good time to look for such work is during the Christmas holiday season. Door-to-door selling is another way to gain retail experience. Occasionally experience in a retail store can be found through special high school programs.

EMPLOYERS

Buyers work for a wide variety of businesses, both wholesale and retail, as well as for government agencies. Employers range from small stores, where buying may be only one function of a manager's job, to multinational corporations, where a buyer may specialize in one type of item and buy in enormous quantity.

Of the approximately 536,000 purchasing managers, buyers, and purchasing agents employed throughout the country, more than 50 percent work in wholesale trade and manufacturing. Approximately 17 percent work in retail trade, such as for grocery stores and department stores. Others work in businesses that provide services and in government agencies.

STARTING OUT

Most buyers find their first job by applying to the personnel office of a retail establishment or wholesaler. Because knowledge of retailing is important, buyers may be required to have work experience in a store.

Most buyers begin their careers as retail sales workers. The next step may be *head of stock*. The head of stock maintains stock inventory records and keeps the merchandise in a neat and well-organized fashion both to protect its value and to permit easy access. He or she usually supervises the work of several employees. This person also works in an intermediate position between the salespeople on the floor and the buyer who provides the merchandise. The next step to becoming a buyer may be assistant buyer. For many department stores, promotion to full buyer requires this background.

Large department stores or chains operate executive training programs for college graduates who seek buying and other retail executive positions. A typical program consists of 16 successive weeks of work in a variety of departments. This on-the-job experience is supplemented by formal classroom work that most often is conducted by senior executives and training department personnel. Following this orientation, trainees are placed in junior management positions for an additional period of supervised experience and training.

ADVANCEMENT

Buyers are key employees of the stores or companies that employ them. One way they advance is through increased responsibility, such as more authority to make commitments for merchandise and more complicated buying assignments.

Buyers are sometimes promoted to *merchandise manager*, which requires them to supervise other buyers, help develop the store's merchandising policies, and coordinate buying and selling activities with related departments. Other buyers may become vice presidents in charge of merchandising or even store presidents. Because buyers learn much about retailing in their job, they are in a position to advance to top executive positions. Some buyers use their knowledge of retailing and the contacts they have developed with suppliers to set up their own businesses.

EARNINGS

How much a buyer earns depends on various factors, including the employer's sales volume. Mass merchandisers, such as discount or chain department stores, pay among the highest salaries.

The U.S. Department of Labor reports the median annual income for wholesale and retail buyers was $37,200 in 2000. The lowest paid 10 percent of these buyers made less than $21,570 yearly, and at the other end of the pay range, the highest paid 10 percent earned more than $70,750 annually. The Department also reports that buyers working for the federal government had median annual earnings of $53,010 in 2000.

Most buyers receive the usual benefits, such as vacation, sick leave, life and health insurance, and pension plans. Retail buyers may receive cash bonuses for their work and may also receive discounts on merchandise they purchase from their employer.

WORK ENVIRONMENT

Buyers work in a dynamic and sometimes stressful atmosphere. They must make important decisions on an hourly basis. The results of their work, both successes and failures, show up quickly on the profit and loss statement.

Buyers frequently work long or irregular hours. Evening and weekend hours are common, especially during the holiday season, when the retail field is at its busiest. Extra hours may be required to bring records up to date, for example, or to review stock and to become familiar with the store's overall marketing design for the coming season. Travel may also be a regular part of a buyer's job, possibly requiring several days away from home each month.

Although buyers must sometimes work under pressure, they usually work in pleasant, well-lit environments. They also benefit from having a diverse set of responsibilities.

OUTLOOK

According to the U.S. Department of Labor, employment of wholesale and retail buyers is projected to decline through the next several years. Reasons for this decrease include the large number of business mergers and acquisitions, which results in the blending of buying departments and the elimination of redundant jobs. In addition, the use of computers, which increases efficiency, and the trend of some large retail companies to centralize their operations will both contribute to fewer new jobs for buyers. Some job openings will result from the need to hire replacement workers for those who leave the field.

FOR MORE INFORMATION

For career information, contact:
American Purchasing Society
8 East Galena Boulevard, Suite 203
Aurora, IL 60506
Tel: 630-859-0250
http://www.american-purchasing.com

For information on the magazine, Your Future Purchasing Career, *lists of colleges with purchasing programs, and interviews with people in the field, contact the ISM:*
Institute for Supply Management (ISM)
PO Box 22160
Tempe, AZ 85285-2160
Tel: 800-888-6276
http://www.ism.ws

For an information packet on purchasing careers in the government, contact:
National Institute of Government Purchasing
151 Spring Street
Herndon, VA 20170-5223
Tel: 800-367-6447
http://www.nigp.org

For materials on educational programs in the retail industry, contact:
National Retail Federation
325 7th Street, NW, Suite 1100
Washington, DC 20004
Tel: 800-673-4692
http://www.nrf.com

CITY MANAGERS

QUICK FACTS

School Subjects Business Government Mathematics	**Certification or Licensing** None available
	Outlook Little change or more slowly than the average
Personal Skills Communication/ideas Leadership/management	**DOT** 188
Work Environment Primarily indoors Primarily multiple locations	**GOE** 11.05.03
Minimum Education Level Bachelor's degree	**NOC** 0414
Salary Range $50,860 to $78,840 to $174,600	**O*NET-SOC** 11-1011.01

OVERVIEW

A *city manager* is an administrator who coordinates the day-to-day running of a local government. Usually an appointed position, the manager directs the administration of city or county government in accordance with the policies determined by the city council or other elected authority.

HISTORY

There have been all sorts of governments and political theories in our world's history, and much of the structure of U.S. government is based on the theories and practices of other nations. The *council-manager* form of government, however, is truly American in origin. With government reforms of the early 1900s came government managers. Before the reform, city councils or boards of aldermen ran cities. Because of rigged elections and other corruption by aldermen, a mayoral form of government was brought into practice. The council-manager form of government also evolved. Though a mayor is elected and holds political power, the council appoints the city manager. When the elected officials develop policies, the city managers use their administrative and management skills to put these policies into action. Some Southern towns began to develop council-manager forms of government as early as 1908; Dayton, Ohio, became the first large city to put the council-manager form into place in 1913. According to the International City/County Management Association (ICMA), 3,312 municipalities (communities with 2,500 people or more) operate in the council-manager form today. More than 80.4 million people live in these communities.

THE JOB

Have more bus routes been added to provide transportation to a new shopping area? Has the small park near the lake been cleaned up so children can play safely there? Will a new performing arts center be built downtown? These are the kinds of questions a city manager faces on the job. Even the smallest community has hundreds of concerns, from quality day care options for its citizens to proper housing for the elderly, from maintaining strong law enforcement in the city to preserving the surrounding environment. Every day, local newspapers feature all the changes underway in their communities. The mayor introduces these developments, speaking to reporters and appearing on the TV news and at city meetings. But, it's the city manager who works behind the scenes to put these changes into effect. A city manager uses managerial experience and skills to determine what programs are needed in the community, to design the programs, and to implement them. The council-manager form of government is somewhat like a smooth-running business: The executives make the decisions about a company, while the managers see that these decisions are put into practice efficiently and effectively.

A city has many different departments in place to collect and disburse taxes, enforce laws, maintain public health and a ready fire department, construct public works such as parks and other recreational facilities, and purchase supplies and equipment. The city manager prepares budgets of the costs of these services and submits estimates to the elected officials for approval. The manager is also responsible for providing reports of ongoing and completed work and projects to the representatives of the residents. The city manager keeps in touch with the community in order to understand what is most important to the people of the city. A city manager also needs to stay several steps ahead of local trends in order to plan for growth, population expansion, and public services. To oversee planning for population growth, crime prevention, street repairs, law enforcement, and pollution and traffic management problems, the manager prepares proposals and recommends zoning regulations. The manager then presents these proposals at meetings of the elected authorities as well as at public meetings of citizens.

In addition to developing plans and budgets, city managers meet with private groups and individuals who represent special interests. Managers explain programs, policies, and projects. They may also seek to enlist the aid of citizen groups in a variety of projects that help the public as a whole. They work closely with urban planners to coordinate new and existing programs. In smaller cities that have no planning staff, this work may be done entirely by the manager. Additional staff may be provided for the city manager of a large city, including an assistant city manager, department head assistants, administrative assistants, and management analysts.

A city manager's staff comprises a variety of titles and responsibilities. Changes in administration are studied and recommended by *management analysts*. Administrative and staff work, such as compiling statistics and planning work procedures, is done by *administrative assistants*, also called *executive assistants*. *Department head assistants* may work in several areas, such as law enforcement, finance, or law, but they are generally responsible for just one area. *Assistant city managers* are responsible for specific projects, such as developing the annual budget, as well as organizing and coordinating programs. They may supervise city employees and perform other administrative tasks, such as answering correspondence, receiving visitors, preparing reports, and monitoring programs.

REQUIREMENTS
High School

Take courses in government and social studies to learn about the nature of cities and counties. Math and business courses are important because you'll be working with budgets and statistics and preparing financial reports. English and composition courses and speech and debate teams are also very important, as you'll need good communication skills for presenting your thoughts and ideas to policy-makers, special interest groups, and the community. Computer science is an important tool in any administrative profession. Take journalism courses and report for your school newspaper to learn about research and conducting polls and surveys.

Postsecondary Training

You'll need at least a bachelor's degree to work as a city manager. As an undergraduate, you'll major in such programs as public administration, political science, sociology, or business. The ICMA notes that an increasing number of local governments are requiring job candidates for manager positions to have master's degrees in public administration or business. Programs resulting in a master's of public administration (M.P.A) degree are available all across the country; some schools offer dual degrees, allowing you to pursue a master's of business administration or master's of social work along with the M.P.A. The National Association of Schools of Public Affairs and Administration (NASPAA) offers voluntary accreditation to schools with degree programs in public affairs and administration. The association has a membership of approximately 250 schools, of which slightly more than half are accredited. The NASPAA website (http://www.naspaa.org) provides a roster of accredited programs, which is updated annually.

Course work in public administration programs covers topics such as finance, budgeting, municipal law, legal issues, personnel management, and the political aspects of urban problems. Degree requirements in some schools also include completion of an internship program in a city manager's office that may last from six months to a year, during which time the degree candidate observes local government operations and does research under the direct supervision of the city manager.

People planning to enter city management positions frequently must pass civil service examinations. This is one way to become eligible for appointments to local government. Other requirements will vary from place to place. Most positions require knowledge of computerized tax and utility billing, electronic traffic control, and applications of systems analysis to urban problems.

Other Requirements

"You have to have the will, desire, and strength to want to lead an organization," says Michael Roberto, former city manager of Clearwater, Florida. He emphasizes that, as manager, you're the person held primarily responsible for the administration of the city. You should have a thick skin: "You'll be yelled at a lot," he says. In addition to handling the complaints, you must be able to handle the stress of the job and the long and frequently unpredictable hours that are required. "But you're only limited by your dreams in what you can create," Roberto says.

You'll need to be decisive, confident, and staunch in making managerial decisions. You need to be skilled at solving problems and flexible enough to consider the ideas of others. Managers must also have a knack for working with people, have the ability to negotiate and tactfully debate with co-workers and other officials, and be able to listen to the opinions and concerns of the people they represent.

EXPLORING
You can learn about public administration by becoming involved in student government or by serving as an officer for a school club, such as a business or Internet club. A summer job in a local government office can give you a lot of insight into the workings of a city. Work for the school newspaper and you'll learn about budgets, projects, and school administrators. An internship with a local newspaper or radio or TV station may give you the opportunity to interview the mayor, council members, and the city manager about city administration.

EMPLOYERS
Cities large and small have council-manager forms of government and require city managers for the administration of policies and programs. Counties and suburbs also have managers. The ICMA reports that 63 percent of U.S. cities with a population of 25,000 or more use a council-manager form of government. Those with a master's degree in public administration may find work as a city planner. Other employment possibilities include working as an administrator of a hospital or an association, or in private industry. Some professionals with this background work as instructors for undergraduate public administration programs at universities or community colleges.

STARTING OUT
In addition to college internships with local public administrators, you can apply to the ICMA internship programs. There is heavy competition for these internship positions because they often lead to full-time work. The ICMA also publishes a newsletter announcing job vacancies. Nearly all city managers begin as management assistants. As a new graduate, you'll work as a management analyst or administrative assistant to city managers for several years to gain experience in solving urban problems, coordinating public services, and applying management techniques. Or you may work in a specific department such as finance, public works, civil engineering, or planning. You'll acquire supervisory skills and also work as an

assistant city manager or department head assistant. After a few years of competent service, you may be hired to manage a community.

Other avenues of potential employment include listings in the job sections of newspapers and professional journals. There are also private firms that specialize in filling government job openings. Those willing to relocate to smaller cities at lower salaries should have better job opportunities.

ADVANCEMENT

An assistant to a city manager is gradually given more responsibilities and assignments as he or she gains experience. At least five years of experience are generally necessary to compete for the position of city manager. City managers are often employed in small cities at first, and during their careers they may seek and obtain appointments in growing cities. Experienced managers may become heads of regional government councils; others may serve several small jurisdictions at one time. Those city managers with a master's degree in business management, political science, urban planning, or law stand the best chance for employment.

EARNINGS

City managers' earnings vary according to such factors as the size of the city, the city's geographical location, and the manager's education and experience. The ICMA reports that the annual income for city managers averaged approximately $78,840 in 2000. The organization also notes that salaries ranged from a low of approximately $50,860 annually to a high of approximately $174,600 during that same period.

Salaries are set by the city council, and good city managers are sometimes given higher than average pay as an incentive to keep them from seeking more lucrative opportunities. Benefits for city managers include paid vacations, health insurance, sick leave, and retirement plans. Cities may also pay travel and moving expenses and provide a city car or a car allowance.

WORK ENVIRONMENT

Typically a city manager has an office and possibly a trained staff to assist him or her. But a city manager also spends many hours attending meetings. To provide information to citizens on current government operations or to advocate certain programs, the manager frequently appears at public meetings and other civic functions and often visits government departments and inspects work sites. A city manager often works overtime at night and on weekends reading and writing reports or finishing paperwork. The manager also needs to attend dinners and evening events and go out of town for conferences. Any extra days worked on weekends are usually compensated for in vacation time or additional pay. "The long hours," Michael Roberto says, "can be tough on your home life, tough on your family." A city manager can be called at any hour of the day or night in times of crisis. Managers must be prepared for sometimes stressful interactions with co-workers and constituents, as well as the acclaim that comes to them for completing a job successfully or solving a particularly complex problem. "You're scrutinized by the press," Roberto says, and he emphasizes that a manager shouldn't be too affected by the coverage, whether negative or positive.

OUTLOOK

Although city management is a growing profession, the field is still relatively small. The U.S. Department of Labor predicts that employment at the local government level will increase by approximately 11 percent through 2010, which is at a rate somewhat slower than the average for all occupations. One reason for this is that few new governments are likely to form and, therefore, there will be few new job openings. Applicants with only a bachelor's degree will have the most difficulty finding employment. Even an entry-level job often requires an advanced degree. The ICMA provides funds to those cities wanting to establish the council-manager form of government, as well as to cities where the form is threatened.

City managers are finding that they are sharing more and more of their authority with many different groups, such as unions and special interest groups. "This dilutes the system," Michael Roberto says, "and makes it harder to manage."

The issues that affect a city are constantly changing. Future city managers will need to focus on clean air regulations, promoting diversity, providing affordable housing, creating new policing methods, and revitalizing old downtown areas.

FOR MORE INFORMATION

For statistics and internship opportunities, contact:
International City/County Management Association
777 North Capitol Street, NE, Suite 500
Washington, DC 20002-4201
Tel: 202-289-4262
http://www.icma.org

For more information on finding a school, the M.P.A. degree, and public affairs work, contact:

National Association of Schools of Public Affairs and Administration
1120 G Street, NW, Suite 730
Washington, DC 20005
Tel: 202-628-8965
Email: naspaa@naspaa.org
http://www.naspaa.org

For information on policy and legislative issues, membership, and conferences, contact:

National League of Cities
1301 Pennsylvania Avenue, NW, Suite 550
Washington, DC 20004
Tel: 202-626-3000
http://www.nlc.org

CREDIT ANALYSTS

QUICK FACTS

School Subjects Business Computer science Mathematics	**Certification or Licensing** None available
	Outlook About as fast as the average
Personal Skills Communication/ideas Leadership/management	**DOT** 160
Work Environment Primarily indoors Primarily one location	**GOE** 07.01.04
Minimum Education Level Bachelor's degree	**NOC** N/A
Salary Range $28,475 to $47,174 to $107,940+	**O*NET-SOC** 13-2041.00

OVERVIEW

Credit analysts analyze financial information to evaluate the amount of risk involved in lending money to businesses or individuals. They contact banks, credit associations, and others to obtain credit information and prepare a written report of findings used to recommend credit limits. There are approximately 60,000 credit analysts employed in the United States.

HISTORY

Only 50 or 75 years ago, lending money was based mainly on a person's reputation. Money was lent after a borrower talked with friends and business acquaintances. Now, of course, much more financial background information is demanded. The use of credit cards and other forms of borrowing has skyrocketed in the last several years, and today only accepted forms of accounting are used to determine if a loan applicant is a good risk. As business and financial institutions have grown more complex, the demand for professional credit analysis has also expanded.

THE JOB

Credit analysts typically concentrate on one of two different areas. *Commercial* and *business analysts* evaluate risks in business loans; *consumer credit analysts* evaluate personal loan risks. In both cases an analyst studies financial documents such as a statement of assets and liabilities submitted by the person or company seeking the loan and consults with banks and other financial institutions that have had previous financial relationships with the applicant. Credit analysts prepare, analyze, and approve loan requests and help borrowers fill out applications.

The scope of work involved in a credit check depends in large part on the size and type of the loan requested. A background check on a $3,000 car loan, for example, is much less detailed than on a $400,000 commercial improvement loan for an expanding business. In both cases, financial statements and applicants will be checked by the credit analyst, but the larger loan will entail a much closer look at economic trends to determine if there is a market for the product being produced and the likelihood of the business failing. Because of these responsibilities, many credit analysts work solely with commercial loans.

In studying a commercial loan application, a credit analyst is interested in determining if the business or corporation is well managed and financially secure and if the existing economic climate is favorable for the operation's success. To do this, a credit analyst examines balance sheets and operating statements to determine the assets and liabilities of a company, its net sales, and its profits or losses. An analyst must be familiar with accounting and bookkeeping methods to ensure that the applicant company is operating under accepted accounting principles. A background check of the applicant company's leading officials is also done to determine if they personally have any outstanding loans. An on-site visit by the analyst may also be necessary to compare how the company's operations stack up against those of its competitors.

Analyzing economic trends to determine market conditions is another responsibility of the credit analyst. To do this, the credit analyst computes dozens of ratios to show how successful the company is in relation to similar businesses. Profit-and-loss statements, collection procedures, and a host of other factors are analyzed. This ratio analysis can also be used to measure how successful a particular industry is likely to be, given existing market considerations. Computer programs are used to highlight economic trends and interpret other important data.

The credit analyst always provides a findings report to bank executives. This report includes a complete financial history of the applicant and usually concludes with a recommendation on the loan amount, if any, that should be advanced.

REQUIREMENTS
High School

If you are interested in this career, take courses in mathematics, economics, business, and accounting in high school. You should also take English courses to develop sound oral and written language skills. Computer courses will help you to become computer literate, learn software programs, understand their applications to particular fields, and gain familiarity with accessing electronic information.

Postsecondary Training

Credit analysts usually have at least a bachelor's degree in accounting, finance, or business administration. Those who want to move up in the field often go on to obtain master's degrees in one of these subjects. Undergraduate course work should include business management, economics, statistics, and accounting. In addition, keep honing your computer skills. Some employers provide new hires with on-the-job training involving both classroom work and hands-on experience.

Other Requirements

To be a credit analyst, you should have an aptitude for mathematics and be adept at organizing, assessing, and reporting data. You must be able to analyze complex problems and devise resourceful solutions. Credit analysts also need strong interpersonal skills. You must be able to interview loan applicants and communicate effectively, establish solid working relationships with customers as well as co-workers, and clearly relate the results of your work.

EXPLORING

For the latest information on the credit management industry, check out newsgroups and Web pages on the Internet that are related to this field. The Credit Management Information and Support website, http://www.creditworthy.com, offers informative interviews with people in the field and advice for breaking into the business. This site also has a section that describes educational resources and offers an online course on the basics of business credit. The National Association of Credit Management website, http://www.nacm.org, has links to other industry sites.

Consider a position as treasurer for student council or other student-run organizations. This will introduce you to the responsibilities associated with managing money. Or explore a part-time job as a bank clerk, teller, or customer service representative that will familiarize you with banking procedures. This is also a good way to network with professionals in the banking field. Various clubs and organizations may have opportunities for volunteers to develop experience working with budgets and financial statements. Join or start a business club at your school. Local institutions and small or single-owner businesses may welcome students interested in learning more about financial operations.

EMPLOYERS

Credit analysts are employed by banks, credit unions, credit agencies, business credit institutions, credit bureaus, corporations, and loan companies. They are also employed by hotels, hospitals, and department stores. Approximately 60,000 credit analysts are employed in the United States.

STARTING OUT

Although some people enter the field with a high school diploma or two-year degree, most entry-level positions go to college graduates with degrees in fields such as accounting, finance, economics, and business administration. Credit analysts receive much of their formal training and learn specific procedures and requirements on the job. Many employees also rise through the ranks via other positions such as teller or customer service representative prior to becoming a credit analyst. Newspaper want ads, school placement services, and direct application to specific employers are all ways of tracking down that first job.

ADVANCEMENT

Credit analysts generally advance to supervisory positions. However, promotion and salary potential are limited, and many employees often choose to leave a company for better paying positions elsewhere. After three to five years of credit work, a skilled credit analyst can expect a promotion to credit manager and ultimately chief credit executive. Responsibilities grow to include training other credit personnel, coordinating the credit department with other internal operations, and managing relations with customers and financial institutions.

EARNINGS

Salaries of credit analysts depend on the individual's experience and education. The size of the financial institution is also a determining factor: large banks tend to pay more than smaller operations. Salaries also increase with the number of years in the field and with a particular company. According to the U.S. Bureau of Labor Statistics' *2001 National Occupational Employment and Wage Estimates,* credit analysts had a mean annual income of $47,174 in 2001. Salary.com, a Web-based recruiting firm providing salary information, reports that in 2002 a credit analyst just starting out earned approximately $28,475 per year and with up to two years' experience may earn a median annual salary of $32,895. Salary.com also reports that analysts with at least five years of experience had a median annual income of approximately $44,920. Senior credit analysts or credit analysis managers had median earnings of approximately $84,725 nationwide, with the top quarter earning about $107,940 or more per year. Those in senior positions often have advanced degrees.

As an added perk, many banks offer their credit analysts free checking privileges and lower interest rates on personal loans. Other benefits include health insurance, sick and vacation pay, and retirement plans.

WORK ENVIRONMENT

Most credit analysts work in typical corporate office settings that are well lighted and air conditioned in the summertime. Credit analysts can expect to work a 40-hour week, but they may have to put in overtime if a project has a tight deadline. A commercial credit analyst may have to travel to the business or corporation that is seeking a loan in order to prepare the agreement. Credit analysts can expect heavy caseloads. Respondents to the annual survey of the National Association of Credit Management reported handling 250 to 2,000 active accounts per year.

A credit analyst should be able to spend long hours behind a desk quietly reading and analyzing financial reports. Attention to detail is critical. Credit analysts can expect to work in high-pressure situations, with loans of millions of dollars dependent on their analysis.

OUTLOOK

As the field of cash management grows along with the economy and the population, banks and other financial institutions will need to hire credit analysts. According to the U.S. Department of Labor, employment in this field is expected to grow about as fast as the average. Credit analysts are crucial to the success and profitability of banks, and the number, variety, and complexity of credit applications are on the rise. Opportunities should be best for those with strong educational backgrounds and those living in urban areas that tend to have the largest and greatest number of banks and other financial institutions.

Credit analysts are particularly busy when interest rates drop and applications surge. Job security is influenced by the local economy and business climate. However, loans are a major source of income for banks, and credit officers are less likely (than most workers) to lose their jobs in an economic downturn.

Information technology is affecting the field of credit analysis as public financial information, as well as economic and market research, becomes more accessible via the Internet. Credit professionals now have a broader range of data available upon which to base decisions.

FOR MORE INFORMATION

For general banking industry information, contact:
American Bankers Association
1120 Connecticut Avenue, NW
Washington, DC 20036
Tel: 800-226-5377
http://www.aba.com

For publications and information on continuing education and training programs for financial institution workers, contact:
Bank Administration Institute
One North Franklin, Suite 1000
Chicago, IL 60606-3421
Tel: 800-224-9889
Email: info@bai.org
http://www.bai.org

For information on the industry, contact:
Credit Research Foundation
8840 Columbia 100 Parkway
Columbia, MD 21045
Tel: 410-740-5499
Email: crf_info@crfonline.org
http://www.crfonline.org

For information on certification, continuing education, and the banking and credit industry, contact:
National Association of Credit Management
8840 Columbia 100 Parkway
Columbia, MD 21045
Tel: 410-740-5560
Email: nacm_info@nacm.org
http://www.nacm.org

CULTURAL ADVISERS

QUICK FACTS

School Subjects	Certification or Licensing
Business	None available
Foreign language	**Outlook**
Speech	Faster than the
Personal Skills	average
Communication/ideas	**DOT**
Helping/teaching	N/A
Work Environment	**GOE**
Primarily indoors	N/A
Primarily multiple locations	**NOC**
Minimum Education Level	N/A
Bachelor's degree	**O*NET-SOC**
Salary Range	N/A
$65 to $100 to $265 per hour	

OVERVIEW

Cultural advisers, also known as *bilingual consultants*, work with businesses and organizations to help them communicate effectively with others who are from different cultural and language backgrounds. Cultural advisers usually have a specialty such as business management, banking, education, or computer technology. They help bridge both language and cultural barriers in our increasingly global business world.

HISTORY

Communication has always been a challenge when cultures come into contact with each other. In the early days of the United States, settlers and explorers relied on interpreters to assist them. One of those famous interpreters, Sacajawea (1787–c. 1812), a member of the Shoshone Indian tribe, was a precursor of the cultural advisers of today. As she helped guide Meriwether Lewis (1774–1809) and

William Clark (1770–1838) across the West to the Pacific Ocean, she acted as interpreter when they encountered Native American tribes. She also helped the explorers adapt to the different cultures and customs.

Today's cultural advisers work with companies or organizations that need to communicate effectively and do business with other cultures. Cultural advisers are becoming even more valuable because it is now relatively quick and easy to travel throughout the world. Each year, more trade barriers are broken down by legislation, such as the North American Free Trade Agreement, implemented in 1994.

THE JOB

Cultural advisers work to bridge gaps in communication and culture. They usually have a second specialty that is complimented by their bilingual skills. For example, a banking and finance expert who has traveled extensively in Japan and is familiar with Japanese language and customs would have the marketable skills to become a cultural adviser for American companies interested in doing business in Japan.

Cultural advisers work in a wide variety of settings. They may hold full-time staff positions with organizations or they may work as independent consultants providing services to a number of clients. Cultural advisers work in education. They provide translation services and help foreign or immigrant students adjust to a new culture. They also educate teachers and administrators to make them aware of cultural differences, so that programs and classes can be adapted to include everyone. Colleges and universities that have large international student populations often have cultural advisers on staff.

In industry, cultural advisers train workers in safety procedures and worker rights. The health care industry benefits from the use of advisers to communicate with non-English-speaking patients. Cultural advisers also hold training sessions for health care professionals to teach them how to better understand and instruct their patients.

Large business enterprises that have overseas interests hire cultural advisers to research new markets and help with negotiations. Some advisers work primarily in employment, finding foreign experts to work for American businesses or finding overseas jobs for American workers. In addition to advising American business leaders, cultural advisers sometimes work with foreign entities who

Best Cities for a Job in Business in 2002

1. San Diego, CA	9. Brownsville, TX
2. Santa Rosa, CA	10. Orange County, CA
3. Las Vegas, NV	11. Riverside, CA
4. Ventura, CA	12. West Palm Beach, FL
5. McAllen, TX	13. Boulder, CO
6. Boise, ID	14. Dallas, TX
7. San Luis Obispo, CA	15. Vallejo, CA
8. Oakland, CA	

Source: *Forbes* and Milken Institute

want to do business in the United States. They provide English language instruction and training in American business practices.

Cultural advisers also work in the legal system, the media, advertising, the travel industry, social services, and government agencies. Whatever the setting, cultural advisers help their clients—foreign and American—understand and respect other cultures and communicate effectively with each other.

REQUIREMENTS
High School

Classes in business, speech, and foreign language will give you an excellent head start to becoming a cultural adviser. In addition, take other classes in your high school's college prep curriculum. These courses should include history, mathematics, sciences, and English. Accounting classes and computer science classes will also help prepare you for working in business.

Postsecondary Training

If you are planning a career as a cultural adviser, fluency in two or more languages is a requirement, so college courses in those languages are necessary. Courses in business, world history, world geography, and sociology would be useful as well. You will need at least a bachelor's degree to find work as a cultural adviser, and you may want to consider pursuing a master's degree to have more job opportunities. Many universities offer programs in cultural studies, and there are master's programs that offer a concentration in international business.

Take advantage of every opportunity to learn about the people and area you want to work with, whether Latin America, Europe, Japan, or another region or country. Studying abroad for a semester or year is also recommended.

Other Requirements

Cultural sensitivity is the number one requirement for an adviser. Knowing the history, culture, and social conventions of a people as well as the language is a very important part of the job. Also, expertise in another area, such as business, education, law, or computers, is necessary to be a cultural adviser.

EXPLORING

A good way to explore this field is to join one of your high school's foreign language clubs. In addition to using the foreign language, these clubs often have activities related to the culture where the language is spoken. You may also find it helpful to join your school's business club, which will give you an opportunity to learn about business tactics and finances, as well as give you an idea of how to run your own business.

Learn as much as you can about people and life in other parts of the world. You can do this by joining groups such as American Field Service International (AFS) and getting to know a student from another country who is attending your school. There are also study and living aboard programs you can apply to even while in high school. Rotary International and AFS offer such opportunities; see the end of the article for contact information.

EMPLOYERS

Cultural advisers are employed on a contract or project basis by businesses, associations, and educational institutions. Large global companies are the most significant source of employment for cultural advisers as they seek to serve the global population. Small- to medium-sized companies that do business in a particular region also employ cultural advisers. Companies in large cities offer the most opportunities for cultural advisers, especially those cities that border other countries and their economies.

Miguel Orta is a cultural adviser in North Miami Beach, Florida. He works with Latin American companies and American companies doing business in Central America and South America. He also has a background in law and business management. Orta is fluent in English, Spanish, and Portuguese. He uses his location in Florida to help businesses in the United States interact with a growing Hispanic population. His Florida location also allows him to be only a short plane flight from his Latin American clients.

STARTING OUT

Most cultural advisers do not begin this career right after college. Some real life experience is necessary to be qualified to fill the cultural adviser's role. "Education is very important," says Miguel Orta. "But first you need some work in the trenches." Once that experience is obtained, you will be ready to try advising.

After graduating with a law degree, Orta spent several years as a private attorney representing many Latin American clients. He practiced corporate, international, and labor law. When the opportunity came to serve one of his Venezuelan clients as a cultural adviser, Orta enjoyed the work and decided to become an adviser to others in need of those services.

ADVANCEMENT

Working with larger companies on more extensive projects is one way for a cultural adviser to advance. If an adviser decides to trade in the flexibility and freedom of the job, opportunities to become a salaried employee would most likely be available.

EARNINGS

Cultural advisers are well compensated for the time they spend on projects. Rates can range from approximately $65 to as high as $265 per hour. The median rate is close to $100 per hour. Advisers may incur business expenses, but their clients generally pay many of the expenses associated with the work, such as travel, meals, and lodging.

WORK ENVIRONMENT

The work environment of cultural advisers largely depends on their specialties. A smaller company may offer a more informal setting than a multinational corporation. A cultural adviser who is employed by a large, international bank may travel much more than an adviser who works for an educational institution or association.

While cultural advisers generally work independently on projects, they must also communicate with a large number of people to complete their tasks. In the middle of a project, a cultural adviser may work 50 to 60 hours per week and travel may be necessary. Between projects, cultural advisers manage their businesses and solicit new clients.

OUTLOOK
The field of cultural advising is predicted to grow faster than average in the next decade. Demand will grow as trade barriers are continually loosened and U.S. companies conduct more business on a global scale. Latin America and Asia are two promising areas for American businesses.

Cultural advisers will also be needed to address the interests of the increasingly diverse population of the United States. However, competition is keen, and those with graduate degrees and specific expertise will be the most successful.

FOR MORE INFORMATION
Management consulting firms employ a large number of cultural advisers. For more information on the consulting business, contact:

Association of Career Management Consulting Firms International
204 E Street, NE
Washington, DC 20002
Tel: 202-547-6344
Email: aocfi@aocfi.org
http://www.aocfi.org

For information about cultural exchanges, contact the following:

American Field Service International
71 West 23rd Street, 17th Floor
New York, NY 10010
Tel: 212-807-8686
Email: info@afs.org
Web: http://www.afs.org

Rotary International
One Rotary Center
1560 Sherman Avenue
Evanston, IL 60201
Tel: 847-866-3000
http://www.rotary.org

For information on etiquette and cross-cultural training, contact:

Multi-Language Consultants, Inc.
Tel: 212-726-2164
Email: contact@mlc.com
http://www.mlc.com

Protocol Advisors, Inc.
241 Beacon Street
Boston, MA 02116
Tel: 617-267-6950
http://www.protocoladvisors.com

CUSTOMER SERVICE REPRESENTATIVES

QUICK FACTS

School Subjects
Business
English
Speech

Personal Skills
Communication/ideas
Helping/teaching

Work Environment
Primarily indoors
Primarily one location

Minimum Education Level
High school diploma

Salary Range
$16,690 to $25,430 to
$42,090+

Certification or Licensing
Voluntary

Outlook
Faster than the
average

DOT
205

GOE
07.05.02

NOC
1453

O*NET-SOC
43-4051.00,
43-4051.02

OVERVIEW

Customer service representatives, sometimes called *customer care representatives,* work with customers of one or many companies, assist with customer problems, and answer questions. Customer service representatives work in many different industries to provide front-line customer support. Most customer service representatives work in an office setting though some may work in the field to better meet customer needs. There are approximately 1.9 million customer service representatives employed in the United States.

HISTORY

Customer service has been a part of business for many years, but the formal title of customer service representative is relatively new. More than a decade ago, the International Customer Service Association established Customer Service Week to recognize and promote customer service.

In 1992, President George Bush made the week a national event. "If the United States is to remain a leader in the changing global economy, highest quality customer service must be a personal goal of every employee in business and industry," said the president in his proclamation.

As the world moves toward a more global and competitive economic market, customer service, along with quality control, has taken a front seat in the business world. Serving customers and serving them well is more important now than ever before.

Customer service is about communication, so the progress in customer service can be tied closely to the progress in the communication industry. When Alexander Graham Bell (1847–1922) invented the telephone in 1876, he probably did not envision the customer service lines, automated response messages, and toll-free phone numbers that now help customer service representatives do their jobs.

The increased use of the Internet has helped companies serve and communicate with their customers in another way. From the simple email complaint form to online help files, companies are using the Internet to provide better customer service. Some companies even have online chat capabilities to communicate with their customers instantaneously on the Web.

THE JOB

Julie Cox is a customer service representative for Affina, a call center that handles customer service for a variety of companies. Cox works with each of Affina's clients and the call center operators to ensure that each call-in receives top customer service.

Customer service representatives often handle complaints and problems, and Cox finds that to be the case at the call center as well. While the operators who report to her provide customer service to those on the phone, Cox must oversee that customer service while also keeping in mind the customer service for her client, whatever business they may be in.

"I make sure that the clients get regular reports of the customer service calls and check to see if there are any recurring problems," says Cox.

One of the ways Cox observes the effectiveness of customer service is is by monitoring the actual time spent on each phone call. If an operator spends a lot of time on a call, there is most likely a problem.

"Our customers are billed per minute," says Cox. "So we want to make sure their customer service is being handled well and efficiently."

Affina's call center in Columbus, Indiana handles dozens of toll-free lines. While some calls are likely to be focused on complaints or questions, some are easier to handle. Cox and her staff handle calls from people simply wanting to order literature, brochures, or to find the location of the nearest dealer.

Customer service representatives work in a variety of fields and business, but one element is common to every customer service job: the customer. All businesses depend on their customers to keep them in business, so customer service, whether handled internally or outsourced to a call center like Affina, is extremely important.

Some customer service representatives, like Cox, do most of their work on the telephone. Others may represent companies in the field, where the customer is actually using the product or service. Still other customer service representatives may specialize in Internet service, assisting customers over the World Wide Web via email or online chats.

Affina's call center is available to clients 24 hours a day, seven days a week, so Cox and her staff must keep around-the-clock shifts. Not all customer service representatives work a varied schedule; many work a traditional daytime shift. However, customers have problems, complaints, and questions 24 hours a day, so many companies do staff their customer service positions for a longer number of hours, especially to accommodate customers during evenings and weekends.

REQUIREMENTS
High School

A high school diploma is required for most customer service representative positions. High school courses that emphasize communication, such as English and speech, will help you learn to communicate clearly. Any courses that require collaboration with others will also help to teach diplomacy and tact—two important aspects of customer service. Business courses will help you get a good overview of the business world, one that is dependent on customers and customer service. Computer skills are also very important.

Postsecondary Training

While a college degree is not necessary to become a customer service representative, certain areas of postsecondary training are helpful. Courses in business and organizational leadership will give you a better feel for the business world. Just as in high school, communications classes are helpful in learning to talk with and meet the needs of other people effectively.

These courses can be taken during a college curriculum or may be offered at a variety of customer service workshops or classes. Julie Cox is working as a customer service representative while she earns her business degree from a local college. Along with her college work, she has taken advantage of seminars and workshops to improve her customer service skills.

Bachelor's degrees in business and communications are increasingly required for managerial positions.

Certification or Licensing

Although it is not a requirement, customer service representative can become certified. The International Customer Service Association offers a manager-level certification program. Upon completion of the program, managers receive the Certified Customer Service Professional designation.

Other Requirements

"The best and the worst parts of being a customer service representative are the people," Julie Cox says. Customer service representatives should have the ability to maintain a pleasant attitude at all times, even while serving angry or demanding customers.

A successful customer service representative will most likely have an outgoing personality and enjoy working with people and assisting them with their questions and problems.

Because many customer service representatives work in offices and on the telephone, people with physical disabilities may find this career to be both accessible and enjoyable.

EXPLORING

Julie Cox first discovered her love for customer service while working in retail at a local department store. Explore your ability for customer service by getting a job that deals with the public on a day-to-day basis. Talk with people who work with customers and customer service every day; find out what they like and dislike about their jobs.

There are other ways that you can prepare for a career in this field while you are still in school. Join your school's business club to get a feel for what goes on in the business world today. Doing volunteer work for a local charity or homeless shelter can help you decide if serving others is something that you'd enjoy doing as a career.

Evaluate the customer service at the businesses you visit. What makes that salesperson at The Gap better than the operator you talked with last week? Volunteer to answer phones at an agency in your town or city. Most receptionists in small companies and agencies are called on to provide customer service to callers. Try a nonprofit organization. They will welcome the help, and you will get a firsthand look at customer service.

EMPLOYERS

Customer service representatives are hired at all types of companies in a variety of areas. Because all businesses rely on customers, customer service is generally a high priority for those businesses. Some companies, like call centers, may employ a large number of customer service representatives to serve a multitude of clients, while small businesses may simply have one or two people who are responsible for customer service.

Geography makes little difference when it comes to customer service. Smaller businesses may not be able to hire a person to handle customer service exclusively, but most businesses will have people designated to meet customer's needs. In the United States, approximately 1.9 million workers are employed as customer service representatives.

STARTING OUT

You can become a customer service representative as an entry-level applicant, although some customer service representatives have first served in other areas of a company. This company experience may provide them with more knowledge and experience to answer customer questions. A college degree is not required, but any postsecondary training will increase your ability to find a job in customer service.

Ads for customer service job openings are readily available in newspapers and on Internet job search sites. With some experience and a positive attitude, it is possible to move into the position of customer service representative from another job within the company. Julie Cox started out at Affina as an operator and quickly moved into a customer service capacity.

ADVANCEMENT

Customer service experience is valuable in any business career path. Julie Cox hopes to combine her customer service experience with a business degree and move to the human resources area of her company.

It is also possible to advance to management or marketing jobs after working as a customer service representative. Businesses and their customers are inseparable, so most business professionals are experts at customer relations.

EARNINGS

Earnings vary based on location, level of experience, and size and type of employer. The U.S. Department of Labor reports the median annual income for all customer service representatives as $25,430 in 2001. Salaries ranged from $16,690 to more than $42,090. The Association of Support Professionals, which conducts salary surveys of tech support workers at PC software companies, reports that customer service representatives earned a median of $29,000 in 2001.

Other benefits vary widely according to the size and type of company in which representatives are employed. Benefits may include medical, dental, vision, and life insurance, 401-K plans, or bonus incentives. Full-time customer service representatives can expect to receive vacation and sick pay, while part-time workers may not be offered these benefits.

WORK ENVIRONMENT

Customer service representatives work primarily indoors, although some may work in the field where the customers are using the product or service. They usually work in a supervised setting and report to a manager. They may spend many hours on the telephone, answering mail, or handling Internet communication. Many of the work hours involve little physical activity.

While most customer service representatives generally work a 40-hour workweek, others work a variety of shifts. Many businesses want customer service hours to coincide with the times that their customers are available to call or contact the business. For many companies, these times are in the evenings and on the weekends, so some customer service representatives work a varied shift and odd hours.

OUTLOOK

The U.S. Department of Labor predicts that employment for customer service representatives will grow faster than the average. This is a large field of workers and many replacement workers are needed each year as customer service reps leave this job for other positions, retire, or leave for other reasons. In addition, the Internet and ecommerce should increase the need for customer service representatives to help customers navigate websites, answer questions over the phone, and respond to emails.

For customer service representatives with specific knowledge of a product or business, the outlook is very good, as quick, efficient customer service is valuable in any business. Additional training and education will also make finding a job as a customer service representative an easier task.

FOR MORE INFORMATION

For information on customer service and other support positions, contact:

Association of Support Professionals
122 Barnard Avenue
Watertown, MA 02472-3944
Tel: 617-924-3944
http://www.asponline.com

For information on jobs, training, workshops, and salaries, contact:

Customer Care Institute
17 Dean Overlook, NW
Atlanta, GA 30318
Tel: 404-352-9291
Email: info@customercare.com
http://www.customercare.com

For information about the customer service industry, contact:

Help Desk Institute
6385 Corporate Drive, Suite 301
Colorado Springs, CO 80919
Tel: 800-248-5667
Email: support@thinkhdi.com
http://www.helpdeskinst.com

For information on international customer service careers, contact:

International Customer Service Association
401 North Michigan Avenue
Chicago, IL 60611
Tel: 800-360-4272
Email: icsa@sba.com
http://www.icsa.com

EVENT PLANNERS

QUICK FACTS

<table>
<tr><td>School Subjects
Business
English
Foreign language</td><td>Certification or Licensing
Voluntary</td></tr>
<tr><td>Personal Skills
Communication/ideas
Leadership/management</td><td>Outlook
Faster than the
average</td></tr>
<tr><td>Work Environment
Primarily indoors
One location with
some travel</td><td>DOT
169</td></tr>
<tr><td></td><td>GOE
N/A</td></tr>
<tr><td>Minimum Education Level
Bachelor's degree</td><td>NOC
1226</td></tr>
<tr><td>Salary Range
$30,000 to $54,613 to
$60,230+</td><td>O*NET-SOC
13-1121.00</td></tr>
</table>

OVERVIEW

The duties of *event planners* are varied and may include the following: establishing a site for an event; making travel, hotel, and food arrangements; and planning the program and overseeing guest registration. The planner may be responsible for all of the negotiating, planning, and coordinating for a major worldwide convention, or the planner may be involved with a small, in-house meeting involving only a few people. Some professional associations, government agencies, nonprofit organizations, political groups, and educational institutions hire event planners or have employees on staff who have these responsibilities. Many of these organizations and companies outsource their event planning responsibilities to firms that specialize in these services, such as marketing, public relations, and event planning firms. Many event and meeting planners are independent consultants.

Some event planners' services are also used on a personal level to plan class or family reunions, birthday parties, weddings, or anniversaries. There are approximately 34,000 event planners employed in the United States.

HISTORY

According to the *National Directory of Occupational Titles and Codes*, the meeting management profession was recognized as a career in the early 1990s. As corporations have specialized and expanded their business to include facilities and employees worldwide, company meeting logistics have become more complex. Planning a meeting that brings together employees and directors from around the world requires advanced planning to acquire a site, make travel and hotel arrangements, book speakers and entertainment, and arrange for catering.

Similarly, the growth of the convention and trade show industry has resulted in the need for persons with skills specific to the planning, marketing, and execution of a successful show. Conventions, trade shows, meetings, and corporate travel have become a big business in recent years, accounting for approximately $80 billion in annual spending.

The scope of meetings has changed as well. Technological advances now allow meetings to be conducted via the Internet, through videoconferencing or closed circuit television, or by setting up conference calls.

THE JOB

Event planners have a variety of duties depending on their specific title and the firms they work for or with. Generally, planners organize and plan an event such as a meeting, open house, convention, or a specific celebration.

Meetings might consist of a small inter-department meeting, a board meeting, an all-employee meeting, an in-house training session, a stockholders' meeting, or a meeting with vendors or distributors. When planning for these events, meeting planners usually check the calendars of key executives to establish a meeting time that fits into their schedules. Planners reserve meeting rooms, training rooms, or outside facilities for the event. They visit outside sites to make sure they are appropriate for that specific event. Planners notify people of the time, place, and date of the event and set up registration procedures, if necessary. They arrange for food, room layout, audiovisual equipment, instructors, computers, sound equipment, and telephone equipment as required.

In some cases, a company may employ an in-house meeting planner who is responsible for small- to medium-sized events. When a large meeting, trade show, conference, open house, or convention is planned, the in-house event planner may contract with outside meeting planners to assist with specific responsibilities such as registration, catering, and display setup. Some companies have their own trade show or convention managers on staff.

Convention, trade show, or conference managers negotiate and communicate with other enterprises related to the convention or trade show industry such as hotel and catering sales staff, speakers' bureaus, and trade staff such as *electricians* or *laborers* who set up convention display areas. They may also be responsible for contracting the transportation of the equipment and supplies to and from the event site. The manager usually works with an established budget and negotiates fees with these enterprises and enters contracts with them. Managers may also negotiate contracts with professionals to handle registration, marketing, and public relations for the event.

Managers and planners need to be aware of legal aspects of trade show setups, such as fire code regulations, floor plan, and space limitations, and make sure they are within these guidelines. They often need to obtain written approval for these arrangements. Good record-keeping and communication skills are daily essentials. The convention manager may have staff to handle the sales, registration, marketing, logistics, or other specific aspects of the event, or these duties may be subcontracted to another firm.

Some convention planners are employed specifically by convention and visitors' bureaus, the tourism industry, or by exhibit halls or convention facilities. Their job responsibilities may be specific to one aspect of the show, or they may be required to do any or all of the above-mentioned duties. Some convention and trade show managers may work for the exposition center or association and be responsible for selling booth space at large events.

Special event coordinators are usually employed by large corporations who hold numerous special events, or by firms who contract their special event planning services to companies, associations, or religious, political, or educational groups. A special event coordinator is responsible for planning, organizing, and implementing a special event such as an open house, an anniversary, the dedication of a new facility, a special promotion or sale, an ordination, a political rally, or a victory celebration. This coordinator works with the company or organization and determines the purpose of the special event, the type of celebration desired, the site, the budget, the attendees, the food and entertainment preferences, and the anticipated outcome. The special event planner then coordinates the vendors and equipment necessary to make the event successful. The coordinator works closely with the client at all times to ensure that the event is being planned as expected. Follow-up assessment of the event is usually part of the services offered by the special event coordinator.

Party planners are often employed by individuals, families, or small companies to help them plan a small party for a special occasion. Many party planners are independent contractors who work out of their homes or are employees of small firms. Party planners may help plan weddings, birthdays, christenings, bar or bat mitzvahs, anniversaries, or other events. They may be responsible for the entire event including the invitations, catering, decorating, entertainment, serving, and cleanup, or planners may simply perform one or two duties, such as contracting with a magician for a children's birthday party, recommending a menu, or greeting and serving guests.

REQUIREMENTS
High School

If you are interested in entering the field of event planning, you should take high school classes in business, English, and speech. Because many conferences and meetings are international in scope, you may also want to take foreign language and geography courses. In addition, computer science classes will be beneficial for the large amount of record-keeping involved in this field.

Postsecondary Training

Almost all coordinators and planners must have a four-year college degree to work for a company, corporation, convention, or travel center. Some institutions offer bachelor's degrees in meeting planning; however, degrees in business, English, communications, marketing, public relations, sales, or travel would also be a good fit for a career as a meetings manager, convention planner, or special event coordinator. Many directors and planners who become company heads have earned graduate degrees.

Some small firms, convention centers, or exhibit facilities may accept persons with associate degrees or travel industry certification for certain planning positions. Party planners may not always need education beyond high school, but advancement opportunities will be more plentiful with additional education.

Certification or Licensing

There are some professional associations for planners that offer certification programs. For example, Meeting Professionals International offers the Certification in Meeting Management designation. The International Association for Exhibition Management offers the Certified in Exhibition Management designation. (See "For More Information" at the end of this article for contact information.)

Other Requirements

To be an event planner, you must have excellent organizational skills, the ability to plan projects and events, and the ability to think creatively. You must be able to work well with people and anticipate their needs in advance. You should be willing to pitch in to get a job done even though it may not be part of your duties. In a situation where there is an unforeseen crisis, you need to react quickly and professionally. Planners should have good negotiating and communication skills and be assertive but tactful.

EXPLORING

High school guidance counselors can supply information on event planners or convention coordinators. Public and school librarians may also be able to provide useful books, magazines, and pamphlets. Searching the Internet for companies that provide event-planning services can give you an idea of the types of services that they offer. Professional associations related to the travel, convention, and meeting industries may have career information for students. Some of these organizations are listed at the end of this article.

Attending local trade shows and conventions will provide insight into the operations of this industry. Also, some exhibit and convention halls may hire students to assist with various aspects of trade show operations. You can learn more about this profession by subscribing to magazines such as *Meetings & Conventions* (http://www.meetings-conventions.com).

You can also gain business experience through school activities. Join the business club, run for student council, or head up the prom committee to learn how to plan and carry out events.

EMPLOYERS

Many large corporations or institutions worldwide hire meeting managers, convention managers, or event planners to handle their specific activities. Although some companies may not have employees with the specific title of event planner or meeting manager, these skills are very marketable and these duties may be part of another job title. In many companies, these duties may be part of a position within the marketing, public relations, or corporate communications department.

Convention facilities, exhibit halls, training and educational institutions, travel companies, and health care facilities also hire event planners. Hotels often hire planners to handle meetings and events held within their facilities. Large associations usually maintain an event planning staff for one or more annual conventions or business meetings for their members.

Job opportunities are also available with companies that contract out event and meeting planning services. Many of these companies have positions that specialize in certain aspects of the planning service, such as travel coordinator, exhibit planner, or facilities negotiator, or they have people who perform specific functions such as trade show display setup, registration, and follow-up reporting.

Experienced meeting planners or convention managers may choose to establish their own businesses or independently contract out their services. Party planning may also be a good independent business venture. Approximately 34,000 event planners are employed in the United States.

STARTING OUT

An internship at a visitors and convention bureau, exhibit center, or with a travel agency or meeting planning company is a good way to meet and network with other people in this field. Attending trade shows might offer a chance to speak with people about the field and to discuss any contacts they might have.

Some colleges and universities may offer job placement for people seeking careers in meeting planning or in the convention and trade show industries. Professional associations related to these industries are also good contacts for someone starting out. Classified ads and trade magazines may also offer some job leads.

ADVANCEMENT

Advancement opportunities for people in the event planning field are good. Experienced planners can expect to move into positions of increased responsibility. They may become senior managers and executive directors of private businesses, hotels, convention facilities, exhibit halls, travel corporations, museums, or other facilities. They can advance within a corporation to a position with more responsibilities or they may go into the planning business for themselves. Planners who have established a good reputation in the industry are often recruited by other firms or facilities and can advance their careers with these opportunities.

EARNINGS

According to a salary survey by *Special Events* magazine online, the average annual base salary for event planners was $36,079 in 2000. Nearly 40 percent of event planners were offered bonuses or commission, and the average bonus was $4,187.

Meeting Professionals International reports that in 2000, the average salary for U.S. meeting planners was $54,613. In the Northeast, meeting planners earned an average $58,146; in the West, $57,136; in the Midwest, $51,650; and in the South, $51,164. Corporate meeting planners earned an average of $56,120; association meeting professionals earned $46,539; and independent planners earned an average of $60,230.

Benefits may vary depending on the position and the employer but generally include vacation, sick leave, insurance, and other work-related benefits.

WORK ENVIRONMENT

Work environments vary with the planner's title and job responsibilities, but generally planners can expect to work in a business setting as part of a team. Usually, the planner's initial planning work is done in a clean environment with modern equipment prior to the opening of a convention or trade show. Working in convention and trade show environments, however, can be noisy, crowded, and distracting. In addition, the days can be long and may require standing for hours. If the planner is involved with supervising the setup or dismantling of a trade show or convention, the work can be dirty and physically demanding.

Although most facilities have crews that assist with setup, meeting planners occasionally get involved with last-minute changes and may need to do some physical lifting of equipment, tables, or chairs.

Event planners can usually expect to work erratic hours, often putting in long days prior to the event and the day the event is actually held. Travel is often part of the job requirements and may include working and/or traveling nights and on the weekends.

OUTLOOK

Job opportunities for event planners will continue to grow at a faster-than-average rate. The introduction of new technology enables more meetings to take place than ever before. Conventions, trade shows, meetings, and incentive travel support more than 1.5 million American jobs, according to the Professional Convention Management Association (PCMA). These events account for more than $80 billion in annual spending.

FOR MORE INFORMATION

For information on careers in the field of event planning, contact the following organizations.

International Association for Exposition Management
8111 LBJ Freeway, Suite 750
Dallas, TX 75251-1313
Tel: 972-458-8002
http://www.iaem.org

International Association of Assembly Managers
4425 West Airport Freeway, Suite 590
Irving, TX 75062-5835
Tel: 972-255-8020
http://www.iaam.org

Meeting Professionals International
4455 LBJ Freeway, Suite 1200
Dallas, TX 75244-5903
Tel: 972-702-3000
http://www.mpiweb.org

Professional Convention Management Association
2301 South Lake Shore Drive, Suite 1001
Chicago, IL 60616-1419
Tel: 312-423-7262
Email: students@pcma.org
http://www.pcma.org

EXECUTIVE RECRUITERS

QUICK FACTS

School Subjects Business Psychology Speech	**Certification or Licensing** None available
	Outlook Faster than the average
Personal Skills Communication/ideas Leadership/management	**DOT** 166
Work Environment Primarily indoors Primarily multiple locations	**GOE** N/A
Minimum Education Level Bachelor's degree	**NOC** N/A
Salary Range $50,000 to $175,000 to $250,000+	**O*NET-SOC** 13-1071.02

OVERVIEW

Executive recruiters are hired by businesses to locate, research, and interview candidates for hard-to-fill employment positions, mainly on the junior to senior management level. Such recruiters work for executive search firms and are paid by clients on a commission basis, or flat fee. There are approximately 10,000 executive recruiters employed by search firms located throughout the United States.

HISTORY

Although most companies have competent in-house human resource departments, a search for a top management position is often lengthy and difficult. Many times, human resource departments are not able to reach, or identify, the most qualified candidates. Also, a measure of privacy is lost if an entire department is aware of the need for a replacement. Companies are increasingly turning to a third party for their employment needs: the executive recruiter.

Executive search firms fall into one of two categories: retained or contingency. *Retainer recruiters* work with upper-level management positions, such as CEOs or CFOs, with salary expectations averaging $150,000 or higher. Companies or other entities contract these firms exclusively to bring new executives on board. Retainer recruiters work on a flat-fee basis or, more commonly, for a percentage of the candidate's first-year salary and bonus. Commission percentages can range anywhere from 10 to 35 percent, although the industry standard is about a third of the candidate's proposed salary package. Executive recruiters, because of the high-level management positions they are assigned to fill and the exclusivity of their contract, usually take longer to complete their task—anywhere from three to six months or more. The more qualities the company is looking for in a candidate, the longer the search.

The *contingency recruiter* deals with junior- to mid-level executive positions paying $50,000 to $150,000. Such recruiters are paid only if the candidate they present is hired for the job; pay is usually a percentage of the first-year salary package. Many times, however, a company will have more than one contingency firm working to fill a single position. Because of this, contingency recruiters are not guaranteed a fee and they may spend less time on their search. Some contingency recruiters also charge on an hourly basis or may work for a flat fee.

THE JOB

Most companies—from *Fortune 500* firms to colleges and universities to small businesses—at one time or another have come across the need to replace an important executive or administrator. Because of restraints such as time, privacy, or resources, many businesses opt to use the services of an executive recruiter. The task begins once the search firm is retained, or notified of the job opening, and is asked to find the best possible candidate.

The recruiter first evaluates the needs and structure of the company and the specifications of the open position. Then a written draft of the job description is made, detailing the title, job definition, responsibilities, and compensation. At this time, a wish list is composed of every possible quality, talent, skill, and educational background the perfect job candidate should possess. It is up to the recruiter to match these specifications as closely as possible.

Once the client approves a written contract the real work begins. The three traditional job functions in the recruitment industry are researcher, associate, and consultant. *Researchers* conduct research to find possible candidates. They look through directories and databases and network with contacts familiar with the field. They read trade papers and magazines as well as national newspapers such as the *Wall Street Journal* and the *New York Times*. Business sections of newspapers often include write-ups of industry leaders. Recruiters also receive resumes from people looking to change employment, which they may use for future reference. Recruiters must stay current with the field they specialize in; they need to be familiar with the key players as well as important technological advances that may change the scope of the industry. They must also have a solid understanding of the workings of their specialty field so they can assess a candidate's ability to meet the demands of a position.

Once a long list is assembled, *associates* contact the prospective candidates, usually by telephone. Candidates who are interested and qualified are screened further and their references are checked fully. *Consultants* conduct personal interviews with promising candidates who make the short list of hopefuls. Consultants also manage client relationships and develop new business for the firm.

The goal of retainer executive recruiters is to present three to five of the best candidates to a client for final interviews. Contingency recruiters, on the other hand, present many qualified candidates to the client to better their chance of filling the position. Executive recruiters will not edit resumes or coach on the interview process, but some will offer information on where candidates stand after the initial interview and give advice on strengths and perceived weaknesses.

A search for the perfect executive is a lengthy process. Most searches take anywhere from one month to a year or more. Once the position is filled, recruiters conduct one or more follow-ups to make sure the employee's transition into the company is smooth. Any conflicts or discrepancies are addressed and often mediated by, or along with, the search firm. Some executive search firms offer some kind of guarantee with their work. If the hired employee leaves a firm within a specified period of time or does not work out as anticipated, then the recruiter will find a replacement for a reduced fee or at no charge.

REQUIREMENTS
High School

To prepare for a career as an executive recruiter, you should take business, speech, English, and mathematics classes in high school.

Psychology and sociology courses will teach you how to recognize personality characteristics that may be key in helping you determine which job candidates would best fit a position.

Postsecondary Training

You will need at least a bachelor's degree and several years of work experience to become an executive recruiter. Postsecondary courses helpful for this career include communications, marketing, and business administration. Some colleges offer undergraduate degrees in human resources management or business degrees with a concentration in human resources management. To have more job opportunities, you may also consider getting a master's degree in one of these fields. Most recruiters move into this industry after successful careers in their particular areas of expertise (for example, health care, finance, publishing, or computers) and they come to the field with a variety of educational backgrounds.

Certification or Licensing

There are no certification or licensing requirements for this industry. Most executive search professionals belong to the Association of Executive Search Consultants or the National Association of Executive Recruiters.

Other Requirements

Executive recruiters need to possess strong people skills. Good communicators are in demand, especially those who can maintain a high level of integrity and confidentiality. Recruiters are privy to sensitive company and employee information that may prove disastrous if leaked to the public.

The most powerful tool in this industry is a network of good contacts. Since executive recruiters come on board after working in the field for which they are now recruiting, they are usually familiar with who's who in the business.

EXPLORING

Familiarize yourself with business practices by joining or starting a business club at your school. Being a part of a speech or debate team is a great way to develop excellent speaking skills, which are necessary in this field. Hold mock interviews with family or friends, and get work and volunteer experience in your specialized field (for example, health care or publishing). Professional associations, such as The International Association of Corporate and Professional Recruiters, are also good sources of information. Visit this association's website at http://www.iacpr.org to learn more.

EMPLOYERS

Executive search firms of all sizes are located throughout the United States. Most specialize in placement in a particular field, for example, chemical engineering or advertising. For a list of search firms, you may want to refer to the *Directory of Executive Recruiters*, also known in the industry as the "Red Book." Search firms in the United States employ approximately 10,000 executive recruiters, according to an estimate by *Executive Recruiter News*.

STARTING OUT

A common starting point in this industry is a position at a contingency search firm, or even an outplacement center. Responsibilities may be limited at first, but a successful, and consistent track record should lead to bigger clients, more placements, and higher commissions. Many executive recruiters were recruited into the field themselves, especially if they were well known in their industry. It is important to market yourself and your accomplishments while you work in entry-level positions. Circulate among the movers and shakers of your company, as well as those of the competition. They may prove to be valuable contacts for the future. Most importantly, cultivate relationships with any recruitment firms that may call; you'll never know when you may need their assistance.

ADVANCEMENT

A typical advancement path in this industry would be a transfer to a retainer-based search firm. Retained search firms deal with the upper-echelon administrative positions that pay top salaries, translating to higher commissions for the recruiter.

Let's say you've already paid your dues and worked successfully at a retainer search firm. What next? You may want to negotiate for partnership or opt to call the shots and start a firm of your own.

EARNINGS

Executive recruiters are paid well for their efforts. Contingency recruiters, who are paid only if their candidate is hired, typically charge a fee from 25 percent to 35 percent of the candidate's first-year cash compensation.

Retained recruiters average fees of one-third of the candidate's first-year cash compensation. Any expenses incurred by the recruiter are usually paid by the employer. According to *U.S. News & World Report,* average entry-level positions pay from $50,000 to $100,000 annually, while mid-level recruiters earn from $100,000 to $250,000. Top earners, those working for larger retainer recruiting firms, can make more than $250,000 a year. Along with their salary, all recruiters are offered a benefit package including health insurance, paid vacations, and sick time or paid disability.

WORK ENVIRONMENT
Many recruiters work 50 to 70 hours a week; it's not uncommon for recruiters to spend several days a week on the road meeting clients, interviewing, or doing candidate research. Also, aspiring recruiters should expect to spend most of their day on the phone.

OUTLOOK
The executive search industry should have a good future. Potential clients include not only large international corporations but also universities, the government, and smaller businesses. Smaller operations are aware that having a solid executive or administrator may make the difference between turning a profit or not being in business at all. Many times, search firm services are used to conduct industry research or to scope out the competition. Executive search firms now specialize in many fields of employment—health care, engineering, or accounting, for example.

The era of company loyalty and employment for life is over in the corporate world. Many savvy workers campaign aggressively, and will transfer given a larger salary, improved benefits, and stock options—in short, a better employment future. Employers, on the other hand, realize the importance in having qualified and experienced employees at the helm of their business. Most companies are willing to pay the price, whether a retainer fee or commission, to find just the right person for the job.

According to the Association of Executive Search Consultants, it is becoming more important for executive recruiters to operate on a global basis. They must be able to conduct searches for clients and candidates in other countries. Peter Felix, president of AESC, says, "Today, the retained executive search business is a $10 billion industry operating in all the major economies of the world. In this era of the knowledge society where executive talent is so important, executive search is seen increasingly as a critical management tool."

FOR MORE INFORMATION

For industry information, contact:

The Association of Executive Search Consultants
500 Fifth Avenue, Suite 930
New York, NY 10110-0900
Tel: 212-398-9556
Email: aesc@aesc.org
http://www.aesc.org

For more industry information, or membership information, contact:

National Association of Executive Recruiters
20 North Wacker Drive, Suite 550
Chicago, IL 60606
Tel: 312-701-0744
http://www.naer.org

For a copy of the industry newsletter, Executive Recruiter News, or the Directory of Executive Recruiters, contact:

Kennedy Information
One Phoenix Mill Lane, 5th Floor
Peterborough, NH 03458
Tel: 800-531-0007
Email: bookstore@kennedyinfo.com
http://www.kennedyinfo.com

FINANCIAL ANALYSTS

QUICK FACTS

School Subjects Business Computer science Mathematics	**Certification or Licensing** Recommended
	Outlook Faster than the average
Personal Skills Communication/ideas Leadership/management	**DOT** N/A
Work Environment Primarily indoors Primarily one location	**GOE** N/A
Minimum Education Level Bachelor's degree	**NOC** 1112
Salary Range $29,499 to $55,130 to $107,720+	**O*NET-SOC** 13-2051.00

OVERVIEW

Financial analysts analyze the financial situation of companies and recommend ways for these companies to manage, spend, and invest their money. Financial analysts' goal is to help their employer or clients make informed, lucrative, financial decisions. They assemble and evaluate the company's financial data and assess investment opportunities. They look at the company's financial history, the direction that company wants to take in the future, the company's place in the industry, and current and projected economic conditions. Financial analysts also conduct similar research on companies that might become investment opportunities. They write reports and compile spreadsheets that show the benefits of certain investments or selling certain securities.

Among the businesses employing financial analysts are banks, brokerage firms, government agencies, mutual funds, and insurance and investment companies. There are approximately 239,000 financial analysts and *personal financial advisers* employed in the United States, and about six out of 10 are financial analysts.

HISTORY

U.S. securities markets date back to the early years of the nation. The first U.S. stock exchanges were created in the 1790s. The New York Stock Exchange (which did not get its present name until 1863) was one of these. It started as a group of men who did their trading under a tree at 68 Wall Street. The markets grew as the country's industries developed. The unregulated U.S. securities markets flourished just following World War I. According to the U.S. Securities and Exchange Commission (SEC), some 20 million people "took advantage of post-war prosperity and set out to make their fortunes in the stock market." The stock market crash of 1929, however, wiped out the savings of many investors. Consumers became wary of the markets and hesitated to invest again. Congress created the SEC in 1934 to keep watch over the markets and institute rules and regulations in the industry. The goal was to ensure that companies and stockbrokers divulged truthful information about their businesses, the investments offered, and the potential risk involved.

The Financial Analysts Federation (FAF), a group for investment professionals, was created in 1947. The FAF brought some prestige and respect to the profession. Then in 1959 the Institute of Chartered Financial Analysts (ICFA) was developed. Financial analysts who successfully completed the ICFA examination received the designation Chartered Financial Analyst (CFA). In June 1963, 268 analysts became the first group of CFA charterholders. The FAF and ICFA went on to merge in 1990, creating the Association for Investment Management and Research (AIMR).

Deregulations in the 1970s and 1980s brought about greater competition in the industry and more crossover between finance and banking. Knowledgeable professionals like financial analysts were in greater demand to help businesses keep up with the growing number and complexity of investment options. Financial analysts who forecast the rapid rise of technology stocks in the late-1990s were hailed in the industry and the media. But the steep decline of many of those same stocks by 2000-01 led to questions and concerns about the truthfulness of the information reported by certain financial analysts. In late 2000 the SEC instituted the Regulation Fair Disclosure rule, calling for fuller and more honest public disclosure of investment information.

Not only have technology stocks affected the business conducted by financial analysts, but so have changes in technology itself. Spreadsheet and statistical software programs afford financial analysts many improved and sophisticated options in compiling and presenting data. What in its early days was little more than deal making among a small group of men beneath a tree has evolved into a worldwide, high-tech, competitive industry, and financial analysts play an integral role in it.

THE JOB

Financial analysts are sometimes called *investment analysts* or *security analysts*. The specific types, direction, and scope of analyses performed by financial analysts are many and varied, depending on the industry, the employer or client, and the analyst's training and years of experience. Financial analysts study their employer's or client's financial status and make financial and investment recommendations. To arrive at these recommendations, financial analysts examine the employer's or client's financial history and objectives, income and expenditures, risk tolerance, and current investments. Once they understand the employer's or client's financial standing and investment goals, financial analysts scout out potential investment opportunities. They research other companies, perhaps in a single industry, that their employer or client may want to invest in. This in-depth research consists of investigating the business of each company, including history, past and potential earnings, and products. Based on their findings, financial analysts may recommend that their employer or client buy stock in these companies. If the employer or client already holds stock in a particular company, financial analysts' research may indicate that stocks should be held or sold, or that more should be purchased.

Financial analysts work for companies in any number of industries, including banking, transportation, health care, technology, telecommunications, and energy. While investment options and concerns differ among these, financial analysts still apply the same basic analytic tools in devising investment strategies. They try to learn everything they can about the industry they're working in. They study the markets and make industry comparisons. They also research past performances and future trends of bonds and other investments.

Financial analysts compile many types of reports on their employer or client and on investment opportunities, such as profit-

and-loss statements and quarterly outlook statements. They help develop budgets, analyze and oversee cash flow, and perform cost-benefit analyses. They conduct risk analyses to determine what the employer or client can risk at a given time and/or in future. Another responsibility is to ensure that their employer or client meets any relevant tax or regulatory requirements. Financial analysts compile their work using various software programs, often developing financial models, such as charts or graphs, to display their data.

Companies that want to go public (sell company shares to individual investors for the first time) often ask financial analysts to make projections of future earnings as well as presentations for potential investors. Financial analysts also make sure that all paperwork is in order and compliant with Securities and Exchange Commission rules and regulations.

Entry-level financial analysts, usually working under direct supervision, mainly conduct research and compile statistical data. After a few years of experience, they become more involved in presenting reports. While a financial analyst generally offers recommendations, a senior financial analyst often has the authority to actually decide purchases or sales. Senior financial analysts implement a company's business plan. In larger companies, they also assist different departments in conducting their own financial analyses and business planning. Those in senior positions become supervisors as well, training junior financial analysts.

Many specialties fall under the job title of financial analyst. These specialties vary from employer to employer, and duties overlap between different types of analysts. In smaller firms a financial analyst may have extensive responsibility, while at larger firms a financial analyst may specialize in one of any number of areas. *Budget analysts,* often called *accountants* or *controllers,* look at the operating costs of a company or its individual departments and prepare budget reports. *Credit analysts* examine credit records to determine the potential risk in extending credit or lending money. *Investment analysts* evaluate investment data so they can make suitable investment recommendations. *Mergers and acquisitions analysts* conduct research and make recommendations relating to company mergers and acquisitions. *Money market analysts* assess financial data and investment opportunities, giving advice specifically in the area of money markets. *Ratings analysts* explore a company's financial situation to determine whether or not it will be able to repay debts. *Risk analysts* focus on evaluating the risks of investments. The intent is to identify and then minimize a company's risks and losses. *Security analysts* specialize in studying securities, such as stocks and bonds. *Tax analysts* prepare, file, and examine federal, state, and local tax payments and returns for their employer or client and perhaps also for local affiliates. They analyze tax issues and keep up with tax law changes. *Treasury analysts* manage their company's or client's daily cash position, prepare cash journal entries, initiate wire transfers, and perform bank reconciliations.

Analysts are considered either *buy-side analysts,* who usually work for money management firms, or *sell-side analysts,* sometimes called *sales analysts* or *Wall Street analysts,* who usually work for brokerage firms.

Personal financial advisors have many similar responsibilities (assessing finances, projecting income, recommending investments), but these are performed on behalf of individuals rather than companies.

REQUIREMENTS
High School
Since financial analysts work with numbers and compile data, you should take as many math classes as are available. Accounting, business, and computer classes will be helpful as well. A good grasp of computer spreadsheet programs such as Microsoft Excel is vital. Take extra care as you research and write reports in any subject matter or in public speaking, and it will pay off later when you must conduct investment research and write and present investment recommendations.

Postsecondary Training
Most employers require that financial analysts hold a bachelor's degree in accounting, business administration, finance, or statistics. Other possible majors include communications, international business, and public administration. Some companies will hire you if you hold a bachelor's degree in another discipline as long as you can demonstrate mathematical ability. In college, take business, economics, and statistics courses. Since computer technology plays such a big role in a financial analyst's work, computer classes can be helpful as well. English composition classes can prepare you for the writing you will need to do when preparing reports. Some employers require a writing sample prior to an interview.

Financial analysts generally continue to take courses to keep up with the ongoing changes in the world of finance, including international trade, state and federal laws and regulations, and computer technology. Proficiency in certain databases, presentation graphics, spreadsheets, and other software is expected. Some employers require their employees to have a master's degree.

Many top firms offer summer internship programs. Check company websites for the particulars, such as assignments and qualifications. An internship can provide you with helpful contacts and increase your chances of landing a job when you finish college.

Certification or Licensing

Financial analysts can earn the title Chartered Financial Analyst (CFA). While certification is not required, it is recommended. The CFA program, which is administered by the Association for Investment Management and Research (AIMR), consists of three levels of examinations. These rigorous exams deal with such topics as economics, financial statement analysis, corporate finance, and portfolio management. AIMR states that a candidate may need to spend 250 hours studying to prepare for each level. The Motley Fool, a financial education company (http://www.fool.com), reported that about 50 percent of the candidates fail the first level. A candidate can take only one level per year, so a minimum of three years is required to become a CFA charterholder. If a candidate fails a level, it can be taken the next year. Candidates who do not successfully complete all three levels within seven years must reregister.

Before taking the exams, you must already have a bachelor's degree. There is no required course of study. Prior to earning the CFA charter, you must have spent three years in a related field working in the investment decision-making process and you must first apply to become a member of AIMR as well as a local society.

The CFA charter is recognized around the world as a standard in the finance industry. Many employers expect job seekers to be CFA charterholders. According to AIMR, more than 35,000 people have become CFA charterholders since the program was first administered in 1963.

For certain upper-level positions, some firms require that you have a Certified Public Accountant license.

Other Requirements

Research, organizational, and communication skills are crucial for this job. Financial analysts conduct in-depth research, often looking for hard-to-find data. Organizational skills are important when it comes to compiling and presenting this data. Once you have explored a company's financial situation, you must communicate complicated ideas through presentations and/or written reports. You should be able to clearly communicate ideas, both verbally when making presentations and on paper when writing reports.

The work requires strong analytic skills, so a knack for numbers and attention to detail are also helpful. An interest in solving problems will go a long way. It is important that a financial analyst be accurate and thorough in preparing financial statements.

You should enjoy reading and be able to retain what you read, since it is important to keep up with what's happening in the industry and take it into account when offering financial solutions to employers or clients. Since many financial analysts must travel at a moment's notice to conduct research or complete a deal, flexibility is another important characteristic.

Financial analysts should be able to work well under pressure, as this line of work often demands long hours and entails strict deadlines. You should have good interpersonal skills and enjoy interacting with others. Deals or important contacts can be made at social functions or business conferences.

EXPLORING

There are many sources of information dealing with the financial services industry. Read publications such as *Barron's* (http://www.barrons.com), *Wall Street Journal* (http://www.wsj.com), *Forbes* (http://www.forbes.com), *BusinessWeek* (http://www.businessweek.com), *Fortune* (http://www.fortune.com), and *Financial Times* (http://www.ft.com). In the print or online versions, you will find a wealth of information on stocks, mutual funds, finance, education, careers, salaries, global business, and more. You can also conduct company research. You might have to become a subscriber to access certain sections online.

AnalystForum (http://www.analystforum.com) is a resource for Chartered Financial Analysts and CFA candidates. While this site won't be of much use to you until you've launched your career, you can find links to financial, investment, and security analyst society sites. From within these societies, you can perhaps track down a professional who would be willing to do an information interview with you.

While in high school, you might volunteer to handle the bookkeeping for a school club or student government, or help balance the family checking account to become familiar with simple bookkeeping practices. Your school may have an investment club you can join. If not, ask a parent or teacher to help you research and analyze investment opportunities. Choose a specific industry (e.g., telecommunications, technology, or health care), study companies in that industry, and select and track several stocks that appear to have growth potential.

EMPLOYERS
Financial analysts work in the public and private sectors. Employers include banks, brokerage and securities firms, corporations, government agencies, manufacturers, mutual and pension funds, and financial management, insurance, investment, trust, and utility companies. Many financial analysts are self-employed.

According to the *Occupational Outlook Handbook,* about 25 percent of financial analysts work for security and commodity brokers, exchanges, and investment services firms, and 20 percent work for depository and nondepository institutions, including banks, credit institutions, and mortgage bankers and brokers. The rest work mainly for insurance carriers, computer and data processing services, and management and public relations firms.

Since financial analysts often work in Wall Street companies, many employers are found in New York City. They are also concentrated in other large cities but work in smaller cities as well. Approximately 239,000 financial analysts and personal financial advisors are employed in the United States (financial analysts make up about 60 percent of this total).

STARTING OUT
Representatives from hiring companies, e.g., banks, brokerage firms, or investment companies, may visit college campuses to meet with students interested in pursuing careers as financial analysts. College placement offices will have details on such visits. Company websites may also offer campus recruiting schedules.

Gaining an entry-level position can be difficult. Some companies offer in-house training, but many don't. Beginning as a research assistant might be one way to break into the business. Read member profiles at association sites to see where members have worked as financial analysts. Explore those companies that look appealing.

Make contacts and network with other financial analysts. Your local AIMR society or chapter will probably hold regular meetings, affording ample networking opportunities. You can become an AIMR member whether or not you are a CFA charterholder, but charterholders enjoy full member benefits, such as access to job postings. (Complete details, including listings for local societies and chapters, can be found at the AIMR website, http://www.aimr.org.) Also, internships can be an excellent way to make contacts and gain experience in the field.

The New York Society of Security Analysts suggests that you compile an investment recommendation for potential clients to give them an idea of the kind of research you're capable of and how you present your data. This can prove to be a valuable interview tool.

You can search for job ads online. One resource is the Jobsin-themoney.com network (http://www.jobsinthemoney.com). If you know what companies you'd like to work for, visit their websites. Chances are you will find online job listings there.

ADVANCEMENT

Financial analysts who accurately prepare their employer's or client's financial statements and who offer investment advice that results in profits will likely be rewarded for their efforts. Rewards come in the form of promotions and/or bonuses. Successful financial analysts may become senior financial analysts, sometimes in only three or four years. Some become portfolio or financial managers. Rather than simply making recommendations on their company's or client's investment policies, those who advance to a senior position have more decision-making responsibility.

Some financial analysts move on to jobs as investment bankers or advisors. Others become officers in various departments in their company. Positions include chief financial officer and vice president of finance. In time, some cultivate enough contacts to start their own consulting firms.

EARNINGS

The 2001 National Occupational Employment and Wage Estimates, compiled by the U.S. Department of Labor, reports that median annual earnings of financial analysts were $55,130 in 2001. Top earners made more than $107,720, and the lowest salaries were less than $33,520.

As of January 2002, *BusinessWeek Online,* using Salary.com's Salary Wizard, reports U.S. salary ranges for several different kinds of analysts. Figures for a financial analyst I (an entry-level position) range from a low of $39,826 to a high of $50,694, whereas the figures for a financial analyst III (a more senior position) range from $61,289 to $76,955. Earnings for a credit analyst I are $29,499 to $39,146, and for a credit analyst III, $40,165 to $52,317. A treasury analyst I earns $33,283 to $40,983, while a treasury analyst III earns $51,641 to $70,803.

If the investments of financial analysts' employers or clients perform well, it is not uncommon for those financial analysts to receive a bonus in addition to their salary. With bonuses, skilled financial analysts can make much more than their base salary.

Benefits include paid vacation, health, disability, life insurance, and retirement or pension plans. Some employers also offer profit-sharing plans. Tuition reimbursement may also be available.

WORK ENVIRONMENT

Most financial analysts work in an office in a corporate setting. Frequently, they work alone (e.g., when conducting research or talking on the phone to clients). Some may work out of their homes. Much time is spent working on a computer, doing research and compiling data. Travel is frequently required—there are meetings and social functions to attend, clients to meet, and companies to research at their place of business. Because financial analysts spend much of their normal business hours talking or meeting with clients, they often conduct research after hours and generally work long days. It is not uncommon for financial analysts to clock well in excess of 50 hours per week.

OUTLOOK

The state of the economy and the stock market has a direct effect on the employment outlook for financial analysts. When the economy is doing well, companies are more likely to make investments, resulting in a need for financial analysts. When the economy is doing poorly, investment and career trends run in the opposite direction. The *Occupational Outlook Handbook (OOH)*, anticipating an increase in business investments, predicts a faster-than-average employment growth in this field. The *OOH* notes, too, that international securities markets, the complexity of financial products, and business mergers and acquisitions demand financial analysts to sort through all the issues involved. Because of the close scrutiny analysts have been under, it might become more desirable for financial analysts to hold the CFA charter.

Individual investing will also affect the need for financial analysts, in that the more people invest in mutual funds (often through

401-K plans), the greater the need there will be for financial analysts to recommend financial products to the mutual fund companies.

FOR MORE INFORMATION

This organization's website offers an E-Library containing a helpful dictionary of financial terminology. Industry news and certification information is also available.

Association for Financial Professionals, Inc.
7315 Wisconsin Avenue, Suite 600 West
Bethesda, MD 20814
Tel: 301-907-2862
http://www.afponline.org

For complete AIMR information, including lists of AIMR societies, publications, news, conference details, and certification information, contact:

Association for Investment Management and Research (AIMR)
PO Box 3668
560 Ray C. Hunt Drive
Charlottesville, VA 22903-0668
Tel: 800-247-8132
Email: info@aimr.org
http://www.aimr.org

The NYSSA website includes a list of top employers of financial analysts as well as an article on becoming a security analyst.

New York Society of Security Analysts (NYSSA)
1601 Broadway, 11th Floor
New York, NY 10019-7406
Tel: 800-248-0108
Email: staff@nyssa.org
http://www.nyssa.org

For information on laws and regulations pertaining to investors and the securities markets, contact:

U.S. Securities and Exchange Commission
Office of Investor Education and Assistance
450 Fifth Street, NW
Washington, DC 20549
Tel: 202-942-7040
Email: help@sec.gov
http://www.sec.gov

This website has links to financial, investment, and security analyst societies.
AnalystForum
http://www.analystforum.com

For issues of interest to senior finance executives, see:
CFO.com
http://www.cfo.com

FINANCIAL INSTITUTION OFFICERS AND MANAGERS

QUICK FACTS

School Subjects
Business
Mathematics

Personal Skills
Communication/ideas
Leadership/management

Work Environment
Primarily indoors
Primarily one location

Minimum Education Level
Bachelor's degree

Salary Range
$36,050 to $55,960 to
$131,120+

Certification or Licensing
Recommended

Outlook
About as fast as the average

DOT
186

GOE
11.06.05

NOC
0122

O*NET-SOC
11-3031.01, 11-3031.02,
13-2071.00, 13-2072.00

OVERVIEW

Financial institution officers and managers oversee the activities of banks and personal credit institutions such as credit unions and finance companies. These establishments serve business, government, and individuals. They lend money, maintain savings, enable people and businesses to write checks for goods and services, rent safe-deposit boxes for storing valuables, manage trust funds, advise clients on investments and business affairs, issue credit cards and traveler's checks, and take payments for gas and electric bills. There are approximately 658,000 financial managers (including those working outside of financial institutions) employed in the United States.

HISTORY

The modern concept of bank notes, or currency, developed in the 17th century. Goldsmiths in London began to issue paper receipts for gold and other valuables that were deposited in their warehouses. The paper money we use today is a modern version of these 17th-century receipts.

The first bank in the United States, Bank of North America, was chartered by the Continental Congress in 1781. By the early 1900s, banks had become so numerous that need arose for federal control of banks. The Federal Deposit System, as we know it today, is the result of the efforts to coordinate the activities of the many banks throughout the nation. As banks grew in number and competed for new customers, financial professionals developed a variety of new services for banks to offer. Advancements in technology made many of these new services possible and, often, changed the way people thought about money. For example, banks introduced the first credit cards that were accepted by multiple vendors (cards that we know as Visa, MasterCard, etc.) in the late 1950s and 1960s. The introduction of these credit cards was made possible by bank computers that were able to track transactions and signal when spending limits were reached. Today, credit cards have become so commonplace that CardWeb.com estimates that there are approximately 6,000 credit card issuers. The average American has eight credit cards and the average debt per household is $8,000 on all cards.

The banking industry continues to use technology developments to expand its services. For example, the American Bankers Association reports that nearly two-thirds of the country's community banks had websites by 2000. As the 21st century began, online banking was quickly becoming an expected option. Within the past 25 years, the number of banks and other financial institutions has grown extensively, and many financial professionals are needed to run the banking industry.

THE JOB

Financial institutions include the following: commercial banks, which provide full banking service for business, government, and individuals; investment banks, which offer their clients financial counseling and brokering; Federal Reserve Banks, whose customers are affiliated banks in their districts; or other organizations such as credit unions and finance companies.

These institutions employ many officers and managers whose duties vary depending on the type and size of the firm as well as on their own area of responsibility. All financial institutions operate under the direction of a president, who is guided by policies set by the board of directors. Vice presidents are department heads who are sometimes also responsible for certain key clients. Controllers handle bank funds, properties, and equipment. Large institutions may also have treasurers, loan officers, and officers in charge of departments such as trust, credit, and investment. A number of these positions are described in more detail in the following paragraphs.

The *financial institution president* directs the overall activities of the bank or consumer credit organization, making sure that its objectives are achieved without violating government regulations or overlooking any legal requirements. The officers are responsible for earning as much of a return as possible on the institution's investments within the restrictions demanded by government and sound business practices. They help set policies pertaining to investments, loans, interest, and reserves. They coordinate the activities of the various divisions and delegate authority to subordinate officers, who administer the operation of their own areas of responsibility. Financial institution presidents study financial reports and other data to keep up with changes in the economy that may affect their firm's policies.

The *vice president* coordinates many of the operations of the institution. This person is responsible for the activities of a regional bank office, branch bank, and often an administrative bank division or department. As designated by the board of directors, the vice president supervises programs such as installment loan, foreign trade, customer service, trust, and investment. The vice president also prepares studies for management and planning, like workload and budget estimates and activity and analysis reports.

The *administrative secretary* usually writes directions for supervisory workers that outline and explain policy. The administrative secretary acts, in effect, as an intermediary between minor supervisory workers and the executive officers.

The *financial institution treasurer* directs the bank's monetary programs, transactions, and security measures in accordance with banking principles and legislation. Treasurers coordinate program activity and evaluate operating practices to ensure efficient operations. They oversee receipt, disbursement, and expenditure of money and sign documents approving or affecting monetary transactions. They direct the safekeeping and control of assets and securities and maintain specified legal cash reserves. They review financial and operating statements and present reports and recommendations to bank officials or board committees.

Controllers authorize the use of funds kept by the treasurer. They also supervise the maintenance of accounts and records, and analyze these records so that the directors or other bank officials will know how much the bank is spending for salaries, operating expenses, and other expenses. Controllers often formulate financial policies.

The *financial institution manager* establishes and maintains relationships with the community. This person's responsibility is to supervise accounting and reporting functions and to establish operating policies and procedures. The manager directs several activities within the bank. The assets, records, collateral, and securities held by the financial institution are in the manager's custody. Managers approve loans of various types, such as credit, commercial, real estate, and consumer loans. They also direct personnel in trust activities.

The *loan officer* and the *credit and collection manager* both deal with customers who are seeking or have obtained loans or credit. The loan officer specializes in examining and evaluating applications for lines of credit, installment credit, or commercial, real estate, and consumer loans and has the authority to approve them within a specified limit or recommend their approval to the loan committee. To determine the feasibility of granting a loan request, the officer analyzes the applicant's financial status, credit, and property evaluation. The job may also include handling foreclosure proceedings. Depending on training and experience, officers may analyze potential loan markets to develop prospects for loans. They negotiate the terms of transaction and draw up the requisite documents to buy and sell contracts, loans, or real estate. Credit and collection managers make up collection notices for customers who already have credit. When the bank has difficulty collecting accounts or receives a worthless check, credit and collection managers take steps to correct the situation. Managers must keep records of all credit and collection transactions.

Loan counselors study the records of the account when payments on a loan are overdue and contact the borrower to discuss payment of the loan. They may analyze the borrower's financial problems and make new arrangements for repayment of the loan. If a loan account is unable to be collected, they prepare a report for the bank or institution's files.

Credit card operations managers are responsible for the overall credit card policies and operations of a bank, commercial establishment, or credit card company. They establish procedures for verifying the information on application forms, determine applicants' credit worthiness, approve the issuance of credit cards, and set a credit limit on each account. These managers coordinate the work involved with reviewing unpaid balances, collecting delinquent accounts, investigating and preventing fraud, voiding lost or stolen credit cards, keeping records, and exchanging information with the company's branches and other credit card companies.

The *letter of credit negotiator* works with clients who hold letters of credit used in international banking. This person contacts foreign banks, suppliers, and other sources to obtain documents needed to authorize the requested loan. Then the negotiator checks to see if the documents have been completed correctly so that the conditions set forth in the letter of credit meet with policy and code requirements. Before authorizing payment, the negotiator verifies the client's credit rating and may request increasing the collateral or reducing the amount of purchases, amending the contract accordingly. The letter of credit negotiator specifies the method of payment and informs the foreign bank when a loan has gone unpaid for a certain length of time.

The *trust officer* directs operations concerning the administration of private, corporate, and probate trusts. Officers examine or draft trust agreements to ensure compliance with legal requirements and terms creating trusts. They locate, inventory, and evaluate assets of probated accounts. They also direct realization of assets, liquidation of liabilities, payment of bills, preparation of federal and state tax returns on trust income, and collection of earnings. They represent the institution in trust fund negotiations.

Reserve officers maintain the institution's reserve funds according to policy and as required by law. They regulate the flow of money through branches, correspondent banks, and the Federal Reserve Bank. They also consolidate financial statements, calculate the legal reserve, and compile statistical and analytical reports of the reserves.

Foreign-exchange traders maintain the balance that the institution has on deposit in foreign banks to ensure its foreign-exchange position and determine the prices at which that exchange will be purchased and sold. Their conclusions are based on an analysis of demand, supply, and the stability of the currency. They establish local rates of exchange based upon money market quotations or the customer's financial standing. They also buy and sell foreign-exchange drafts and compute the proceeds.

The *securities trader* performs securities investment and counseling service for the bank and its customers. They study financial background and future trends and advise financial institution officers

Do M.B.A.'s Still Pay Off?

According to an annual study by *Business Week*, the average starting salary for a recent business school graduate fell from $75,900 in 2000 to $75,000 in 2002. Other years held much different results. Between 1996 and 1998, earnings jumped 30 percent; between 1998 and 2000, earnings increased by 15 percent. Despite this compensation cool off, business school graduates still earn more than their bachelor's counterparts because of their increased skills and marketable knowledge.

and customers regarding investments in stocks and bonds. They transmit buy-and-sell orders to a trading desk or broker as directed and recommend purchase, retention, or sale of issues. They compute extensions, commissions, and other charges for billing customers and making payments for securities.

The *operations officer* is in charge of the internal operations in a department or branch office of a financial institution. This person is responsible for the smooth and efficient operation of a particular area. Duties include interviewing, hiring, and directing the training of employees, as well as supervising their activities, evaluating their performance, and making certain that they comply with established procedures. Operations officers audit accounts, records, and certifications and verify the count of incoming cash. They prepare reports on the activities of the department or branch, control the supply of money for its needs, and perform other managerial tasks of a general nature.

The *credit union manager* directs the operations of credit unions, which are chartered by the state or federal government to provide savings and loan services to their members. This manager reviews loan applications, arranges automatic payroll deductions for credit union members wishing to make regular savings deposits or loan payments, and assists in collecting delinquent accounts. Managers prepare financial statements, help the government audit credit union records, and supervise bookkeeping and clerical activities. Acting as management representative of the credit union, credit union managers have the power to sign legal documents and checks on behalf of the board of directors. They also oversee control of the credit union's assets and advise the board on how to invest its funds.

REQUIREMENTS
High School

You will need at least a bachelor's degree if you want to work as a financial institution officer or manager. While you are in high school, therefore, you should take classes that will give you a solid preparation for college. These classes include mathematics, such as algebra and geometry, science, history, and a foreign language. Take English courses to improve your researching, writing, and communication skills. Also, take computer classes. Computer technology is an integral part of today's financial world. Finally, if your high school offers classes in economics, accounting, or finance, be sure to take these courses. The course work will not only give you an opportunity to gain knowledge but also allow you to see if you enjoy working with numbers and theories.

Postsecondary Training

Possible majors for you to take in college include accounting, economics, finance, or business administration with an emphasis on accounting or finance. You will need to continue honing your computer skills during this time. Also, you will probably have exposure to business law classes. It is important for you to realize that federal and state laws regarding business and finances change, so you will need to become familiar with current regulations.

Financial institutions increasingly seek candidates with master's degrees in business administration for positions as managers. So keep in mind that you may have to pursue further education even after you have completed your bachelor's degree. No matter what level of degree you obtain, however, you will also need to keep up your education even as you work. Many financial management and banking associations offer continuing education programs in conjunction with colleges or universities. These programs are geared toward advancing and updating your knowledge of subjects such as changing banking regulations, financial analysis, and international banking.

Certification or Licensing

Certification is one way to show your commitment to the field, improve your skills, and increase your possibilities for advancement. Professional certification is available in specialized fields such as investment and credit management. Requirements for earning the designation Chartered Financial Analyst, which is conferred by the Association for Investment Management and Research, include having the educational background to be able to do master's level work, passing three levels of tests, and having three or more years of experience in the field. The National Association of Credit Management offers business credit professionals a three-part certification program that consists of work experience and examinations. Financial managers pass through the level of Credit Business Associate to Credit Business Fellow to Certified Credit Executive. The Association for Financial Professionals confers the Certified Cash Manager designation. Applicants must pass an examination and have working experience in the field. In partnership with the University of Michigan Business School, the Association for Financial Professionals also offers the Certificate in Finance and Treasury Management for advanced professionals who complete education through a series of institutes.

Other Requirements

In the banking business, the ability to get along well with others is essential. You should be able to show tact and convey a feeling of understanding and confidence. Honesty is perhaps the most important qualification for this job. These officers and managers handle large sums of money and have access to confidential financial information about the individuals and business concerns associated with their institutions. Therefore, if you are interested in this career, you must have a high degree of personal integrity.

EXPLORING

Except for high school courses that are business oriented, you will find few opportunities for experience and exploration during high school. Ask your teacher or guidance counselor to arrange a class tour of a financial institution. This will at least give you a taste of how banking services work. You can gain the most valuable experience by finding a part-time or a summer job in a bank or other institution that sometimes hires qualified high school or college students. Finally, to gain some hands-on experience with managing money, consider joining a school or local club in which you could work as the treasurer.

EMPLOYERS

Financial managers and related workers hold approximately 658,000 jobs. They primarily work for banks and personal credit institutions such as credit unions and finance companies.

STARTING OUT

One way to enter banking as a regular employee is through part-time or summer employment. Anyone can apply for a position by writing to a financial institution officer in charge of personnel or by arranging for an interview appointment. Many institutions advertise in the classified section of local newspapers. The larger banks recruit on college campuses. An officer will visit a campus and conduct interviews at that time. Student placement offices can also arrange interviews.

ADVANCEMENT

There is no one method for advancement among financial institution officers. Advancement depends on the size of the institution, the services it offers, and the qualifications of the employee. Usually, the smaller the employer the slower the advancements.

Financial institutions often offer special training programs that take place at night, during the summer, and in some special instances during scheduled working hours. People who take advantage of these opportunities usually find that advancement comes more quickly. The American Banking Institute (part of the American Bankers Association), for example, offers training in every phase of banking through its own facilities or the facilities of the local universities and banking organizations. The length of this training may vary from six months to two years. Years of service and experience are required for a top-level financial institution officer to become acquainted with policy, operations, customers, and the community. Similarly, the National Association of Credit Management offers training and instruction.

EARNINGS

Those who enter banking in the next few years will find their earnings are dependent on their experience, the size of the institution, and its location. In general, starting salaries in financial institutions are not usually the highest, although among larger financial institutions in big cities, starting salaries often compare favorably with salaries in large corporations. After five to 10 years' experience, the salaries of officers usually are slightly higher than those in large corporations for people of comparable experience.

Financial managers in commercial banks earned a median annual salary of $55,960 in 2000, according to the U.S. Department of Labor. Also according to the Department, the lowest paid 10 percent of financial managers made approximately $36,050 in 2000, while the highest paid 10 percent earned $131,120 or more in 2000.

Group life insurance, paid vacations, profit-sharing plans, and health care and retirement plans are some of the benefits offered to financial officers and managers.

WORK ENVIRONMENT
Working conditions in financial institutions are generally pleasant. They are usually clean, well maintained, and often air-conditioned. They are generally located throughout cities for the convenience of customers and employees, too. Working hours for financial institution officers and managers may be somewhat irregular as many organizations have expanded their hours of business.

OUTLOOK
The number of job openings for financial institution officers and managers is expected to increase about as fast as the average for all other occupations, according to predictions by the U.S. Department of Labor. The need for skilled professionals will increase primarily as a result of greater domestic and foreign competition, changing laws affecting taxes and other financial matters, and a growing emphasis on accurate reporting of financial data for both financial institutions and corporations.

Competition for these jobs will be strong, however, for several reasons. Financial institution officers and managers are often promoted from within the ranks of the organization, and, once established in their jobs, they tend to stay for many years. Also, more qualified applicants are becoming available each year to fill vacancies; workers who have earned a master's degree in business administration will enjoy the lowest unemployment rates. Chances for employment will be best for workers who are familiar with a range of financial services, such as banking, insurance, real estate, and securities, and for those experienced in computers and data processing systems.

FOR MORE INFORMATION
This organization has information about the banking industry and continuing education available through the American Institute of Banking. It also has information on the Stonier Graduate School of Banking.

American Bankers Association
1120 Connecticut Avenue, NW
Washington, DC 20036
Tel: 800-226-5377
http://www.aba.com

For certification, industry news, and career information, contact:
Association for Financial Professionals
7315 Wisconsin Avenue, Suite 600 West
Bethesda, MD 20814
Tel: 301-907-2862
http://www.afponline.org

For information on the Chartered Financial Analyst designation, contact:
Association for Investment Management and Research
PO Box 3668
560 Ray C. Hunt Drive
Charlottesville, VA 22903-0668
Tel: 800-247-8132
Email: info@aimr.org
http://www.aimr.org

FT Knowledge Financial Learning offers continuing education courses. Its website also links to FT.com, a provider of information on financial markets and related news.
FT Knowledge Financial Learning
New York Institute of Finance
1330 Avenue of the Americas, 10th Floor
New York, NY 10019
Tel: 212-641-6616
http://www.ftkfinance.com

For information on certification, continuing education, and general information on the banking and credit industry, contact:
National Association of Credit Management
8840 Columbia 100 Parkway
Columbia, MD 21045
Tel: 410-740-5560
Email: nacm_info@nacm.org
http://www.nacm.org

FRANCHISE OWNERS

QUICK FACTS

School Subjects Business Mathematics	**Certification or Licensing** Required by certain franchisers (certification) Required by certain states (licensing)
Personal Skills Following instructions Leadership/management	**Outlook** About as fast as the average
Work Environment Primarily indoors Primarily one location	**DOT** N/A
Minimum Education Level Some postsecondary training	**GOE** N/A
	NOC N/A
Salary Range $0 to $30,000 to $100,000+	**O*NET-SOC** N/A

OVERVIEW

A *franchise owner* enters into a contract with a company to sell the company's products or services. After paying an initial fee and agreeing to pay the company a certain percentage of revenue, the franchise owner can use the company's name, logo, and guidance. McDonald's, Subway, and KFC are some of the top franchised companies with locations all across the country. However, franchises are not limited to the fast food industry. Franchises are available in a wide variety of business areas including computer service, lawn care, real estate, and hair salons. According to industry expert FranchiseHelp, franchises account for more than 40 percent of all retail sales in the United States and these sales total approximately $1 trillion a year.

HISTORY

Know anybody with an antique Singer sewing machine? Chances are, it was originally sold by one of the first franchise operations.

During the Civil War, the Singer Sewing Machine Company recognized the cost-efficiency of franchising and allowed dealers across the country to sell its sewing machines. Coca-Cola, as well as the Ford Motor Company and other automobile manufacturers, followed Singer's lead in the early 20th century by granting individuals the rights to sell their products. Franchising, however, didn't quite catch on until after World War II, when the needs for products and services across the country boomed, right along with the population. Ray Kroc (1902–1984) jumped on the bandwagon with his McDonald's restaurants in the 1950s. Since then, the McDonald's franchise has become one of the top money-making franchise opportunities of all time.

Franchises have changed somewhat over the last 20 to 30 years. Abuses of the franchise system brought new government regulations in the 1970s, and the government has been actively involved in protecting the rights of franchisers and franchisees. Also, single-unit ownership, the "mom and pop" operations, is giving way to multiple-unit ownership. A majority of franchisees own more than one of the franchiser's units.

THE JOB

Get off the subway at Hobby Town, then take the Candy Express to the Children's Orchard. No, this isn't some strange journey in a franchise fever dream—it could be any shopping mall or main street in the United States. Industry experts report that franchises are responsible for almost 50 percent of all retail sales in the United States, and this figure is expected to grow through the 21st century. Franchisers (those companies that sell franchise businesses) and franchisees (those who buy the businesses) are sharing in the almost one trillion dollars a year that franchise businesses take in. While everyone probably has a favorite business or two—maybe the neighborhood Krispy Kreme with its fresh crullers or the 7-Eleven down the street with its gallon-sized sodas—not everyone may realize that these are franchised establishments. For those people interested in starting their own businesses, becoming franchisees may offer just the right mix of risk and security. Any new business venture comes with a certain amount of risk, but franchises offer the new owners the security of a name and product that customers are used to and are willing to seek out. Someone with money to invest, the willingness to work hard and sometimes long hours, and the desire to be in the retail world may just be the person able to become the successful franchisee, sharing in the franchiser's success.

There's a franchise for practically every type of product and service imaginable. McDonald's and Burger King are two of the more familiar franchises, but there are many franchise opportunities in today's market, such as businesses that offer temporary employment, maid services, weight control centers, and custom picture framing, to name a few. The International Franchise Association (IFA) reports that there are approximately 75 different industries that use of the franchise system. There is most likely a franchise opportunity to suit every interest.

Depending on the size and nature of the franchise, owners' responsibilities differ. Those who are able to make a large initial investment may also be able to hire managers and staff members to assist them. Those running a smaller business will need to handle most, if not all, of the job responsibilities themselves. Though there should be assistance from the franchiser in terms of training, marketing guidance, and established business systems, the business is essentially the franchisee's own. The franchisee pays an initial franchise fee, makes royalty payments to the franchiser, purchases equipment, and rents business space. Any franchisee must handle administrative details, such as record-keeping, creating budgets, and preparing reports for the franchiser. A franchisee is also responsible for hiring (and firing) employees, scheduling work hours, preparing payroll, and keeping track of inventory. Using the franchiser's marketing methods, the franchisee advertises the business. The practices and systems of franchisers differ, so those interested in this work need to carefully research the franchise before buying into it.

Some owners work directly with the clientele. Of course, someone who owns multiple units of the McDonald's franchise probably won't be taking orders at the counter; but someone who owns a single unit of a smaller operation, like a pool-maintenance service, may be actively involved in dealing with customers on a personal level.

Donna Weber of Redmond, Washington, owns a Jazzercise franchise. Jazzercise is the world's largest dance fitness franchise corporation, with over 5,000 instructors leading almost half a million participants each year. "I own and teach seven Jazzercise classes a week in two suburbs around the Seattle area," Weber says. After investing with an initial low franchise fee, Weber went through considerable training and testing; the training involves instruction on exercise physiology, dance/exercise technique, and safety issues, as well as instruction on the business aspect of owning a franchise. After training, Weber received certification and started her business. She pays a monthly fee to Jazzercise and in return receives choreography notes to new songs and videos demonstrating the exercises.

In addition to conducting classes, Weber spends some part of every workday preparing paperwork for the corporate headquarters. "I keep track of my students' attendance and write personal postcards to those I haven't seen in a while, those who are having birthdays, those who need some personal recognition for a job well done, etc.," says Weber, who must also regularly learn new routines. "I teach three different formats each week," she says, "regular aerobics, step, and a circuit-training classes, so there is a lot of prep to do a good, safe class."

The franchisee's experience will be affected by the name recognition of the business. If it's a fairly new business, the franchisee may have to take on much of the responsibility of promoting it. If it is a well-established business, customers and clients already know what to expect from the operation.

REQUIREMENTS
High School

Business, math, economics, and accounting courses will be the most valuable to you in preparing for franchise ownership. Before buying into a franchise, you'll have to do a lot of research into the company, analyzing local demographics to determine whether a business is a sound investment. English classes will help you develop the research skills you'll need. In addition, you will need to hone your communication skills that will be essential in establishing relationships with franchisers and customers. Take computer classes since it is virtually impossible to work in today's business world without knowing how to use a computer or the Web. If you already know of a particular area that interests you—such as food service, fashion, or fitness—take classes that will help you learn more about it. Such classes may include home economics, art, dance, or physical education.

Postsecondary Training

Because there is such a wide variety of franchise opportunities available, there is no single educational path to take on the road to owning a franchise. Keep in mind, however, that when franchisers review your application for the right to purchase a unit, they'll take into consideration your previous experience in the area. Obviously, a real estate company is unlikely to take a risk on you if you've never had any experience as a broker. In addition, there are some franchise opportunities that require degrees; for example, to own an environmental consulting agency, a business that helps companies meet government environmental standards, you must be an engineer or geologist. But there are also many companies willing to sell to someone wanting to break into a new business. Franchisers will often include special training as part of the initial franchise fee.

Experts in the field stress the importance of gaining work experience before starting your own business. Hone your sales, management, and people skills and take the time to learn about the industry that interests you. Even if you don't plan on getting a college degree, consider taking some college-level courses in subjects such as business and finance. One recent survey of franchisees found that over 80 percent had attended college or had a college degree. This reflects the fact that many franchisees have worked for many years in other professions in order to have the money and security needed for starting new businesses. Some organizations and schools, for example, the Institute for Franchise Management at the University of St. Thomas (http://www.stthomas.edu/franchise), offer courses for prospective franchisees.

Certification or Licensing

Some franchisers have their own certification process and require their franchisees to go through training. You may also want to receive the certification Certified Franchise Executive offered by the Institute of Certified Franchise Executives, an organization affiliated with the IFA's Education Foundation. This certification involves completing a certain number of courses in topics such as economics and franchise law, participating in events such as seminars or conventions, and work experience. Although this certification is voluntary, it will show your level of education and commitment to the field as well as give you the opportunity to network with other franchise professionals.

You may also need to obtain a small business license to own a franchise unit in your state. Regulations vary depending on the state and the type of business, so it is important that you check with your state's licensing board for specifics before you invest in a franchise.

Other Requirements

As with any small business, you need self-motivation and discipline in order to make your franchise unit successful. Although you'll have some help from your franchiser, the responsibilities of ownership are your own. You'll also need a good credit rating to be eligible for a bank loan, or you'll need enough money of your own for the initial investment. You should be a fairly cautious person, as many people are taken every year in fraudulent franchise schemes. But at the same time you should feel comfortable taking some risks.

EXPLORING

One relatively easy way to learn about franchising is by doing some research on the Web. The IFA, for example, hosts a very informative website (http://www.franchise.org). The association offers the free online newsletter *Franchise-Enews* as well as the magazine *Franchising World*. Both have information of interest to potential franchisees. Also, check out your public library or bookstores for the many business magazines that report on small business opportunities. Many of these magazines, such as *Entrepreneur* (http://www.entrepreneurmag.com), publish special editions dealing specifically with franchises.

Join your high school's business club, a group that may give you the opportunity to meet business leaders in your community. Find a local franchise owner and ask to meet with him or her for an informational interview. Discuss the pros and cons of franchise ownership, find out about the owner's educational and professional background, and ask them for general advice. Also, most franchise companies will send you brochures about their franchise opportunities. Request some information and read about what's involved in owning a franchise unit.

Think about what industry interests you, such as services, fast food, health and fitness, or computers. Come up with your own ideas for a franchise business and do some research to find out if this business already exists. If it does, there may be a part-time or summer job opportunity there for you. If it doesn't, keep the idea in mind for your future but go ahead and get some work experience now. Many franchises hire high school students, and even if you end up working at a restaurant when lawn care is your main interest, you'll still be gaining valuable experience dealing with customers, handling sales, and working with others.

EMPLOYERS

There are a number of franchise directories available that list hundreds of franchise opportunities in diverse areas. While some franchisers sell units all across the country, others only do business in a few states. Some of the most successful franchises can guarantee a franchisee great revenue, but these franchise units can require hundreds of thousands of dollars in initial investment.

Many franchisees own more than one franchise unit with a company; some even tie two different franchises together in a practice called "cross-branding." For example, a franchisee may own a pizza franchise, as well as an ice cream franchise housed in the same restaurant. Another popular combination is a convenience store that also houses a fast food outlet.

STARTING OUT

Before you invest a cent or sign any papers, you should do an extensive amount of research into the franchise, particularly if it's a fairly new company. There are many disreputable franchise operations, so you need to be certain of what you're investing in. Lawyers and franchise consultants offer their services to assist people in choosing franchises; some consultants also conduct seminars. The Federal Trade Commission (FTC) publishes *The FTC Consumer Guide to Buying a Franchise* and other relevant publications. IFA also provides free franchise-buying advice.

You'll need money for the initial franchise fee and for the expenses of the first few years of business. You may pursue a loan from a bank, from business associates, or you may use your own savings. In some cases your start-up costs will be very low; in others you'll need money for a computer, rental of workspace, equipment, signs, and staff. According to the IFA, total start-up costs can range from $20,000 or less to over 1 million dollars, depending on the franchise selected and whether it is necessary to own or lease real estate to operate the business. Moreover, the initial franchise fee for most franchisers is between $20,000 and $28,000. Some franchises can cost much less. Donna Weber's Jazzercise franchise required an initial $600 franchise fee. Though her business has been successful, she must share her gross income. "Twenty percent of that goes back to Jazzercise each month as a fee, I pay about 23 percent of the gross for monthly rent, and 8.6 percent to the state of Washington for sales tax collected on the price of my tickets. There are lots of women grossing $75,000 a year doing this, and there are some who choose to do this for fun and make nothing in return. It's all in how you make it work for you."

ADVANCEMENT

A new franchise unit usually takes a few years to turn profitable. Once the business has proven a success, franchisees may choose to invest in other franchise units with the same company. Franchise owners may also be able to afford management and other staff to take on some of the many responsibilities of the business.

EARNINGS

The earnings for franchisees vary greatly depending on such factors as the type of franchise they own, the amount of money a franchisee was able to initially invest without taking a loan, the franchise's location, and the number of franchise units the franchisee owns. An IFA survey of 1,000 franchise owners found that the average yearly salary of this group was $91,630. Approximately 24 percent made more than $100,000 annually.

Since franchisees run their own businesses, they generally do not have paid sick days or holidays. In addition, they are typically responsible for providing their own insurance and retirement plans.

WORK ENVIRONMENT

Owning a franchise unit can be demanding, requiring work of 60 to 70 hours a week, but owners have the satisfaction of knowing that their business's success is a result of their own hard work. Some people look for franchise opportunities that are less demanding and may only require a part-time commitment. "I'm not getting rich," Donna Weber says, "but I love my job, and I love being my own boss. I can schedule my vacations when I want; we usually don't close our classes down, so we hire certified Jazzercise substitutes."

Franchise owners who handle all the business details personally may consider this work to be very stressful. In addition, dealing with the hiring, management, and sometimes firing of staff can also be difficult. In some situations, much of a franchisee's work will be limited to an office setting; in other situations, such as with a home inspection service or a maid service, the franchisee drives to remote sites to work with clients. Some franchises are mobile in nature, and these will involve a lot of traveling within a designated region.

OUTLOOK

While some experts say that the success rate of franchises is very high and a great deal of money can be made with a franchise unit, others say franchising isn't as successful as starting an independent business. According to the Department of Commerce, less than 5 percent of franchised outlets have failed each year since 1971. However, when reporting figures, franchisers don't always consider a unit as failing if it is under different ownership, but still in operation. The employment outlook will depend on factors such as the economy—a downturn in the economy is always most difficult for new businesses—as well as the type of franchise. Overall, though, growth should be steady and about as fast as the average.

FOR MORE INFORMATION

For information about buying a franchise and a list of AAFD-accredited franchisers, contact:

American Association of Franchisees and Dealers (AAFD)
PO Box 81887
San Diego, CA 92138-1887
Tel: 800-733-9858
http://www.aafd.org

Contact the FTC for publications regarding franchising. The website also provides the text of some publications as well as current franchise news.

Federal Trade Commission (FTC)
Franchises and Business Opportunities
CRC-240
Washington, DC 20580
Tel: 202-326-2222
http://www.ftc.gov

For more information on franchising as well as a free newsletter, contact:

FranchiseHelp
101 Executive Boulevard, 2nd Floor
Elmsford, NY 10523
Tel: 800-401-1446
Email: company@franchisehelp.com
http://www.franchisehelp.com

For general information about franchising, specific franchise opportunities, and the publications Franchise-Enews and Franchise NewsBriefs, contact the IFA:

International Franchise Association (IFA)
1350 New York Avenue, NW, Suite 900
Washington, DC 20005-4709
Tel: 202-628-8000
Email: ifa@franchise.org
http://www.franchise.org

GRANT COORDINATORS AND WRITERS

QUICK FACTS

School Subjects Business English	**Certification or Licensing** None available
	Outlook Little change or more slowly than the average
Personal Skills Communication/ideas Leadership/management	
	DOT 169
Work Environment Primarily indoors Primarily one location	**GOE** 11.05.02
Minimum Education Level Bachelor's degree	**NOC** N/A
Salary Range $21,250 to $64,643 to $78,000+	**O*NET-SOC** N/A

OVERVIEW

Grant coordinators are responsible for managing all grant-funded programs for nonprofit organizations. *Grant writers* handle the actual creation and preparation of proposals to potential funders. In smaller organizations, one person may handle both jobs. Both grant coordinators and grant writers may work for schools, local governments, social service agencies, and other organizations to oversee all aspects of grant funding. The Association of Fundraising Professionals reports that it has over 25,000 members employed at a variety of nonprofit organizations, including those in the arts, social service, health care, and educational fields, as well as at private consulting firms around the country.

HISTORY

The first recorded government research grant was given to the inventor Samuel Morse in 1842. In the United States, the amount of grants funding has grown consistently and dramatically since that time. More private foundations began bestowing grants when it became clear how much help they could provide to all types of nonprofit groups. Government agencies have increased grants funding, especially in the sciences, recognizing that these grants help U.S. scientists and inventors stay on the cutting edge of new technology.

The positions of grant coordinator and grant writer have come into being only in the last few decades. Organizing and writing grant proposals were usually assigned to various employees (who had other job duties) in each nonprofit agency. Now more agencies are recognizing the value of having separate grant coordinators and writers who work solely on grants for the agency.

THE JOB

The number of grants awarded each year in the United States is very large, and so is the competition among grants-seekers; hundreds of institutions may apply for the same grant. Furthermore, organizations that award grants have very specific rules and requirements that must be satisfied for a proposal even to be considered.

Grant coordinators must be familiar with all applicable funding organizations and their requirements. They often make the difference in securing the grant for their organizations. Grant coordinators plan and organize all grant-funded programs for their agency or organization. They conduct extensive research on foundations and grant-offering agencies by ordering their publications and contacting officials at the foundations.

To determine which grants the organization should apply for, coordinators work with other officers in their own agency. Grant coordinators participate in many of the planning stages for the agency. For instance, they may sit in on meetings in which budgets are planned and financial officials determine operating budgets, anticipate income, and forecast expenditures. Employees of the nonprofit organization may suggest programs, equipment, or materials that they would like to have funded by a grant, and the grant coordinator determines the best sources of funding for each need.

Before applying for a grant, a grant coordinator maps out a proposal for how the funding would be used. Often these proposals are long and complex. Other employees may help the grant coordinator write up a proposal justifying the need for the program or equipment.

Some nonprofit organizations are fortunate enough to have one or more employees whose primary function is grant writing. In these cases the grant coordinator does not write the grant proposal. The grant writer creates the proposal document and develops the vocabulary and overall structure. Working with the staff whose programs require funding, the grant writer devises a strategy, translating the program to make it relevant to the funder's interests. In the proposal, the grant writer also must communicate both the short-term and long-term goals of the organization so an outsider could understand them. The grant writer also may be responsible for assembling supporting documents that accompany the proposal, such as the organization's budget, board of directors, history, mission, and executive biographies. The grant writer must create different proposals for different kinds of funding, for example, general operating support for the organization overall versus funding for a specific program or project. Additionally, if a grant is received, the grant writer often has to prepare a final report required by many funders.

When an organization does not have a separate grant writer on staff, the writer may be a financial officer in the organization, a teacher in the school, or an employee in charge of a particular project.

Drafts of the proposal usually pass through many hands, including fiscal officers or other executives, before being sent to foundations or grant-offering agencies. Once a final draft has been approved, the grant coordinator or writer prepares the grant proposal using the format required by the funding agency. The proposal then is submitted to the foundation or funding agency. It is the responsibility of the grant coordinator or writer to follow up on the application and meet with agency or foundation representatives if necessary.

Once an organization receives its grant, the coordinator makes sure to meet all of the requirements of the grant-giver. For example, if the grant covers the purchase of equipment, the coordinator confirms receipt of the correct equipment and completes follow-up reports for the foundation or agency. In some instances, the grant coordinator hires an outside agency to monitor the implementation of a grant-funded program. The outside agency then may submit its periodic monitoring reports both to the funding agency and to the grant coordinator.

A large part of the grant coordinator's work involves maintaining files and overseeing paperwork, which is usually done on computer. A thorough grant coordinator must keep the literature published by funding agencies for reference and file copies of all applications and proposals.

Grant coordinators are essentially *project managers*. They must understand the overall work of their organization while focusing on finding and obtaining the best grants. They see to it that their organization presents itself to funding agencies in the best possible way.

REQUIREMENTS
High School

High school courses in English, journalism, and creative writing, will develop your written communication skills. Courses in history and the other humanities also are useful as background reference, and a solid background in mathematics will help you feel comfortable dealing with budgets and other financial documents.

Postsecondary Training

A survey by the Association of Fundraising Professionals reports that 90 percent of respondents hold a bachelor's degree and 43 percent hold a master's degree or higher. The degree can be a bachelor of arts, bachelor of science, or an equivalent degree from a four-year college or university. Grant coordinators and writers can have any of several kinds of educational backgrounds. Some study liberal arts, some have business degrees, and some have studied in management-training programs.

Regardless of your educational background, you will need the ability to communicate clearly and effectively in writing. Much paperwork is involved in applying for a grant; the funding agency's instructions must be followed precisely, and the proposal must state the institution's goals and objectives in a clear and persuasive way.

Certification or Licensing

There is no licensing requirement or specific test that grant coordinators or writers must pass. Although not required, different levels of certification programs exist for fund-raising professionals. Requirements include filling out an application, passing a written examination, and pledging to uphold a code of ethics. Contact the Association of Fundraising Professionals for more information.

Other Requirements

Most grant coordinators learn their work on the job. Experience in the workplace helps the coordinator locate the best sources of grants funding and learn the best ways to pursue those sources. For example, if the ideals of a foundation match the intent of the grant coordinator's agency, an ongoing relationship may develop between the agency and the foundation. The grant coordinator learns about these connections in the day-to-day work.

Grant coordinators must have good administrative skills and be detail-oriented. Good communication skills are essential. They work with a wide range of people and must express themselves easily.

Coordinators direct and supervise others, so they must be comfortable in management situations. They should be able to influence and persuade others, including their associates and foundation employees. The more grant coordinators and writers understand about the operations of the foundations that they will be applying to, the more successful they will be in writing the grant proposals and securing the requested funding. Grant coordinators and writers must also work well under pressure. There are deadlines to meet, and the responsibility for meeting those deadlines falls squarely on their shoulders. The financial pressure on an organization that does not receive an expected grant can be enormous, and the grant coordinator may bear the responsibility for the loss.

EXPLORING

Volunteering for nonprofit organizations is a good way to find out about a grant coordinator's work firsthand. Contact local churches or synagogues, charities, health organizations, or social service agencies. In nonprofit organizations that have grant coordinators, the ideal internship or volunteer experience involves assisting with a grant-application project. Sometimes schools have their own grant-application projects several times a year. You can get an understanding of all of the work involved by seeing the application or proposal process through from start to finish.

Several organizations sponsor intensive workshops on grant coordination and fund-raising. The Grantsmanship Center (http://www.tgci.com) conducts seminars and workshops in cities across the United States more than 200 times a year. It helps grant coordinators and writers with proposal writing and other aspects of their jobs. Its publication *The Grantsmanship Center Magazine* and guide *Program Planning and Proposal Writing* are good resources for grant writers and coordinators. The Grantsmanship Center also maintains a reference library. The National Network of Grantmakers (http://www.nng.org) also runs seminars and offers publications.

Many fund-raising organizations also have helpful publications for the potential grant coordinator. An annual almanac, *Giving USA* (http://www.aafrc.org/giving) is published by the American Association of Fundraising Counsel.

Some colleges and universities offer courses in fund-raising. These may even include business lectures or seminars on the grant-application process. Many colleges also offer courses in arts management or in nonprofit work that would help potential grant coordinators and writers understand the type of work required in this occupation.

EMPLOYERS

Grant writers and coordinators work for nonprofit organizations and agencies, such as social service agencies, arts organizations, museums, educational institutions, and research foundations. Grant writers also work independently as freelancers. They contract their services to smaller nonprofit agencies or individuals who might seek funding for an arts program or a scientific research project, for example.

STARTING OUT

After earning your bachelor's degree, apply for a job at a nonprofit organization. Keep in mind that you will probably be hired by an agency to do tasks other than grant writing or coordinating. You first need to learn how the organization operates and understand its goals before beginning to work with grants. In these first years, many prospective coordinators and writers sign up for management-training programs or courses in technical writing, psychology, sociology, and statistical methods.

ADVANCEMENT

Since grant coordinators almost always begin their careers in other work, they advance into grant positions by showing an understanding of the organization's goals. Once the organization moves a person into a grant position, advancement comes with successful work on grant proposals and obtaining the necessary funding. If the grant coordinator and writer positions are separate, usually grant writers advance to grant coordinators, having gained expertise and familiarity with the funding community. But because nonprofit organizations often employ only one person responsible for grant writing and coordination, a grant administrator advances by moving into a position with a larger nonprofit organization that requires higher level skills.

EARNINGS

According to the National Association of Colleges and Employers, the average starting salary for those with a bachelor's degree working in fund-raising and development was $21,250 in 2000. Entry-level writers and editors earned average salaries of $30,441 and those in social service administration positions earned $27,029. Nonprofit employers paid starting salaries between $26,500 and $33,500 for those with bachelor's degrees. Grant coordinators and writers with master's degrees start from $35,000 to $48,000 a year.

The average salaries of surveyed members of the Association of Fundraising Professionals were much higher: $64,643 a year in 2001. The median salary was $56,000, and the top 25 percent of members earned more than $78,000. The salary survey noted that earnings varied among members based on position, organization, location, and experience. Pay differences based on gender and ethnic background were also discovered.

Freelance grant coordinators usually charge separate fees for research and grant writing. The International Alliance of Grantwriters and Nonprofit Consultants charges $1,500 for a grant search, $5,000 for grant writing for private and corporate funds, and $10,000 for grant writing for public funds. An individual might expect to pay $500 to $800 for a prospect search and $2,500 to $5,000 for grant writing.

Benefits for grant coordinators and writers often are equivalent to other professional business positions, including paid vacation, group insurance plans, and paid sick days.

WORK ENVIRONMENT

Grant coordinators work primarily in comfortable office environments. Some nonprofit agencies have cramped or inadequate facilities, while others may be quite luxurious. The grant coordinator usually works during regular office hours unless a deadline must be met. When grant coordinators approach the deadlines for submitting grant proposals, overtime work, including nights or weekends, may be required. Meetings with foundation representatives may take place outside the office or before or after regular hours. Benefits packages and vacation time vary widely from agency to agency, but most nonprofit organizations are flexible places to work. Grant coordinators are often most satisfied with their jobs when they believe in the goals of their own agency and know they are helping the agency do its work.

OUTLOOK

The outlook for grant coordinators and writers is steady. However, reports by the *Chronicle of Philanthropy* say that corporate giving is leveling off, partly due to an uncertain economy. Hundreds of agencies are applying for the same grants, and a top grant coordinator or writer can make the difference between the organization that gets the funding and the one that does not. A grant coordinator who has proven success in coordinating grants proposals and obtaining grants, as well as a grant writer who has written successful proposals, should be able to find work. Many people who work in nonprofit organizations believe that more grant coordinators and writers will be hired as more of these organizations realize that a professional grant administrator may help them get funding they have been missing. The grant coordinator's knowledge of how to choose the most appropriate sources of grant funding and implement funding programs is invaluable to nonprofit organizations.

FOR MORE INFORMATION

For statistics on charitable donations, contact:
American Association of Fundraising Counsel
10293 North Meridian Street, Suite 175
Indianapolis, IN 46290
Tel: 800-462-2372
Email: info@aafrc.org
http://www.aafrc.org

For information on fundraising careers, educational programs, and other resources, contact:
Association of Fundraising Professionals
1101 King Street, Suite 700
Alexandria, VA 22314-2967
Tel: 703-684-0410
http://www.afpnet.org

The following organization provides assistance on proposal writing, offers 200 seminars annually, and publishes The Grantsmanship Center Magazine.
Grantsmanship Center
1125 West Sixth Street, Fifth Floor
PO Box 17220
Los Angeles, CA 90017
Tel: 213-482-9860
http://www.tgci.com

HOTEL AND MOTEL MANAGERS

QUICK FACTS

School Subjects Business Mathematics Speech	**Certification or Licensing** Voluntary
	Outlook Little change or more slowly than the average
Personal Skills Helping/teaching Leadership/management	**DOT** 187
Work Environment Primarily indoors Primarily one location	**GOE** 11.11.01
Minimum Education Level Associate's degree	**NOC** 0632
Salary Range $19,890 to $32,860 to $57,460+	**O*NET-SOC** 11-9081.00

OVERVIEW

Hotel and motel managers, sometimes called *lodging managers,* are ultimately responsible for the business of running their hotel or motel smoothly and efficiently. Larger establishments may have several managers accountable for different departments. In turn, these departmental managers report to the general manager. The general manager's many duties include managing personnel, financial operations, and promotional activities. Lodging managers hold approximately 68,000 jobs in the United States.

HISTORY

As travel became more frequent in the United States and around the world, the idea of a comfortable place for travelers to stay and rest became a reality. The earliest lodging places were probably simple shelters with no food or running water available. Better roads and means of transportation allowed more people the luxury of travel, which in turn raised the standard of lodging. The early inns, called *mansiones*, were often located along roads. They offered a bed and, sometimes, a meal. The first hotel and motel managers were the owners themselves. They were responsible for maintaining the rooms, collecting payment, and providing food and drink to guests.

As hotels and motels began to consolidate and chains were built, managers became more important. Many times, a single person, or family, would own numerous hotel or motel properties, and hire reliable people to help manage the business. Managers were trusted to run the establishments properly, turn a profit, and make sure rooms were filled.

THE JOB

Hotel and motel managers are responsible for the overall supervision of their establishment, the different departments, and their staff. They follow operating guidelines set by the owners, or if part of a chain, by the main headquarters and executive board. A *general manager,* often abbreviated to *GM,* allocates funds to all departments, approves expenditures, sets room rates, and establishes standards for food and beverage service, decor, and all guest services. GMs tour their property every day, usually with the head of the housekeeping department, to make certain everything is clean and orderly. GMs are responsible for keeping their establishment's accounting books in order, doing or approving the advertising and marketing, maintaining and ordering supplies, and interviewing and training new employees. However, in large hotels and motels, the GM is usually has one or more assistants.

Some hotels and motels still employ *resident managers,* who live on the premises and are on call 24 hours a day, in case of emergencies. Resident managers work regular eight-hour shifts daily, attending to the duties of the hotel or motel. In many modern establishments, the general manager has replaced the resident manager.

In large hotels and motels, departmental managers include the following:

Front office managers supervise the activity and staff of the front desk. They direct reservations and sleeping room assignments. Front office managers make sure that all guests are treated courteously and check-in and check-out periods are managed smoothly. Any guest complaints or problems are usually directed to the front desk first—front office managers are responsible for rectifying all customer complaints before they reach the general manager.

Executive housekeepers are managers who supervise the work of the room attendants, housekeepers, janitors, gardeners, and the laundry staff. Depending on the size and structure of the hotel, they may also be in charge of ordering cleaning supplies, linens, towels, and toiletries. Some executive housekeepers may be responsible for dealing with suppliers and vendors.

Personnel managers head human resources or personnel departments. They hire and fire employees and work with other personnel employees, such as employee relations managers, to protect employee rights and address grievances.

Restaurant managers oversee the daily operation of hotel or motel restaurants. They manage employees such as waiters, buspersons, hosts, bartenders, and cooks and bakers. They also resolve customer complaints. They are responsible for all food service operations in the hotel or motel—from restaurants, cocktail lounges, and banquets to room service. They supervise food and service quality and preparation, order supplies from different vendors, and estimate food costs.

Large hotels and motels can profit by marketing their facilities for conventions, meetings, and special events. *Convention services managers* are in charge of coordinating such activities. The convention services manager takes care of all necessary details, such as blocking sleeping rooms for the group, arranging for meeting rooms or ballrooms, and resolving any problems that arise.

REQUIREMENTS
High School
It's a good idea to begin preparing for a career in hotel management while in high school. Concentrate on a business-oriented curriculum, with classes in finance, accounting, and mathematics. Since computers are widely used in the hotel setting for reservations, accounting, and management of supplies, it is important that you become computer literate. Brush up on your communication skills while in high school: You'll need them when giving direction and supervision to a large and diverse staff. Take English classes and other courses, such as speech or drama, that will give you the chance to polish grammar and speaking skills. A second language, especially Spanish, French, or Japanese, will be very helpful to you in the future.

Postsecondary Training
While you should be able to get a starting position at a hotel or motel with only a high school diploma, many companies now require management trainees to have a minimum of a bachelor's

degree in hotel and restaurant management. Numerous community and junior colleges and some universities offer associate's, bachelor's, or graduate degree programs in hotel or restaurant management. In addition, technical, vocational, and trade schools and other institutions offer hotel business programs resulting in a formal recognition of training, such as a certificate.

Classes in hotel management cover topics such as administration, marketing, housekeeping, hotel maintenance, and computer skills. To complement class instruction, most programs require students to work on site at a hotel.

Many hotels and motels will also consider candidates with liberal arts degrees or degrees in such fields as business management and public relations if they are highly qualified and talented.

Certification or Licensing

Certification for this job is not a requirement, though it is recognized by many as a measurement of industry knowledge and job experience. Programs are offered by industry trade associations, such as the Educational Institute of the American Hotel and Lodging Association.

Other Requirements

Managers are strong leaders who have a flair for organization and communication and, most important, work well with all types of people. To keep the hotel or motel running smoothly, general managers need to establish policies and procedures and make certain their directions are followed. Managing can sometimes be stressful, and managers need to keep a cool demeanor when dealing with difficult situations that come their way.

Vlato Lemick, general manager and owner of several hotels in the Chicago area, considers dealing with customer complaints to be one of his most challenging job duties. "Problems do reach my desk, and I have to take care of them." Does he only give attention to the important problems? "No," he says firmly. "No complaint or request should be considered unimportant."

EXPLORING

You can test your interest in this career firsthand by visiting a local hotel or motel and spending a day at the front desk, or better yet, with the general manager. Working in hospitality is really the best way to explore the field. Part-time jobs in any department, no matter how small, will give you important business experience. Here's a success story to inspire you. Keith Pierce's first hotel job was loading dishwashers at the Waldorf Astoria. Many dishes later, armed with a college degree and work experience, Pierce is now a vice president of Wingate Hotels.

EMPLOYERS

There are approximately 68,000 hotel and motel managers working in the United States. Half of these workers own their own hotel or motel.

Some major employers in the industry are Comfort Inn, based in Newark, Delaware; the Hilton Hotels, based in Carrollton, Texas; and Mirage Resorts of Las Vegas, which is noted for its quality of management. These companies have properties located nationwide and abroad. Host Marriott Corporation, another international player, offers a fast-track management program for qualified employees and has been known to encourage career advancement for minorities and women.

Long-term experience is important in this industry. It is wise to work at least one year at a company before moving to another. Employers are likely to question applicants who have had more than four employers in less than two years.

STARTING OUT

The position of general manager is one of the top rungs on this career ladder. It's unlikely this would be your first industry job. In today's highly technical age, experience, though still important, is not enough for job advancement. Most candidates have some postsecondary education; many have at least a bachelor's degree in hotel and restaurant management. Graduates entering the hotel industry usually pay their dues by working as assistant managers, assistant departmental managers, or shift managers. Many hotels and motels have specific management training programs for their management-bound employees. Employees are encouraged to work different desks so they will be knowledgeable about each department.

Your school's career center, the local library, and the Internet can all be helpful when researching college programs or specific businesses.

ADVANCEMENT

The average tenure of a general manager is between six and seven years; those who have worked as a GM for 10 years or more usually view their job as a lifetime commitment. Managers who leave the profession usually advance to the regional or even national area of hotel and motel management, such as property management or the administrative or financial departments of the lodging chain. Some may opt to open their own hotel or motel franchises or even operate a small inn or bed and breakfast. The management skills learned as a general manager can be successfully utilized in any avenue of business.

EARNINGS

Salary figures vary according to the worker's level of expertise, the lodging establishment, the duties involved, the size of the hotel or motel, and its location. General managers working in large urban areas can expect to have more responsibilities and higher compensation than those at smaller inns in rural areas.

According to the U.S. Department of Labor, lodging managers reported a median yearly income of $32,860 in 2001. The lowest paid 10 percent earned less than $19,890 annually, and the highest paid 10 percent made more than $57,460 per year. Managers may receive bonuses of 20 to 25 percent of their base salary when conditions are favorable, such as during a strong economy and when managers have increased business. These bonuses can often boost earnings by thousands of dollars.

Managers receive paid vacation and sick days and other benefits, such as medical and life insurance, and pension or profit-sharing plans. They may also receive lodging, meals, parking, laundry, and financial assistance with education.

WORK ENVIRONMENT

Don't expect to manage a 200-room hotel sitting behind a desk. General managers make at least one property walk-through a day, inspecting the condition of the hotel. The rest of the day is spent returning phone calls, meeting with clients, and running from one department to another. Managers do not have nine-to-five days; they usually work an average of 55 hours a week. Weekends and holidays are no exceptions. Off-duty managers are sometimes called back to work in cases of emergency—night or day—and they don't go home until the problem is solved. Managers have a lot of interaction with many different people, such as those on the hotel or motel staff, tourists in town to see the sights, business people attending conventions, and numerous other professionals in the hospitality industry. Not everyone is polite or reasonable, and managers must be able to "think on their feet" and work calmly in difficult situations.

OUTLOOK

Overall, the employment outlook for lodging managers is predicted to grow more slowly than the average through the next decade, according to the U.S. Department of Labor. Many factors influence the employment of managers, including hotel consolidations that mean layoffs for redundant workers and the increasing number of budget hotels and motels with fewer extras, such as a restaurant or room service. Hotels and motels with fewer offerings need fewer managers.

Additionally, the travel and hospitality industry is very sensitive to economic developments. During weak economic times, people travel less often for pleasure, which means fewer tourists in need of lodging. Businesses also cut back on their expenses by limiting or eliminating business travel and using other methods, such as teleconferencing, to meet with clients who are in different locations. This also means fewer customers for hotels and motels.

World events also have a major influence on the travel and hospitality industry. The terrorist attacks in the United States in 2001 dramatically reduced the number of people willing to travel for business and pleasure. A lack of customers translated into layoffs in the industry. According to the publication *National Hotel Executive*, approximately 360,000 people in the hotel sector alone lost their jobs in the three months after the attacks.

Nevertheless, industry experts predict a rebound from such slow times. Hotels and other places of lodging continue to be built, and managers are needed to run them. College graduates with degrees in hotel or restaurant management, or a similar business degree, will have the best opportunities, as will managers with excellent work experience and those with certification. Other opportunities will become available as current managers move to other occupations, retire, or leave the work force for other reasons.

FOR MORE INFORMATION

For information on careers in hotel management, contact:
American Hotel and Lodging Association
1201 New York Avenue, NW, Suite 600
Washington, DC 20005-3931
Tel: 202-289-3100
Email: info@ahla.com
http://www.ahlaonline.org

For information on internships, scholarships, or certification requirements, contact:

Educational Institute of the American Hotel & Lodging Association
800 North Magnolia Avenue, Suite 1800
Orlando, FL 32803
Tel: 800-752-4567
http://www.ei-ahla.org

For information and a listing of hostels worldwide, contact:

Hostelling International-USA
American Youth Hostels
8401 Colesville Road, Suite 600
Silver Spring, MD 20910
Tel: 301-495-1240
http://www.hiayh.org

For publication offering information on sales and marketing in hospitality, contact:

Hospitality Sales and Marketing Association International
8201 Greensboro Drive, Suite 300
McLean, VA 22102
Tel: 703-610-9024
http://www.hsmai.org

For education information and a list of available school programs, contact:

International Council on Hotel, Restaurant, and Institutional Education
2613 North Parham Road, 2nd Floor
Richmond, VA 23294
Tel: 804-346-4800
Email: info@chrie.org
http://chrie.org

For information on careers, education, and certification programs, contact:

International Executive Housekeepers Association
1001 Eastwind Drive, Suite 301
Westerville, OH 43081-3361
Tel: 800-200-6342
Email: excel@ieha.org
http://www.ieha.org

INSURANCE UNDERWRITERS

QUICK FACTS

School Subjects Business Mathematics	**Certification or Licensing** Recommended
Personal Skills Following instructions Leadership/management	**Outlook** Little change or more slowly than the average
Work Environment Primarily indoors Primarily one location	**DOT** 169
	GOE 11.06.03
Minimum Education Level Bachelor's degree	**NOC** 1234
Salary Range $27,720 to $44,060 to $76,750+	**O*NET-SOC** 13-2053.00

OVERVIEW

Insurance underwriters review individual applications for insurance coverage to evaluate the degree of risk involved. They decide whether the insurance company should accept an applicant, and, if the applicant is accepted, underwriters determine the premium that the policyholder will be charged. There are approximately 107,000 underwriters employed in the United States.

HISTORY

Lloyd's of London is generally considered to be the first insurance underwriter. Formed in the late 1600s, Lloyd's subscribed marine insurance policies for seagoing vessels. Over the years, the principles of insurance were adopted by various fraternal and trade unions.

In the United States, fire and life insurance companies date from colonial times. Benjamin Franklin helped start the Philadelphia

Contributionship for the Insurance of Houses, a fire insurance company, in 1752. The first life insurance company was established in 1759 by the New York and Philadelphia synods of the Presbyterian Church.

Industrial insurance began in the late 19th century, offering life insurance to millions of industrial workers. In 1910, the first workers' compensation policy was issued. Group coverage was introduced in the life insurance field in 1911, and has since been broadened to include disability, hospitalization, and pension benefits. Group hospitalization insurance was pioneered by the Blue Cross organization in 1936. Private insurance companies began to furnish insurance protection in the early 1900s.

Package insurance, such as automobile and homeowners insurance, which includes a variety of types of insurance, developed on a large scale in the 1950s. Health maintenance organizations were first established during the early 1970s in an attempt to stem the rising cost of health care. Judgments in liability lawsuits had drastically increased by 1980, resulting in rapid growth in purchases of liability insurance. Today, insurance packages and managed care companies provide many options and levels of coverage.

THE JOB

People buy insurance policies to protect themselves against financial loss resulting from injuries, illnesses, or lost or damaged property; policyholders transfer this risk of loss from themselves to their insurance companies. As a result, insurance companies assume billions of dollars in risks each year. Underwriters are responsible for evaluating the degree of risk posed by each policy application to determine whether the insurance company should issue a policy.

Underwriters base their decisions on a number of factors, including the applicant's health, occupation, and income. They review and analyze information in insurance applications, medical reports, reports from loss control specialists, and actuarial studies. If an applicant appears to be at a greater risk level than normal, the underwriter may decide that an extra premium is needed. Underwriters must exercise sound judgment when deciding whether to accept an applicant and in deciding upon the premium; their decisions are crucial to the financial success of the insurance company.

Insurance underwriting is a very competitive business. If the underwriter evaluates risks too conservatively and quotes prices that are too high, the insurance company may lose business to competitors. If the underwriters evaluate risks too liberally and accept applications at inadequate prices, the company will have to pay more claims and will ultimately lose money. It is essential that underwriters evaluate applications very carefully.

Many underwriters specialize in life, property, or health insurance; many further specialize in individual or group policies. *Property or casualty underwriters* may specialize by the type of risk involved, such as fire or automobile. Some underwriters work exclusively with business insurance. These *commercial account underwriters* must often evaluate the firm's entire business operation.

Group contracts are becoming increasingly popular. In a group policy, life or health insurance protection is given to all persons in a certain group at uniform rates. Group contracts may also be given to specified groups as individual policies reflecting individual needs. A labor union, for example, may be given individual casualty policies covering automobiles.

Business Education for Women Needs to Start Early

The study *Teen Girls on Business: Are They Being Empowered?*, sponsored in part by the Simmons School of Management, found that 97 percent of young girls expect to work outside the home when they grow up, but only 9 percent want to work in the business world, as opposed to 15 percent of the boys surveyed. Girls' low level of interest in business is due in part to a common misconception: According to Patricia O'Brien, president of Simmons College, most girls want to work in a career where they can help people, and business is not the first field that comes to mind. But business presents many opportunities to make a positive impact on people, such as offering technological assistance, humanitarian services, and quality-of-life improvements, to name just a few. Thus, schools and businesses need to educate young girls and women about both the potential for money-making and the humanitarian opportunities inherent in the business arena.

The survey also found that a higher percentage of minority girls were interested in business than white girls (39 percent). Fifty-six percent of African American girls, 50 percent of Hispanic girls, and 41 percent of Asian girls surveyed said they were interested in starting their own business someday.

Underwriters must assess the acceptability of risk from a variety of policy applications. They must be able to review and analyze complex technical information.

REQUIREMENTS
High School
Small insurance companies may hire people without a college degree for trainee positions, and high school graduates may be trained for underwriting work after working as underwriting clerks. In general, however, a college education is advantageous, if not required, for employment. In high school you should take mathematics, business, and speech classes to help prepare you for work in this field. A basic knowledge of computers is also necessary.

Postsecondary Training
Most insurance companies prefer to hire college graduates for beginning underwriting jobs. Many different majors are acceptable, but a degree in business administration or finance may be particularly helpful. Accounting classes and business law classes will help to round out your educational background for this field. In addition, keep up your computer skills in college. The computer is a tool you will use throughout your professional career.

Certification or Licensing
Underwriters who become certified, or designated, show commitment to their profession and increase their possibilities for advancement. Several designations are available to underwriters. The Insurance Educational Association offers the Associate in Underwriting (AU) designation, which was originally developed by the Insurance Institute of America. Requirements for the AU include completion of designated course work (usually lasting two years) and the passage of a comprehensive examination.

The American Institute for Chartered Property Casualty Underwriters offers a more advanced professional certification, the Chartered Property and Casualty Underwriter (CPCU) designation. Course work for the CPCU usually takes five years, and a candidate must pass 10 examinations covering such subjects as accounting, finance, business law, and commercial risk management.

For life insurance underwriters, The American College offers the Chartered Life Underwriter (CLU) designation. Like the CPCU, the CLU requires completing a comprehensive series of courses and passing examinations. In addition, the College recently teamed up with The Life Underwriter Training Council (LUTC) to offer the more extensive LUTC Fellow designation. To receive this certification, individuals must meet or exceed qualifications and continuing education requirements determined by the College. Visit the College's website (http://www.amercoll.edu/mainlutc) for more details.

Other Requirements

Underwriting work requires great concentration and mental alertness. Underwriters must be analytical, logical, and detail oriented. They must be able to make difficult decisions based on technical, complicated information. Underwriters must also be able to communicate well both in speech and in writing. Group underwriters often meet with union employees or employer representatives. The ability to communicate well is vital for these underwriters.

Keep in mind that advancement in this career comes through continuing your education. While insurance companies often pay tuition for their employees taking underwriting courses, the underwriters themselves must have the desire to learn continuously.

EXPLORING

There are many different ways to explore the underwriting profession. You may visit insurance companies to talk with underwriters and other insurance employees. Many insurance organizations, such as those listed at the end of this article, will send basic information on underwriting jobs to interested people. You might also consider applying for a part-time or summer job at an insurance company. Even if you handle phones or help file records for the office, you are still gaining basic business experience.

High school graduates may decide to work at insurance companies before going to college to determine their interest in and aptitude for underwriting work. In addition, many insurance companies are willing to hire and train college students during the summer months.

EMPLOYERS

Most of the approximately 107,000 underwriters in the United States work for property and casualty insurance companies. Insurance agents, brokers, and services and life insurance companies are the next two largest employers of underwriters. Opportunities are often best in large cities such as New York, Chicago, San Francisco, Dallas, Philadelphia, and Hartford. Finally, some underwriters work in independent agencies, banks, mortgage companies, or regional offices.

STARTING OUT
The most effective way to enter the underwriting profession is to seek employment after earning a college degree. Most insurance companies prefer to hire college graduates, and college placement offices often assist students in securing employment.

It is possible to enter this field without a college degree. Underwriting clerks who show exceptional promise may be trained for underwriter positions. In addition, some insurance companies will hire people without a college degree for trainee jobs.

ADVANCEMENT
Advancement opportunities for underwriters depend on an individual's educational background, on-the-job performance, and leadership abilities. Continuing education is also very important.

Experienced underwriters who have taken continuing education courses may be promoted to chief underwriter or underwriting manager. Underwriting managers may advance to senior management positions.

EARNINGS
According to the Bureau of Labor Statistics, the median annual salary for underwriters was $44,060 in 2001. At the low end of the scale, 10 percent of underwriters earned less than $27,720 per year. The top 10 percent earned $76,750 or more. Experience, certification, and position within the company are all factors influencing salary levels. In addition, most insurance companies have generous employee benefits, normally including liberal vacation allowances and employer-financed group life and retirement plans.

WORK ENVIRONMENT
Underwriters generally work at a desk in pleasant offices; their jobs entail no unusual physical activity, although at times they may have to work under stressful conditions. The normal work week is 40 hours; overtime may be required from time to time. Occasionally, underwriters may travel away from home to attend meetings or continuing education classes.

OUTLOOK

The U.S. Department of Labor predicts little or no change in employment for underwriters through the next decade. Most job openings will occur as a result of underwriters leaving the field for other professions or retirement. The increasing use of underwriting software programs and the increasing numbers of businesses that self-insure will limit job growth in this field.

There will always be a need for underwriters. New businesses will seek protection for new plants and equipment, insurance for workers' compensation, and product liability. The public's growing security consciousness and the increasing importance of employee benefits will result in more opportunities in this field. And, finally, the increasing number of Americans over the age of 65 who utilize long-term health care and pension benefits will create a demand for underwriters.

FOR MORE INFORMATION

For information regarding the LUTC program and the CLU designation and distance education programs, contact:

The American College
270 South Bryn Mawr Avenue
Bryn Mawr, PA 19010-2196
Tel: 888-263-7265
Email: StudentServices@Amercoll.Edu
http://www.amercoll.edu

For information regarding the CPCU certification, contact:

American Institute for Chartered Property Casualty Underwriters
720 Providence Road
PO Box 3016
Malvern, PA 19355-0716
Tel: 800-644-2101
Email: cserv@cpcuiia.org
http://www.aicpcu.org

For information about the Insurance Institute of America's *AU certification and other programs, contact:*

Insurance Educational Association
100 California Street, Suite 650
San Francisco, CA 94111

Tel: 800-655-4432
Email: info@ieatraining.com
http://www.ieatraining.com

For information on continuing education and general information about health underwriting, contact:
National Association of Health Underwriters
2000 North 14th Street, Suite 450
Arlington, VA 22201
Tel: 703-276-0220
Email: info@nahu.org
http://www.nahu.org

For information on life underwriting, contact:
National Association of Insurance and Financial Advisors
2901 Telestar Court
PO Box 12012
Falls Church, VA 22042-1205
Tel: 877-TO-NAIFA
http://www.naifa.org

This organization is associated with The American College and has information on industry news and events.
Society of Financial Service Professionals
270 South Bryn Mawr Avenue
Bryn Mawr, PA 19010-2195
Tel: 610-526-2500
http://www.financialpro.org

INTERNET CONSULTANTS

QUICK FACTS

School Subjects Business Computer science	**Certification or Licensing** Voluntary
Personal Skills Communication/ideas Technical/scientific	**Outlook** Faster than the average
Work Environment Primarily indoors Primarily multiple locations	**DOT** N/A
	GOE N/A
Minimum Education Level Bachelor's degree	**NOC** N/A
Salary Range $35,000 to $65,000 to $100,000+	**O*NET-SOC** N/A

OVERVIEW

Internet consultants use their technological and computer skills to help people or businesses access and utilize the Internet. Their work may include implementing or refining a networking system, creating a website, establishing an online ordering or product-support system, or training employees to maintain and update their newly established website. Some consultants work independently, and others may be employed by a consulting agency.

HISTORY

The Internet as we know it has only been around a little longer than a decade. In this short amount of time, the Internet has brought new ways of communicating and selling products and services to customers, without the presence of an actual store or office. With the fast growth of Internet sales and services, companies with a Web presence need people who can help create and manage sites to fit the company's business goals. This created the need for the Internet consultant. Because of constantly evolving technology, the future will require even more specialized and complex skills of Internet consultants.

THE JOB

The job of an Internet consultant can vary from day to day and project to project. The duties can also vary depending on the consultant's areas of expertise. For example, an Internet consultant specializing in creative work may design a website and help a company create a consistent visual message, while a consultant who is a "techie" may get involved with setting up the company's Intranet or Internet connections. The entrepreneurial Internet consultant may help a business establish an online storefront and an online ordering and processing system. Some Internet consultants who have considerable business experience may work with CEOs or other company heads to analyze the company's current use of the Internet and determine what markets the company is reaching.

Some consultants work independently (running their own businesses) and are paid for their work by the hour; others may be paid by the project. Those who work for consulting firms may be salaried employees of the firm. Some businesses may require that the consultants be on-site; this means that they work on a particular project at the company's office for several days, weeks, or months. Many consultants work out of their home offices and only visit the company occasionally, such as when meetings are necessary.

Frank Smith, an Internet consultant in San Diego, California, started working in this career, because, as he puts it, "I was essentially a computer geek and a technology freak. I was interested in computer technology early on and just continued to learn." Smith has a degree in business administration and was previously employed as a project manager for a manufacturing firm. However, the appeal of working at different locations, meeting a variety of technological challenges, and working independently drew him to the field of consulting. Smith added to his computer knowledge by learning many software programs and programming languages. He also took classes that focused on special elements of website design, networking, and image manipulation. Internet consultants must constantly update their knowledge to keep abreast of new technological developments.

Smith says it's not difficult to love his job because there are no typical days and no typical projects. "I may work with a company to develop their Web presence, or I may simply analyze what they are currently doing and give them some tips to make their Internet and networking connections more efficient." One of the first things a consultant may do on a new project for a company is to meet with key people at the company. During the meeting the consultant gathers information on the business and finds out what the company hopes to do through the Internet. "I don't simply design a website and get them on the Internet," emphasizes Smith. "I get a feel for their company and their business. I look at their current marketing, advertising, and sales material and make sure their website will be consistent with their printed material."

This means the consultant's work involves researching, analyzing information, and preparing reports based on their findings. As Smith notes, "This takes time and research. Sometimes I go home from a meeting with a stack of material about the company, and I study it to make sure I am familiar with the company and its focus." Internet consultants must know their clients to be successful. Smith adds, "I believe this is an important business aspect that is sometimes overlooked by consultants and company executives when they go on the Internet."

Internet consultants may also develop the entire Internet setup, including the hardware and software, for their client. The client may be a company that is upgrading their equipment or a company that has never been connected to the Internet before. Some consultants also train company employees to monitor, maintain, and enhance their website.

According to Smith, consultants who have business experience and business degrees, as well as some technical training, will be the most highly sought. "A good consultant needs to have a working knowledge of the business world as well as computer and technological expertise." The consultant with an understanding of business is able to offer clients more in terms of service than the consultant who is only a computer whiz. "Many consultants can put together a website for their clients," Smith explains, "however, more and more companies are beginning to look for the consultant who can offer added value, such as business analysis or marketing skills that will enhance their business and its products and services."

Although Smith feels there is currently an abundance of work for Internet consultants, he believes that demand may slow as companies get connected to the Internet and establish their presence. New technologies, however, are constantly being developed. The consultant who keeps up with technical changes will be able to offer new and old clients improved and different services.

Some people may use their computer skills to work as consultants in a sideline business or as a supplement to their part-time or full-time job. Linda McNamara is employed on a part-time basis as a website designer with a local Illinois government agency. In addition to that job, though, she also works as an independent Internet consultant. McNamara partners with another consultant to operate a business that designs and maintains websites for small enterprises in the area.

Although McNamara does not consult on the large scale that Smith does, she also emphasizes that consultants need to have good communication skills. "Everyone has a different idea of how they want their website to look," she says. "This requires that I have the ability to listen, communicate, and perform according to expectations."

REQUIREMENTS
High School

If you are considering a career as an Internet consultant, you should take a general high school curriculum that is college preparatory. Make sure you take computer science courses and business courses. You should also take courses that develop your analytical and problem-solving skills such as mathematics (including algebra and geometry) and sciences (including chemistry and physics). Take English courses to develop the research and communication skills you'll need for this profession.

Postsecondary Training

While a college degree may not be necessary to gain entry into this field, you will find it easier to get the best jobs and advance if you have one. As the high-tech market tightens and becomes more sophisticated, consultants with degrees generally have more opportunities than those with a high school diploma. Some people enter the field with computer-related degrees; others have a liberal arts or business background that includes computer studies. No matter what your major, though, you should take plenty of computer classes, study programming, and play on the Web.

Because consultants are usually responsible for marketing themselves, you should have good business skills and knowledge of marketing and sales, as well as computer knowledge. Therefore, take business and management classes, as well as economics and marketing. The consultant with a broad educational background may have the inside edge in certain situations. More and more clients are looking for consultants who can offer "value-added" services such as business analysis and marketing assistance along with computer skills. As one consultant says, "Just attending college teaches rigorous, valuable lessons that can benefit you and your clients in the real world."

Certification or Licensing

There are numerous certifications and designations available in programming languages, software, and network administration. Some employers may require that consultants have certain certifications. To become certified you will probably have to complete a training course and pass a written exam. Often the company that puts out a new technology, such as new software, will sponsor a training program.

The Institute for Certification of Computing Professionals offers the Certified Computing Professional and the Associate Computing Professional designations, as well as other designations for different professionals in information technology. To become certified, you must pass various written exams and fulfill certain work experience requirements.

Other Requirements

Internet consultants must be lifelong learners. You should have the desire and initiative to keep up on new technology, software, and hardware. You must also have good communication skills, including good listening skills. Creativity and a good eye for graphic design are also desirable. Because Internet consultants deal with many different people in various lines of work, they must be flexible and have good interpersonal skills. To be a successful consultant, you should be self-motivated and have the ability to work alone as well as with groups. You also need to have the patience and perseverance to see projects through.

EXPLORING

You can explore your interest in computers by getting involved with a computer users group or club in your community or school. If a computer trade show comes to your area, be sure to attend. You'll be able to see new advances in technology and talk with others interested in this field. Search the Web for interesting sites, and look at their source code to see how they were developed. Increase your knowledge by experimenting and learning independently. Check out library books about computers and teach yourself some programming or website design skills. Mastering a Web page authoring program is a good introduction to Web design.

Offer to help people you know set up their home computer systems or do upgrades. Gain experience working with people by volunteering to help seniors or others learn how to use computers at a community center. Try to get a summer or part-time job at a computer store. Large retailers, such as Best Buy, also have computer departments where you might find work. The business experience will be beneficial, even if you are not working directly on the Internet.

By simply accessing the Internet frequently and observing different website designs and the increasing number of e-commerce sites, you can gain insight into how rapidly the computer industry is changing. Contact computer consultants, website designers, or programmers in your area and set up an informational interview with them. At the interview you can ask them questions about their educational background, what they like about the work, how they market their business, what important skills someone wanting to enter the field should have, and any other things you are interested in knowing about this work.

EMPLOYERS

Many Internet consultants work independently, running their own consulting businesses. Others may be salaried employees of traditional management consulting firms that have Internet consulting divisions or departments. And still others may be salaried employees of Internet consulting companies.

Independent consultants have the added responsibility of marketing their services and always looking for new projects to work on. Consultants at a firm are typically assigned to work on certain projects.

Clients that hire Internet consultants include small businesses, large corporations, health care facilities, and government institutions. Consultants work all across the country (and world), but large cities may offer more job opportunities. Some consultants specialize in working with a certain type of business such as a hospital or a retail enterprise.

STARTING OUT

Most consultants enter the field by working for an established consulting firm. This way they can gain experience and develop a portfolio and a list of references before venturing out on their own as an independent or moving to a different firm in a higher position. The Internet is a good resource to use to find employment. Many websites post job openings, as do local employment agencies, newspapers, trade magazines, and college career placement offices.

Networking is a key element to becoming a successful consultant and requires getting in touch with previous business and social associates as well as making new contacts.

ADVANCEMENT

Internet consultants have several avenues for advancement. As they become known as experts in their field, the demand for their services will increase. This demand can support an increase in fees. They can also specialize in a certain aspect of computer consulting, which can increase their client base and fees. Those working for consulting firms may move into management or partner positions. Consultants who want to work independently can advance by starting their own consulting businesses. Eventually they may be able to hire consultants to work under them. Some consultants leave the field to head up the computer departments or perform website administration for corporations or other agencies. Because of the continuous developments within the information technology industry, the advancement possibilities for consultants who continually upgrade their knowledge and skills are practically endless.

EARNINGS

Internet consultants' earnings vary widely depending on their geographic location, type of work performed, and their experience and reputation. Beginning consultants may make around $35,000 per year, while many consultants earn around $65,000 annually. Some consultants have salaries that exceed $100,000 a year.

Many independent consultants charge by the hour, with fees ranging from $45 an hour to well above $100 an hour. Consultants who work on contract must estimate the hours needed to complete the project and their rate of pay when determining their contract price. Independent consultants must also realize that not all their work time is "billable" time, meaning that general office work, record keeping, billing, maintaining current client contacts, and seeking new business do not generate revenue. This nonbillable time must be factored into contract or hourly rates when determining annual income.

Although independent consultants may be able to generate good contract or hourly fees, they do not receive benefits that may be typical of salaried employees. For example, independent consultants are responsible for their own medical, disability, and life insurances. They do not receive vacation pay, and when they are not working, they are not generating income. Retirement plans must also be self-funded and self-directed.

WORK ENVIRONMENT

Internet consultants can expect to work in a variety of settings. Depending on the project, independent consultants may work out of their homes or private offices. At other times, they may be required to work on-site at the client's facilities, which may, for example, be a hospital, office building, or factory. Consultants employed by a large or small consulting firm may also spend time working at the consulting firm's offices or telecommuting from home.

Internet consultants generally can expect to work in a clean office environment. Consultants may work independently or as part of a team, depending on the project's requirements.

Consulting can be a very intense job that may require long hours to meet a project's deadline. Some settings where employees or consultants are driven by a strict deadline or where a project is not progressing as planned may be stressful. Many people in the computer field often work over 40 hours a week and may need to work nights and weekends. In addition, Internet consultants must spend time keeping current with the latest technology by reading and researching. Intensive computer work can result in eye strain, hand and wrist injuries, and back pain.

OUTLOOK

According to the Bureau of Labor Statistics, seven out of the 10 fastest growing occupations through 2010 are computer related. There is currently a large demand for Internet consultants; however, as more and more companies become established on the Web, they may hire their own Webmasters and systems specialists. In addition, new software programs are making the development of simple Web pages easier to create without expert help.

Frank Smith notes, "If you don't stay on top of the industry, you quickly become unemployable. The market will mature, and companies will not be struggling to get their website up and running like they are now. Consultants will have to be more competent and offer more to their clients." Good consultants who keep current with technology and who are willing to learn and adapt should have plenty of job opportunities. Clients, Smith adds, "will be looking for consultants who can do more for their business and who can bring them more value, such as business analysis and additional marketing skills."

FOR MORE INFORMATION
This organization's Education Foundation offers a limited number of scholarships and has information on the tech industry. To learn more, contact:
Association of Information Technology Professionals
401 North Michigan Avenue, Suite 2200
Chicago, IL 60611-4267
Tel: 800-224-9371
http://www.aitp.org or http://www.edfoundation.org

For interesting information on the industry, check out the following website:
Association of Internet Professionals
4790 Irvine Boulevard, Suite 105-283
Irvine, CA 92620
Tel: 866-AIP-9700
Email: info@association.org
http://www.association.org

To learn more about consulting, check out the following website:
Independent Computer Consultants Association
11131 South Towne Square, Suite F
St. Louis, MO 63123
Tel: 800-774-4222
Email: info@icca.org
http://www.icca.org

For certification information, contact:
Institute for Certification of Computing Professionals
2350 East Devon Avenue, Suite 115
Des Plaines, IL 60018-4610
Tel: 800-843-8227
Email: office@iccp.org
http://www.iccp.org

For useful IT career links, check out the following website:
Mainfunction.com
http://www.mainfunction.com

INTERNET EXECUTIVES

QUICK FACTS

School Subjects Business Computer science	**Certification or Licensing** None available
Personal Skills Communication/ideas Leadership/management	**Outlook** Faster than the average
Work Environment Primarily indoors One location with some travel	**DOT** N/A **GOE** N/A
Minimum Education Level Bachelor's degree	**NOC** 0611
Salary Range $50,000 to $76,501 to $250,000+	**O*NET-SOC** N/A

OVERVIEW

Internet executives plan, organize, direct, and coordinate the operations of businesses that engage in commerce over the Internet. These upper-level positions include presidents, chief operating officers, executive vice presidents, chief financial officers, chief information officers, and regional and district managers. The majority of Internet executives are employed in large companies in urban areas.

HISTORY

Since the early 1990s, online business, often called e-commerce, has been extended to virtually every industry. Advertising, distance education programs, sales, banking, tax filing, Web conferencing, bill payment, and online auctions are just a few of the business outlets in which the Internet has played a profound role. Companies that have developed a Web presence in these industries, either in addition to or as a replacement to a brick-and-mortar-business, need management executives to run their online business dealings just as a normal business needs a CEO. This is the job of Internet executives.

THE JOB

All businesses have specific goals and objectives that they strive to meet, such as making a certain profit or increasing the client base by a certain amount. Executives devise strategies and formulate policies to ensure that these objectives are met. In today's business world, many companies that first began as brick-and-mortar businesses now have a presence on the Internet. Additionally, many new companies, known as dot-coms, are found only on the Internet. At both types of companies, Internet executives are the professionals who devise ways to meet their companies' objectives—making sales, providing services, or developing a customer base, for example—as they relate to the Internet.

Like executives in traditional companies, Internet executives have a wide range of titles and responsibilities. The positions include president, chairman, chief executive officer (who is sometimes the same person as the president or chairman), chief operating officer, chief financial officer, chief information officer, executive vice presidents, and the board of directors. *Presidents, chairmen,* and *chief executive officers (CEOs)* at companies with an Internet presence are leaders of the companies. They plan business objectives and develop policies to coordinate operations between divisions and departments and establish procedures for attaining objectives. They may review activity reports and financial statements to determine progress and revise operations as needed. They also direct and formulate funding for new and existing programs within their organizations. Public relations plays a big part in the lives of Internet executives as they deal with executives and leaders from other countries or organizations, and with customers, employees, and various special interest groups.

Chief operating officers, or *COOs,* at dot-coms and other companies with an Internet presence are typically responsible for the day-to-day operations of the company. They may work to increase their companies' client base, improve sales, and develop operational and personnel policies. Depending on the type of business, a COO may also serve as head of a department departments, such as marketing, engineering, or sales. Usually the COO directly reports to the top executive, whether it is the CEO, chairman, or president. COOs typically have years of experience working in their industry and may also have worked at their particular company for years, moving up the corporate ranks while gaining knowledge about their companies' products and markets. Additionally, they have extensive knowledge of Internet capabilities and technologies available that will help their companies reach goals.

Some companies have an *executive vice president* who directs and coordinates the activities of one or more departments, depending on the size of the organization. In very large organizations, the duties of executive vice presidents may be highly specialized; for example, they may oversee the activities of business managers of marketing, sales promotion, purchasing, finance, personnel training, industrial relations, administrative services, data processing, property management, transportation, or legal services. In smaller organizations, an executive vice president might be responsible for a number of these departments. Executive vice presidents also assist the CEO in formulating and administering the organization's policies and developing its long-range goals. Executive vice presidents may serve as members of management committees on special studies.

Dot-coms and other companies with a presence on the Internet may also have a *chief financial officer* or *CFO.* In small firms, the CFO is usually responsible for all financial management tasks, such as budgeting, capital expenditure planning, cash flow, and various financial reviews and reports. In larger companies, the CFO may oversee financial management departments to help other managers develop financial and economic policy and oversee the implementation of these policies.

Chief information officers, or *CIOs,* are responsible for all aspects of their company's information technology. They use their knowledge of technology and business to determine how information technology can best be used to meet company goals. This may include researching, purchasing, and overseeing setup and use of technology systems, such as Intranet, Internet, and computer networks. These managers sometimes take a role in implementing a company's website.

In companies that have several different locations, managers may be assigned to oversee specific geographic areas. For example, a large retailer with facilities all across the nation may have a Midwest manager, a Southwest manager, a Southeast manager, a Northeast manager, and a Northwest manager. In the case of Internet companies, whose territory is not limited by geographical boundaries, managerial responsibilities may be assigned by product or client type instead.

All of these executive and management positions may be available at large companies, while the responsibilities of several of these positions may be combined into one role at smaller companies. Internet executives may work in any of these positions for companies that do business exclusively online or traditional businesses that also have an online presence. The common denominator among these executives is that they are all involved to some extent with figuring out how to use the Internet to enhance the capabilities and profitability of their businesses.

Rob Linxweiler, a consultant to a number of Internet companies in the Chicago area, says, "A downside of the industry is that sometimes it's hard to measure success on a daily or even weekly basis. We may accomplish two or three major projects per year, and those are the milestones by which we judge ourselves. It's possible to get mired in the day-to-day and fail to see the larger picture."

Linxweiler is quick to point out that there are many positives to an Internet executive's job, including working with interesting people. He also adds, "The work may not always be fascinating, but the technologies available can be used in some creative ways to overcome obstacles. I like to apply my creativity to problem solving."

Involvement in Internet commerce adds a new dimension for the consideration of executives. While most executives don't get directly involved in the day-to-day operation of the technology that drives their Internet business, an understanding of the technologies at work is crucial to the performance of their jobs. Executives will likely have to work directly with technology experts, so proficiency with the relevant technologies is a necessity. Internet executives' combination of technological and business expertise ranks them among the most sought-after individuals in the executive job market.

REQUIREMENTS
High School

The educational background of Internet executives varies as widely as the nature of their diverse responsibilities. Many have a bachelor's degree in computer science, business administration, or a liberal arts field such as economics or communications. If you are interested in a management career dealing with the Internet, you should plan on going to college after high school. Take a college preparatory curriculum, including classes in science, history, and government. Be sure to take as many computer science classes as possible so that you have a basic understanding of the technology that is available. Because an executive must communicate with a wide range of people, take as many English classes as possible to hone your communication skills. Speech classes are another way to improve these skills. Courses in mathematics and business are also excellent choices to help you prepare for this career. A foreign language may also be helpful in preparing for today's global business market.

Postsecondary Training

Internet executives often have a college degree in a subject that pertains to the department they direct or the organization they administer. For example, chief executive officers may have business administration degrees, chief financial officers often have accounting degrees, chief information officers often have computer science degrees, and directors of research and development often have engineering or science degrees. All Internet executives are expected to have experience with the information technology that applies to their field. While in college, you should keep up with your computer studies in addition to deciding what type of work interests you. Are you drawn to sales and marketing, for example, or does the actual manufacturing of a product interest you? A good way to find out is to get some hands-on experience through an internship or summer job. Your college placement office should be able to help you in locating such a position with a business or organization that appeals to you.

Graduate and professional degrees are common among executives. Many executives in administrative, marketing, financial, and manufacturing activities have a master's degree in business administration. Executives in highly technical manufacturing and research activities often have a master's degree or doctorate in a technical or scientific discipline.

Other Requirements

There are a number of personal characteristics that make a successful executive, depending upon the specific responsibilities of the position. An executive who manages other employees should have good communication and interpersonal skills. Rob Linxweiler advises, "Work on your communication skills. There is a surprising level of ambiguity in the technological arena, and the ability to say what you mean and be understood is crucial." He adds, "Hands-on experience with some technologies is also very important. The technologies change rapidly. It's not really relevant which particular system you have experience with, but an understanding of the basic processes and rules by which computer technologies operate is extremely important."

The ability to delegate work and think on your feet is often key in executive business management. A certain degree of organization is important, since executives often manage many different tasks simultaneously. Other traits considered important for top executives are intelligence, decisiveness, intuition, creativity, honesty, loyalty, and a sense of responsibility. Finally, successful executives should be interested in staying abreast of new developments in their industry and technology.

EXPLORING

To explore your interest in the computer and technology aspect of this work, take every opportunity to work with computers. Surf the Web to visit sites of businesses and organizations and find out what services they offer. Improve your computer skills by joining a users group, setting up your own Web page, and taking extra computer classes at a local community center or tech school.

To get experience as an executive, start with your own interests. Whether you're involved in drama, sports, school publications, or a part-time job, there are managerial and executive duties associated with any organized activity. Look for ways in which you can be involved with planning, scheduling, managing other workers or volunteers, fund-raising, or budgeting. Contact a local business executive—the best source would be one whose company also has a website—and ask for an informational interview during which you can talk with him or her about this career. Some schools or community organizations arrange "job shadowing," where interested young people can spend part of a day following selected employees to see what their job is like. Joining Junior Achievement (http://www.ja.org) is another excellent way to get involved with local businesses and learn about how they work. Finally, get a part-time or summer job at a local business to get hands-on experience working in an office environment. Although your job may only be that of cashier, you'll be able to see how the business is organized and run. You may also find a manager or executive there who can act as a mentor and give you advice.

EMPLOYERS

General managers and executives hold more than three million jobs in the United States, according to the U.S. Department of Labor. These jobs are found in every industry; however, over 60 percent of these jobs are in the manufacturing, retail, and service industries—industries that are now heavily involved in the Internet.

Virtually every business in the United States offers executive and managerial positions. Obviously, the larger the company is, the more executive and managerial positions it is likely to have. In addition, companies that do business in larger geographical territories are likely to have more executive and managerial positions than those with smaller territories. Businesses with an Internet presence are the norm in today's market. Almost all large retail businesses have a website that is essential for customer contact and sales and marketing. Besides working at large retail businesses, Internet executives may work in such areas as not-for-profit organizations, small start-up companies, and corporate consulting firms.

STARTING OUT
Executive positions are not entry-level jobs. Generally, those interested in becoming Internet executives start with a college degree and gain a significant amount of work experience. After you have decided what industry you are interested in, your college placement office should be able to help you locate your first job. Many companies also send representatives to college campuses to interview graduating students as potential hires. You may also want to attend recruitment and job fairs to find job openings. In addition, a past internship or summer work experience may provide you with contacts that lead to employment. You should research the field you are interested in to find out what might be the best point of entry.

After you have gained some work experience you may want to consider returning to school for a graduate degree. You may also be able to work your way up through your organization's management levels. Some organizations have executive management-trainee programs available to their employees; other companies may pay for an employee's graduate schooling as long as the employee continues to work for the company. Many executives have master's degrees in business administration, although higher degrees in computer science and related technology fields are becoming more common.

Once you have considerable training and management experience, you can move into an executive level position by directly applying to the corporate management. In addition, some executive search and placement firms specialize in job hunting for those involved with the Internet. Digital agents, specialists who work only with those seeking technology jobs, may also be a good source of employment leads.

Hiring standards for technology executives are still evolving, but it's clear that simply being well acquainted with the technologies is not enough to land this type of job. You need significant experience in both business management and technology to meet the requirements of most of these positions.

ADVANCEMENT

Most business management and top executive positions are filled by experienced lower level managers and executives who display valuable managerial traits, such as leadership, self-confidence, creativity, motivation, decisiveness, and flexibility. Rob Linxweiler says, "Good interpersonal skills are a must. Patience, enthusiasm, and the ability to listen to employees are indispensable skills that are often underrated. The ability to make good decisions and act on them is also vital. These are the building blocks of a strong leader, which is the most important thing an executive can be."

Advancement in smaller firms may come more slowly than in larger firms. A good way to accelerate advancement is participating in different kinds of educational programs available for managers. These are often paid for by the employer. Managers who participate in company training programs broaden their knowledge of company policy and operations. Training programs sponsored by industry and trade associations and continuing education courses taken at colleges and universities can familiarize managers with the latest developments in management techniques. In recent years, large numbers of middle managers were laid off as companies streamlined operations. An employee's proven commitment to improving his or her knowledge of the business's field and computer information systems is important in establishing a reputation as a top professional.

Business managers may advance to executive or administrative vice president. Vice presidents may advance to peak corporate positions, such as president or chief executive officer. Sometimes executives go on to establish their own firms.

Many CEOs are moving toward the role of chairman and away from day-to-day operations to focus on higher level, visionary strategy. The ability to understand and implement solutions based on Internet technologies is essential at this level.

Regardless of the industry, the advancement path of executives at Internet companies is limited only by their interest, abilities, and willingness to work hard.

EARNINGS

Salary levels for Internet executives vary substantially, depending upon their level of responsibility, length of service, and the type, size, and location of the organization for which they work. Top-level executives in large firms can earn much more than their counterparts in small firms. Also, salaries in large metropolitan areas tend to be higher than those in smaller cities.

According to the *2002 Salary Guide* from Robert Half Technology, chief information officers earned between $123,500 and $202,500 a year. Chief technology officers earned between $96,000 and $155,750. Vice presidents of information systems earned between $112,250 and $168,500, and vice presidents of technology earned between $109,250 and $161,500.

The Association of Internet Professionals' *2000 AIP Compensation and Benefits Survey* reports that the median compensation, including salary and bonus for all executive management was $76,501. Most top executives earn cash bonuses in addition to their salaries. The highest paid executives earn more than $250,000 in salary and bonuses.

Benefit and compensation packages for Internet executives are usually excellent and may include stock awards and options, cash incentives in addition to bonuses, company-paid insurance premiums, use of company cars, club memberships, expense accounts, and generous retirement benefits. According to *Enterprise* magazine, 55 percent of the dot-com workforce hold stock options in their companies.

Top executives at successful Internet companies see few limits to their earnings potential; salaries into the millions of dollars are not uncommon for CEOs and other key executives.

WORK ENVIRONMENT

Internet executives work in comfortable offices near the departments they direct. Top executives at established companies may have spacious, lavish offices with comfortable desks and chairs, PCs, phones, and even personal support staff.

Executives often travel between the company's various offices at the national, regional, or local levels. Top executives may travel to meet with executives in other corporations, both within the United States and abroad. Meetings and conferences sponsored by industries and associations occur regularly and provide invaluable opportunities to meet with peers and keep up with the latest developments. In large corporations, job transfers between the parent company and its local offices or subsidiaries are common, so executives must be prepared to move for their work.

Executives often work long hours under intense pressure to meet corporate goals. A typical workweek might consist of 55 to 60 hours at the office. Some executives, in fact, spend up to 80 hours working each week. These long hours limit time available for family and leisure activities, but the financial rewards can be great.

OUTLOOK

Employment of Internet executives is expected to grow quickly over the next several years as Internet businesses continue to grow and new companies are formed. The demand will be high for candidates with strong managerial skills and a solid understanding of computer and Internet technology. Education and experience will also count for a lot. Many job openings will be the result of promotions, company expansions, or executives leaving their positions to start their own businesses.

The employment outlook for executives is closely tied to the overall economy. In times when the economy is good, businesses expand both in terms of their output and the number of people they employ. This creates a need for more executives. In economic downturns, businesses often lay off employees and cut back on production, which lessens the need for executives.

There were many highly publicized dot-com failures in the early 2000s. Many experts predict that in the next few years, 80 to 90 percent of dot-coms will either close or be acquired by other companies. The statistics, however, are not likely to deter new Web businesses, especially small businesses that are able to find niche markets, anticipate trends, adapt to market and technology changes, and plan for a large enough financial margin to turn a profit. Traditional brick-and-mortar businesses will also have to implement dot-com marketing plans in order to compete and survive. Analysts anticipate that business-to-business e-commerce will become much more important than business-to-consumer transactions.

FOR MORE INFORMATION

For news about management trends, conferences, and seminars, visit the following website:
American Management Association
1601 Broadway
New York, NY 10019-7420

Tel: 212-586-8100
http://www.amanet.org

For information on the industry, networking, legislative activities, and careers, contact:

Association of Internet Professionals
4790 Irvine Boulevard, Suite 105-283
Irvine, CA 92620
Tel: 866-247-9700
Email: info@association.org
http://www.association.org

For information on programs that teach students about free enterprise and business and information on local chapters, contact:

Junior Achievement
One Education Way
Colorado Springs, CO 80906
Tel: 719-540-8000
Email: newmedia@ja.org
http://www.ja.org

For a brochure on management as a career, contact:

National Management Association
2210 Arbor Boulevard
Dayton, OH 45439-1580
Tel: 937-294-0421
http://nma1.org

There are a number of magazines covering the topics of the Internet, computers, and business. Many are available in print form and online. For a sampling of such magazines, check out the following websites:

InfoWorld
http://www.infoworld.com
Internet Week
http://www.internetwk.com
PC World
http://www.pcworld.com
Wired
http://www.wired.com

INTERNET STORE MANAGERS AND ENTREPRENEURS

QUICK FACTS

School Subjects Business Computer science	**Certification or Licensing** Required by certain states
Personal Skills Leadership/management Technical/scientific	**Outlook** Faster than the average **DOT** N/A
Work Environment Primarily indoors Primarily one location	**GOE** N/A
Minimum Education Level Bachelor's degree	**NOC** N/A
Salary Range $0 to $25,000 to $60,000+	**O*NET-SOC** N/A

OVERVIEW

Internet store managers and entrepreneurs use the exciting technology of the Internet to sell products or services. They may research the marketability of a product or service, decide on what product or service to sell, organize their business, and set up their storefront on the Web. Numerous small businesses owners who sell a limited number of products or a specific service have found the Internet a great place to begin their business venture because start-up costs may be less than those for traditional businesses. Internet entrepreneurs run their own businesses. Internet store managers are employed by Internet entrepreneurs and stores.

HISTORY

The Internet became a popular sales tool in the 1990s and continues to grow today. Although many dot-com companies failed in the early 2000s, Internet sales remain an integral part of our economy. From 1995 to 2000, nearly one-third of real economic growth was attributed to Internet sales, according to the U.S. Department of Commerce. Online sales managers have been listed on *U.S. News & World Report*'s Top 20 Hot Job Tracks.

In 2002, lawmakers and tax officials from 30 states agreed to enter a voluntary pact to collect online sales tax. According to washingtonpost.com, this action was taken partially in response to regular "bricks-and-mortar" stores who complained that online retailers had an advantage.

More and more revenue is generated online each year, and some Internet stores, such as Amazon.com, have had tremendous success in this field. As the Internet continues to grow in popularity and importance, more consumers will be exposed to Internet stores on a daily basis. This will create a strong demand for Internet managers and entrepreneurs to research and market potential products and services, as well as manage businesses and employees.

THE JOB

In spite of the failure of many high-profile dot-coms in the early 2000s, many online businesses have continued to survive and thrive. These e-tailers have adapted to the constantly changing technology, economic climate, business trends, and consumer demands, instead of concentrating on fast growth and offering the lowest prices. Reports by research firm Jupiter Communications show that consumers are using Internet stores to do comparison shopping, and a significant number of consumers research products online before buying them at traditional stores. Jupiter Communications predicts that the amount spent by consumers for online purchases and Web-influenced purchases at traditional stores will top $831 billion in 2005.

Because of the vastness of the Internet, the role of an Internet store manager or entrepreneur can vary as much as the numerous websites on the Internet. Expert opinion on what makes one website or one business more successful than another differs, too. E-commerce is a new and relatively unexplored field for entrepreneurs. But, because most entrepreneurs have innovative and creative natures, this uncertainty and uncharted territory is what they love.

Like traditional entrepreneurs, Internet entrepreneurs must have strong business skills. They come up with ideas for an Internet product or service, research the feasibility of selling this product or service, decide what they need to charge to make a profit, determine how to advertise their business, and even arrange for financing for their business if necessary. In addition, Internet entrepreneurs typically are computer savvy and may even create and maintain their own sites.

Some entrepreneurs may choose to market a service such as website design to target the business-to-business market. Other Internet entrepreneurs may decide to market a service such as computer dating to target the individual consumer market. Still others may develop a "virtual store" on the Internet and sell products that target businesses or individual consumers.

Internet stores vary in size, items for sale, and the range of products. Smaller Internet stores, for example, may market the work done by a single craftsperson or businessperson. Many large Internet stores focus on selling a specific product or line of products. As some of these stores have grown they have diversified their merchandise. Amazon.com is one such example. Originally a small, online bookstore, the company now sells music CDs, videos, and other electronic products, along with books. Other Internet stores, such as those of Eddie Bauer and Sears, may be extensions of catalog or traditional brick-and-mortar stores. These large companies are generally so well established that they can employ Internet store managers to oversee the virtual store.

Many Internet businesses begin small, with one person working as the owner, manager, Webmaster, marketing director, and accountant, among other positions. John Axne of Chicago, Illinois, took on all these responsibilities when he developed his own one-person business designing websites for small companies and corporations. "Having my own business allows me more creative freedom," says Axne. The successful Internet entrepreneur, like the successful traditional entrepreneur, is often able to combine his or her interests with work to fill a niche in the business world. "It's a great fit for me," Axne explains. "I have a passion for computers and a love of learning." Dave Wright of Venice, California, is also an Internet entrepreneur and website designer. He, too, combined his interests with computer skills to start his business. "I had a strong interest in art," he says. "I simply married my art and graphic art experience with computers."

Those who want to start their own businesses on the Web must be very focused and self-motivated. Just like any other entrepreneur, they always need to keep an eye on the competition to see what products and services as well as prices and delivery times others offer. While Internet entrepreneurs do not need to be computer whizzes, they should enjoy learning about technology so that they can keep up with new developments that may help them with their businesses. Internet entrepreneurs must also be decision-makers, and many are drawn to running their own businesses because of the control it offers. "I'm a control freak," Wright admits. "This way I can oversee every aspect of my job."

The typical day of the Internet store manager or entrepreneur will depend greatly on the company he or she works for. For example, someone who works for a large company that also has a online store may meet with company department heads to find out about upcoming sales or products that should be heavily advertised on the website. They may do research about the store use and report their findings to company managers. They may work on the site itself, updating it with new information.

The Internet entrepreneur also has varied responsibilities that depend on his or her business. Wright notes, "No two projects and no two days are alike." An entrepreneur may spend one day working with a client to determine the client's needs and the next day working on bookkeeping and advertising in addition to working on a project. Most entrepreneurs, however, enjoy this variety and flexibility.

While the Internet world is appealing to many, there are risks for those who start their own businesses. "The Internet changes so rapidly that in five years it may be entirely different," Wright says. "That's why I started a business that simply sells services and didn't require a major investment. It is a business that I can get into and out of quickly if I find it necessary. There is no product, per se, and no inventory." Despite uncertainties, however, Web stores continue to open and the number of Internet store managers and entrepreneurs continues to grow.

REQUIREMENTS
High School

If you are considering becoming an Internet store manager or entrepreneur, there are a number of classes you can take in high school to help prepare you for these careers. Naturally you should take computer science courses to give you a familiarity with using computers and the Web. Business and marketing courses will also be beneficial for you. Also take mathematics, accounting, or bookkeeping classes because as an entrepreneur you will be responsible for your company's finances. Take history classes to learn about economic trends and psychology classes to learn about human behavior. A lot of advertising and product promotion has a psychological element. Finally, take plenty of English classes. These classes will help you develop your communication skills—skills that will be vital to your work as a store manager or business owner.

Postsecondary Training

Although there are no specific educational requirements for Internet store managers or entrepreneurs, a college education will certainly enhance your skills and chances for success. Like anyone interested in working for or running a traditional business, take plenty of business, economics, and marketing and management classes. Your education should also include accounting or bookkeeping classes. Keep up with computer and Internet developments by taking computer classes. Some schools offer classes on e-commerce. Many schools have undergraduate degree programs in business or business administration, but you can also enter this field with other degrees. Dave Wright, for example, graduated with a degree from art school, while John Axne has degrees in biomedical engineering and interactive media.

Certification or Licensing

Licenses may be required for running a business, depending on the type of business. Since requirements vary, you will need to check with local and state agencies for regulations in your area.

Other Requirements

Internet entrepreneurs and store managers must have the desire and initiative to keep up on new technology and business trends. Because they must deal with many different people in various lines of work, they need to be flexible problem solvers and have strong communication skills. Creativity and insight into new and different ways of doing business are qualities that are essential for a successful entrepreneur. In addition, because the Internet and e-commerce are relatively new and the future of Internet businesses is uncertain, those who enter the field are generally risk-takers and eager to be on the cutting edge of commerce and technology. Dave Wright notes, "This is not a job for someone looking for security. The Internet world is always changing. This is both exciting and scary to me as a businessperson. This is one career where you are not able to see where you will be in five years."

EXPLORING

There are numerous ways in which you can explore your interest in the computer and business worlds. Increase your computer skills and find out how much this technology interests you by joining a computer users group or club at your high school or your community. Access the Internet frequently on your own to observe different website designs and find out what is being sold and marketed electronically. What sites do you think are best at promoting products and why? Think about things from a customer's point of view. How easy are the sites to access and use? How are the products displayed and accessed? How competitive are the prices for goods or services?

Make it a goal to come up with your own ideas for a product or service to market on the Web, then do some research. How difficult would it be to deliver the product? What type of financing would be involved? Are there other sites already providing this product or service? How could you make your business unique?

Talk to professionals in your community about their work. Set up informational interviews with local business owners to find out what is involved in starting and running a traditional business. Your local chamber of commerce or the Small Business Administration may have classes or publications that would help you learn about starting a business. In addition, set up informational interviews with computer consultants, website designers, or Internet store managers or owners. How did they get started? What advice do they have? Is there anything they wish they had done differently? Where do they see the future of e-commerce going?

If your school has a future business owners club, join this group to meet others with similar interests. For hands-on business experience, get a part-time or summer job at any type of store in your area. This work will give you the opportunity to deal with customers (who can sometimes be hard to please), work with handling money, and observe how the store promotes its products and services.

EMPLOYERS

Internet store managers may work for an established traditional business or institution that also has a website dealing with products and services. The manager may also work for a business that only has a presence on the Web or for an Internet entrepreneur. Entrepreneurs are self-employed, and sometimes they may employ people to work under them. Some Internet entrepreneurs may be hired to begin a business for someone else.

STARTING OUT

Professionals in the field advise those just starting out to work for someone else to gain experience in the business world before beginning their own business. The Internet is a good resource to use to find employment. There are many sites that post job openings. Local employment agencies and newspapers and trade magazines also list job opportunities. In addition, your college placement office should be able to provide you with help locating a job. Networking with college alumni and people in your computer users groups may also provide job leads.

ADVANCEMENT

Advancement opportunities depend on the business, its success, and the individual's goals. Internet entrepreneurs or store managers who are successful may enter other business fields or consulting. Or they may advance to higher level management positions or other larger Internet-based businesses. Some entrepreneurs establish a business and then sell it only to begin another business venture. The Internet world is constantly changing because of technological advancements. This state of flux means that a wide variety of possibilities are available to those working in the field. "There is no solid career path in the Internet field," says Dave Wright. "Your next career may not even be developed yet."

EARNINGS

Income for Internet store managers and entrepreneurs is usually tied to the profitability of the business. Internet store managers who work for established traditional businesses are typically salaried employees of the company. Internet entrepreneurs who offer a service may be paid by the project. Entrepreneurs are self-employed and their income will depend on the success of the business. Those just starting out may actually have no earnings, while those with a business that has been existence for several years may have annual earnings between $25,000 and $50,000. Some in the field may earn much more than this amount. John Axne estimates that those who have good technical skills and can do such things as create the database program for a website may have higher salaries, in the $60,000 to $125,000 range.

Entrepreneurs are almost always responsible for their own medical, disability, and life insurances. Retirement plans must also be self-funded and self-directed. Internet store managers may or may not receive benefits.

WORK ENVIRONMENT

Internet entrepreneurs and store managers may work out of a home or private office. Some Internet store managers may be required to work on site at a corporation or small business.

The entrepreneur must deal with the stresses of starting a business, keeping it going, dealing with deadlines and customers, and coping with problems as they arise. They must also work long hours to develop and manage their business venture; many entrepreneurs work over 40 hours a week. Evening or weekend work may also be required, both for the entrepreneur and the store manager.

In addition, these professionals must spend time researching, reading, and checking out the competition in order to be informed about the latest technology and business trends. Their intensive computer work can result in eyestrain, hand and wrist injuries, and back pain.

OUTLOOK

Online commerce is a very new and exciting field with tremendous potential, and it is likely that growth will continue over the long term. However, it is important to keep in mind that the failure rate for new businesses, even traditional ones, is fairly high. Some experts predict that in the next few years, 80 to 90 percent of dotcoms will either close or be acquired by other companies. The survivors will be small businesses that are able to find niche markets, anticipate trends, adapt to market and technology changes, and plan for a large enough financial margin to turn a profit. Analysts also anticipate that the amount of business-to-business e-commerce will surpass business-to-consumer sales.

Internet managers and entrepreneurs with the most thorough education and experience and who have done their research will have the best opportunities for success. For those who are adventurous and interested in using new avenues for selling products and services, the Internet offers many possibilities. The Bureau of Labor Statistics predicts that the top four fastest growing occupations through 2010 will be computer related.

FOR MORE INFORMATION

For information about the information technology industry and e-commerce, contact:

Information Technology Association of America
1401 Wilson Boulevard, Suite 1100
Arlington, VA 22209

Tel: 703-522-5055
http://www.itaa.org

The Small Business Administration offers helpful information on starting a business. For information on state offices and additional references, check out their website:

Small Business Administration
6302 Fairview Road, Suite 300
Charlotte, NC 28210
Tel: 800-827-5722
Email: answerdesk@sba.gov
http://www.sba.gov

Check out the following online magazine specializing in topics of interest to entrepreneurs:

Entrepreneur.com
http://www.entrepreneurmag.com

For resources on information technology careers and computer programming, check out the following website:

Mainfunction.com
http://www.mainfunction.com

LABOR UNION
BUSINESS AGENTS

QUICK FACTS

School Subjects Business English Mathematics	**Certification or Licensing** None available
	Outlook About as fast as the average
Personal Skills Communication/ideas Leadership/management	
	DOT 187
Work Environment Indoors and outdoors Primarily multiple locations	**GOE** 11.05.02
	NOC 1121
Minimum Education Level High school diploma	
	O*NET-SOC N/A
Salary Range $50,000 to $65,000 to $75,000+	

OVERVIEW

Labor union business agents manage the daily business matters of labor unions and act as liaisons between the union and management during contract negotiations. They manage business affairs for the labor unions that employ them and inform the media of labor union happenings. Labor union business agents are also responsible for informing employers of workers' concerns.

HISTORY

The idea of workers or craft workers banding together for their mutual benefit has existed for centuries. In the Middle Ages, groups such as blacksmiths and carpenters organized themselves into guilds, which established product and wage standards, set requirements for entering the trade, and erected barriers to outside competition. The first guilds in the United States were organized around the time of the Revolutionary War.

Unions were first organized in both England and the United States by workers in response to the Industrial Revolution of the 19th century. In 1886, the American Federation of Labor (AFL) was founded. Through collective bargaining tactics, the AFL was able to get higher wages, shorter hours, workers' compensation, and child labor laws. In the beginning of the 20th century, there was a huge growth in union membership, which jumped from less than 800,000 in 1900 to more than 5 million by 1920. Unionism got a further boost from such New Deal federal legislation as the Wagner Act in 1935, which established the National Labor Relations Board. In the same year, the Congress of Industrial Organizations (CIO) was created to bring about a separation between unions representing factory workers and those representing skilled craftsmen. The two groups eventually merged together forming the AFL-CIO, which still exerts a powerful influence on improving working relations today.

Most unions are essentially organized into two types: the *craft union,* whose members are all skilled in a certain craft, such as carpentry or electrical work; and the *industrial union,* whose members work in the various jobs of a certain industry, such as automobiles or steel manufacturing. Companies began to reorganize around the existence of unions. A company that hired only union members was called a *closed shop,* while a *union shop* was one that required newly hired workers to join a union after a certain time period. The closed shop was outlawed in 1947 with the passage of the Taft-Hartley Act. Since then, more than one-third of the states have also outlawed the union shop by passing "right to work" laws.

The economic recession in the early 1980s caused a weakening of many unions' power, as employers in financially troubled industries asked unions for contract concessions in order to save the jobs of existing employees. In 2000, 13.5 percent of wage and salary workers were represented by unions, according to the U.S. Department of Labor.

THE JOB

Union business agents act as representatives for the working members of the union, who are often called the "rank and file." Agents are usually elected by members in a democratic fashion, although sometimes they are appointed by the union's elected officers or executive board. A union agent normally represents a certain number of workers. In an industrial union, an agent could speak for workers in several small plants or a single large plant. In a craft union, an agent will represent a single trade or group of craft workers.

Unions are structured like corporations and government groups in many ways. In the same way that a company will follow the procedures described in its articles of incorporation to conduct meetings and elect its board of directors, a union follows the rules set down by its own constitution and democratically elects its leaders and representatives. Union leaders must be responsive to the wills of their union members, or they may be overruled in union meetings or defeated in their next bid for reelection. In industrial unions, local chapters are directed by a central union, which is led by a regional director and is part of a larger national or international union.

Craft unions are organized somewhat differently. Each craft is represented by a different business agent, and several of these agents work on the staff of a district council. These district councils are like an organization of unions, each governed independently of the others, banding together for bargaining strength.

One of the most important aspects of a union business agent's job is the role as a liaison, or go-between, for workers and employers. This role becomes most apparent at the times when the union and its employers need to negotiate a new contract. The business agent needs to know what the members of the union want in order to talk with management about wages, benefits, pensions, working conditions, layoffs, workers' compensation, and other issues. The agent explains the union's position to management during pre-bargaining talks. During negotiations, the agent keeps the members informed of the progress of contract talks and advises them of management's position.

The business agent needs to be able to drive a hard bargain with employers while at the same time be aware of employer limitations so that an agreement can be reached that is suitable to all parties. If a contract agreement cannot be reached, a third party may be needed. *Conciliators,* or *mediators,* are dispute-resolution specialists that may be brought in to keep the talks moving on both sides. *Arbitrators,* sometimes called *referees* or *umpires,* help decide disputes by drawing up conditions that bind both workers and employers to certain agreements. Only as a last resort will labor union business agents help organize a general strike, which can hurt both labor and management financially. During a strike, workers are not paid and employers lose money from a loss in production.

In addition, the business agent is responsible for making certain that the union is serving its members properly. The agent often handles grievances expressed by union members and, if necessary, will work with people in the company to solve them. It is also the agent's job to make sure that employers carry out the terms of the union's contract. The agent is in constant contact with union members through the *shop steward,* who is the general representative for the union. The steward is either elected by the membership or appointed by the business agent.

Agents are also responsible for much of the public image of the union. This involves everything from contacting newspaper reporters and other members of the media to organizing charity drives. The business agent is often in charge of recruiting new members for the union, finding jobs for members who are out of work, conducting union meetings, and renting meeting halls.

REQUIREMENTS
High School
Union business agents should at least have a high school education. To build a solid background, take courses in business, English, mathematics, public speaking, history, and economics. You should also take technical courses, such as shop and electronics, if they are available at your school.

Top 5 Undergraduate Business Programs of 2003

1. University of Pennsylvania (Wharton)
   http://www.wharton.upenn.edu

2. Massachusetts Institute of Technology (Sloan)
   http://mitsloan.mit.edu

3. University of Michigan at Ann Arbor
   http://www.umich.edu

4. University of California at Berkeley
   http://www.berkeley.edu

5. University of North Carolina at Chapel Hill (Kenan-Flagler)
   http://www.bschool.unc.edu

6. University of Virginia (McIntire)
   http://www.virginia.edu

Source: *U.S. News & World Report*

Postsecondary Training

A college degree can also be very valuable for union business agents. Many colleges now offer curricula in labor and industrial relations. Other useful courses are psychology, business, collective bargaining, labor law, occupational safety and health, economics, and political science. Some unions may offer to reimburse some of the costs of higher education for union members interested in leadership positions. In most cases, business agents will receive additional training on the job while working under experienced union leaders.

Other Requirements

To succeed as a union business agent, you need to have both relevant job skills and leadership qualities. Agents should have previous work experience in the trade, industry, or profession that they represent in order to fully understand and appreciate the problems and concerns of the workers. Most business agents begin as industrial or craft workers, join a union, become involved in its affairs, and progressively move up through the ranks.

Agents must also possess leadership skills and be committed to the cause of the union and to the rights and concerns of the workers. Their role in negotiations requires intelligence, persuasiveness, self-discipline, and patience. They must be able to command the respect of both the employer and the members. A good command of the English language, both written and oral, is essential to vocalize the concerns of the workers, understand the terms of union contracts, and persuade the representatives of the company and the union members to accept an agreement. If the union leadership has reached a decision that may be unpopular, the agent will have to explain the reasoning behind it to the members.

EXPLORING

The career of labor union business agent offers you the opportunity to follow your career interest into such fields as teaching or electronics, and then expand as a leader of others. Whatever your specific interest area, you should also gain experience in policy making and hold positions of leadership to nurture the qualities necessary for a future career as a union business agent. Get involved with the student council, debate society, and other clubs with leadership opportunities. In addition, talking with working business agents can also lend insight into the daily responsibilities of union leadership.

EMPLOYERS

Since union business agents represent the workers in a labor union, they are employed by the various craft and industrial unions, normally representing a particular group of workers. There are active unions in nearly every line of work.

STARTING OUT

Almost all union business agents first work for a number of years in their respective industries and work their way up from the inside. Each type of industry has its own requirements for joining, such as previous experience, training, and apprenticeships. Once they become members of a union, workers can seek opportunities to become involved in union matters, such as serving on committees. Through efforts and dedication to the union's cause, workers attract the attention of union leadership, who may encourage them to run for a local union job in the next election. Initially, prospective agents are usually elected or appointed to the position of shop steward, who is responsible for communicating the members' wishes to the business agent. If popular and effective, the steward may then run for election as union business agent. The process of electing or selecting representatives varies from union to union, but an agent usually serves a term of about three years.

ADVANCEMENT

A labor union business agent is in many ways like a politician. In the same ways that politicians can work their way from local to state government and possibly to Washington, D.C., union business agents can move upward in the ranks of leadership. If business agents do their jobs well, gain respect, and maintain high profiles, they may advance to positions at the council headquarters or at regional union offices. An experienced agent can even advance to represent the union at the international level.

EARNINGS

The earnings of business agents vary depending on the union's membership size and the type of business it represents. Agents' pay is usually prescribed in union bylaws or its constitution. Typically, their wages mirror the earnings of the highest paid worker in the particular field the agent represents. Average starting salaries for agents are about $50,000. After five years' experience, business agents earn about $65,000, and after 10 years, $75,000 or more.

In addition, agents get the same benefits as other union members, such as paid holidays, health insurance, and pension plans. Some agents may drive a car owned by the union and have their expenses paid while they travel on union business.

WORK ENVIRONMENT

An agent's dedication to the union often dictates the amount of hours worked every week. Most agents work a 40-hour week, but often work much longer hours during contract-bargaining talks and membership drives. They are also expected to be available 24 hours a day to handle any possible emergencies.

Agents generally split their time between office work at council or local headquarters and fieldwork. They spend many hours visiting factories and construction sites, meeting with shop stewards, and listening to the opinions of the rank-and-file members. During these visits, they have to deal with the working conditions of their industry. Agents also travel a great deal and can be on the road for long periods of time.

OUTLOOK

The success of union business agents depends to a great extent on the strength and growth prospects of their particular unions as well as of their industries in general. The best opportunities for employment and advancement exist in those industries that are expected to grow in years to come.

In recent years, there has been a strong shift in the U.S. economy away from manufacturing and toward service industries. Such service industries include insurance, banking, legal services, health care, accounting, retailing, data processing, and education. According to the U.S. Department of Labor, the growth of these industries and the industries that support them will provide the greatest opportunities for unionization and union business agents through the next decade. Unions already exist for public workers, such as teachers, police officers, and firefighters. Other opportunities for unionization and business agent employment will arise in health care, representing workers such as physicians, nurses, medical assistants, technicians, and custodians.

The manufacturing sector of the economy, which traditionally has been very highly unionized, is expected to lose jobs because of increasingly efficient technologies and competition from overseas. However, certain areas of opportunity will still exist in manufacturing. Increases are expected in certain durable goods industries, such as computing equipment, medical supplies, plastics, and commercial printing. Construction is the only goods-producing sector of the economy that is expected to show a steady increase in employment in the next decade.

FOR MORE INFORMATION

Following are a handful of national labor unions. For more detailed information about careers in a specific trade or profession, contact the appropriate local unions in your area.

American Federation of Labor and Congress of Industrial Organizations
815 16th Street, NW
Washington, DC 20006
Tel: 202-637-5000
Email: feedback@aflcio.org
http://www.aflcio.org

American Federation of Teachers
555 New Jersey Avenue, NW
Washington, DC 20001
Tel: 202-879-4400
Email: online@aft.org
http://www.aft.org

International Union, United Automobile, Aerospace and Agricultural Implement Workers of America
8000 East Jefferson Avenue
Detroit, MI 48214
Tel: 313-926-5000
Email: uaw@uaw.org
http://www.uaw.org

United Steelworkers of America
Five Gateway Center
Pittsburgh, PA 15222
Tel: 412-562-2400
http://www.uswa.org

LIFE INSURANCE AGENTS AND BROKERS

QUICK FACTS

School Subjects
Business
Mathematics

Personal Skills
Communication/ideas
Leadership/management

Work Environment
Primarily indoors
One location with
some travel

Minimum Education Level
Some postsecondary
training

Salary Range
$20,630 to $38,890 to
$94,040+

Certification or Licensing
Required by all states

Outlook
More slowly than the
average

DOT
250

GOE
08.01.02

NOC
6231

O*NET-SOC
41-3021.00

OVERVIEW

Life insurance agents and brokers sell policies that provide life insurance, retirement income, and various other types of insurance to new clients or to established policyholders. Some agents are referred to as *life underwriters,* since they may be required to estimate insurance risks on some policies. Approximately 378,000 insurance agents and brokers work in the United States; about 16 percent of that number specialize in working for life insurance carriers.

HISTORY

The first life insurance company in the United States was founded in Philadelphia in 1759 and was known as "A Corporation for the Relief of Poor and Distressed Presbyterian Ministers and of Poor and Distressed Widows and Children of Presbyterian Ministers." The company still exists, although its name has been shortened to the Presbyterian Ministers Fund.

In the middle of the 19th century, companies similar to today's life insurance firms began to develop. Two types of organizations grew: mutual companies, which are owned by the policyholders, and stock companies, which are owned by stockholders. The emergence of the profession of full-time insurance agent, who is paid a commission on the basis of what is sold, contributed greatly to the growth of life insurance.

THE JOB

Life insurance agents act as field sales representatives for the companies to which they are under contract. They may be under direct contract or work through a general agent who holds a contract. Insurance brokers represent the insurance buyer and do not sell for a particular company but place insurance policies for their clients with the company that offers the best rate and coverage. In addition, some brokers obtain several types of insurance (automobile, household, medical, and so on) to provide a more complete service package for their clients.

The agent's work may be divided into five functions: identifying and soliciting prospects, explaining services, developing insurance plans, closing the transaction, and following up.

The life insurance agent must use personal initiative to identify and solicit sales prospects. Few agents can survive in the life insurance field by relying solely on contacts made through regular business and social channels. They must make active client solicitation a part of their regular job. One company, for example, asks that each agent make between 20 and 30 personal contacts with prospective customers each week, through which eight to 12 interviews may be obtained, resulting in from zero to three sales. As in many sales occupations, many days or weeks may pass without any sales, then several sales in a row may suddenly develop.

Some agents obtain leads for sales prospects by following newspaper reports to learn of newcomers to the community, births, graduations, and business promotions. Other agents specialize in occupational groups, selling to physicians, farmers, or small businesses. Many agents use general telephone or mail solicitations to help identify prospects. All agents hope that satisfied customers will suggest future sales to their friends and neighbors.

Successful contact with prospective clients may be a difficult process. Potential customers already may have been solicited by a number of life insurance agents or may not be interested in buying life insurance at a particular time. Agents are often hard-pressed to obtain their initial goal, a personal interview to sit down and talk about insurance with the potential customer.

Once they have lined up a sales interview, agents usually travel to the customer's home or place of business. During this meeting, agents explain their services. Like any other successful sales pitch, this explanation must be adapted to the needs of the client. A new father, for example, may wish to ensure his child's college education, while an older person may be most interested in provisions dealing with retirement income. With experience, agents learn how best to answer questions or objections raised by potential customers. The agents must be able to describe the coverage offered by their company in clear, non-technical language.

With the approval of the prospective client, the agent develops an insurance plan. In some cases this will involve only a single standard life insurance policy. In other instances the agent will review the client's complete financial status and develop a comprehensive plan for death benefits, payment of the balance due on a home mortgage if the insured dies, creation of a fund for college education for children, and retirement income. Such plans usually take into account several factors: the customer's personal savings and investments, mortgage and other obligations, Social Security benefits, and existing insurance coverage.

To best satisfy the customer's insurance needs, and in keeping with the customer's ability to pay, the agent may present a variety of insurance alternatives. The agent may, for example, recommend term insurance (the cheapest form of insurance since it may only be used as a death benefit) or ordinary life (which may be maintained by premium payments throughout the insured's life but may be converted to aid in retirement living). In some cases, the agent may suggest a limited payment plan, such as 20-payment life, which allows the insured to pay the policy off completely in a given number of annual premiums. Agents can develop comprehensive life insurance plans to protect a business enterprise (such as protection from the loss resulting from the death of a key partner), employee group insurance plans, or the creation and distribution of wealth through estates. The agent's skill and the variety of plans offered by the company are combined to develop the best possible insurance proposal for customers.

Closing the transaction is probably the most difficult part of the insurance process. At this point, the customer must decide whether to purchase the recommended insurance plan, ask for a modified version, or conclude that additional insurance is not needed or affordable.

After a customer decides to purchase a policy, the agent must arrange for him or her to take a physical examination; insurance company policies require that standard rates apply only to those people in good health. The agent also must obtain a completed insurance application and the first premium payment and send them with other supporting documents to the company for its approval and formal issuance of the policy.

The final phase of the insurance process is follow-up. The agent checks back frequently with policyholders both to provide service and to watch for opportunities for additional sales.

Successful life insurance agents and brokers work hard at their jobs. A majority of agents average over 40 hours of work a week. Because arranging a meeting often means fitting into the client's personal schedule, many of the hours worked by insurance agents are in the evenings or on weekends. In addition to the time spent with customers, agents must spend time in their homes or offices preparing insurance programs for customer approval, developing new sources of business, and writing reports for the company.

REQUIREMENTS
High School

Formal requirements for the life insurance field are few. Because more mature individuals are usually better able to master the complexities of the business and inspire customer confidence, most companies prefer to hire people who are at least 21 years of age. Many starting agents are more than 30 years of age. If this field interests you, there are a number of courses you can take in high school to prepare yourself for college and this type of work. Naturally you should take English classes. These classes will help you improve your research, writing, and speaking skills—all of which you will use in this line of work. Business classes will teach you how to interact professionally with others and deal with customer needs. If your high school offers economics or finance classes, take these as well. Working with insurance means working with money and numbers, and these classes will give you this exposure. You may also benefit from taking sociology and psychology classes, which can give you a greater understanding of people. Finally, take math and computer classes. Undoubtedly you will be using computers in your professional life, so become comfortable with this tool now.

Postsecondary Training

Today most insurance companies and agencies prefer to hire college graduates. Those who have majored in economics or business will likely have an advantage in getting jobs. Classes you can take in college that will help you in this field include math, economics, and accounting. Business law, government, and business administration classes will help you understand the functions of different types of insurance as well as how to successfully run a business. Of course, keep up with your computer work. Knowing how to use software, such as spreadsheet software, will be indispensable in your line of work. You may want to attend a college or university that offers specific courses in insurance; there are more than 60 colleges and universities in the United States that offer such classes.

Certification or Licensing

Life insurance agents must obtain a license in each state in which they sell insurance. Agents are often sponsored for this license by the company they represent, which usually pays the license fee.

In most states, the agent must pass a written test on insurance fundamentals and state insurance laws before they are issued a license. Companies usually provide training programs to help prepare for these examinations. Often, the new agent may sell on a temporary certificate while preparing for the written examination. Information on state life insurance licensing requirements can be easily obtained from the state commissioner of insurance. Agents who sell securities, such as mutual funds, must obtain a separate securities license.

For full professional status, many companies recommend that their agents become chartered life underwriters (CLU) and/or chartered financial consultants (ChFC). To earn these designations, agents must successfully complete at least three years of work in the field and course work offered through the American College (http://www.amercoll.edu/ce). This work will demonstrate the agents' ability to apply their knowledge of life insurance fundamentals, economics, business law, taxation, trusts, and finance to common insurance problems. Only a small percentage of life insurance agents are CLUs and/or ChFCs.

Other Requirements

Personal characteristics of agents are of great importance. The following traits are most helpful: a genuine liking and appreciation for people; a positive attitude toward others and sympathy for their problems; a personal belief in the value of life insurance coverage; a willingness to spend several years learning the business and becoming established; and persistence, hard work, and patience. Sales workers should also be resourceful and organized to make the most effective use of their time.

Requirements for success in life insurance are elusive, and it is this fact that contributes to the high turnover rate in this field. Despite the high rate of failure, life insurance sales offers a rewarding career for those who meet its requirements. It has been said that life insurance offers the easiest way to earn $1,000 to $2,000 a week, but the most difficult way to earn $300 or $400. People with strong qualifications may readily develop a successful insurance career, but poorly qualified people will find it a very difficult field.

EXPLORING

Because of state licensing requirements, it is difficult for young people to obtain actual experience. The most notable exceptions are the student-agency programs developed by several companies to provide college students with practical sales experience and a trial exposure to the field.

To get a general idea of how business transactions take place in the professional world, join or start a business club at your school. Those wishing to learn more about life insurance may be able to get a part-time or summer job as a clerical worker in an insurance agency. This work will provide background information on the requirements for the field and an understanding of its problems and prospects for the future. Formal college or evening school courses in insurance will also provide a clearer picture of this profession's techniques and opportunities.

EMPLOYERS

Life insurance agents and brokers can be found throughout the country, but most work in or near large cities. The majority work out of local offices or in independent agencies; others are employed at insurance company headquarters. There are approximately 378,000 insurance agents and brokers working in the United States, and about 16 percent of these workers specialize in life insurance.

STARTING OUT

Aspiring agents may apply directly to personnel directors of insurance companies or managers of branches or agencies. In most cases, the new agent will be affiliated with a local sales office almost immediately. To increase the agency's potential sales volume, the typical insurance office manager is prepared to hire all candidates who can be readily recruited and properly trained. Prospective life insurance agents should discuss their career interests with representatives of several companies to select the employer that offers them the best opportunities to fulfill their goals.

Prospective agents should carefully evaluate potential employers to select an organization that offers sound training, personal supervision, resources to assist sales, adequate financial compensation, and a recognizable name that will be well received by customers. Students graduating from college should be able to arrange campus interviews with recruiters from several insurance companies. People with work experience in other fields usually find life insurance managers eager to discuss sales opportunities.

In addition to discussing personal interests and requirements for success in the field, company representatives usually give prospective agents aptitude tests, which are developed either by their company or by LIMRA International (formerly the Life Insurance Marketing and Research Association).

Formal job training usually involves three phases. In pre-contract orientation, candidates are provided with a clearer picture of the field through classroom work, training manuals, or other materials. On-the-job training is designed to present insurance fundamentals, techniques of developing sales prospects, principles of selling, and the importance of a work schedule. Finally, intermediate instruction usually provides company training of an advanced nature.

More than 30,000 agents a year take continuing educational courses prepared by the American College. After completing a certain number of courses, an agent may apply for the professional educational designation of Life Underwriter Training Council Fellow.

ADVANCEMENT

Continuing education has become essential for life insurance agents. Several professional organizations offer courses and tests for agents to obtain additional professional certification. Although voluntary, many professional insurance organizations require agents to commit to continuing education on a regular basis. Membership in professional organizations and the accompanying certification is important in establishing client trust. Many states also require continuing education to maintain licensing.

Unlike some occupations, many of the ablest people in the life insurance field are not interested in advancing into management. There can be many reasons for this. In some cases, a successful sales agent may be able to earn more than the president of the company. Experienced agents often would rather increase their volume of business and quality of service rather than their responsibility for the work of others. Others develop by specializing in various phases of insurance.

Still, many successful agents aspire to positions in sales management. At first, they may begin by helping train newcomers to the field. Later, they may become assistant managers of their office. Top agents are often asked by their companies (or even by rival insurance companies) to take over as managers of an existing branch or to develop a new one. In some cases, persons entering management must take a temporary salary cut, particularly at the beginning, and may earn less than successful agents.

There are several types of life insurance sales office arrangements. *Branch office managers* are salaried employees who work for their company in a geographic region. *General agency managers* are given franchises by a company and develop and finance their own sales office. *General agents* are not directly affiliated with their company, but they must operate in a responsible manner to maintain their right to represent the company. *General insurance brokers* are self-employed persons who place insurance coverage for their clients with more than one life insurance company.

The highest management positions in the life insurance field are in company headquarters. Persons with expertise in sales and field management experience may be offered a position with the home office.

EARNINGS

According to the U.S. Department of Labor, in 2001 the median yearly income of insurance agents and brokers was about $38,890. The Department also reported that the lowest paid 10 percent of these workers, which typically includes those just beginning in the field, made less than $20,630. The highest paid 10 percent earned $94,040 or more. Many offices also pay bonuses to agents who sell a predetermined amount of coverage. Beginning agents usually receive some form of financial assistance from the company. They may be placed on a moderate salary for a year or two; often the amount of salary declines each month on the assumption that commission income on sales will increase. Eventually, the straight salary is replaced by a drawing account—a fixed dollar amount that is advanced each month against anticipated commissions. This account helps agents balance out high- and low-earning periods.

Agents receive commissions on two bases: a first-year commission for making the sale (usually 55 percent of the total first-year premium) and a series of smaller commissions paid when the insured pays the annual premium (usually 5 percent of the yearly payments for nine years). Most companies will not pay renewal commissions to agents who resign.

WORK ENVIRONMENT

The job of the life insurance agent is marked by extensive contact with others. Most agents actively participate in groups such as churches, synagogues, community groups, and service clubs, through which they can meet prospective clients. Life insurance agents also have to stay in touch with other individuals to keep their prospective sales list growing.

Because they are essentially self-employed, agents must be self-motivated and capable of operating on their own. In return, the life insurance field offers people the chance to go into business for themselves without the need for capital investment, long-term debt, and personal liability.

When asked to comment on what they liked least about the life insurance field, a group of experienced agents listed the amount of detail work required of an agent, the lack of education by the public concerning life insurance, the uncertainty of earnings while becoming established in the field, and the amount of night and weekend work. The last point is particularly important. Some agents work four nights a week and both days of the weekend when starting out. After becoming established, this may be reduced to three or two evenings and only one weekend day. Agents are often torn between the desire to spend more time with their families and the reality that curtailing evening and weekend work may hurt their income. Most agents work a 40-hour week, although those beginning in the field and those with thriving businesses may work longer, some up to 60 hours.

OUTLOOK

The U.S. Department of Labor predicts slower-than-average employment growth for insurance agents and brokers through the next decade. Despite this prediction, however, there should be opportunities for people with the right skills. The percentage of citizens older than 65 is growing at a much faster rate than that of the general population. Agents will be needed to meet the special needs of this group, converting some insurance policies from a death benefit to retirement income. Also, the 25-to-54 age group is growing. This is the age group that has the greatest need for insurance, and agents will be needed to provide them with services. In addition, more women in the workplace will increase insurance sales. Finally, employment opportunities for life insurance agents will be aided by the general increase in the nation's population, the heavy turnover among new agents, and the openings created by agents retiring or leaving the field.

A number of factors may limit job growth in this field. For example, some life insurance business has been taken over by multi-line insurance agents who handle every type of insurance, thus reducing the need for those specializing in selling life insurance. Department stores and other businesses outside the traditional insurance industry have begun to offer insurance. Also, customer service representatives are increasingly assuming some sales functions, such as expanding accounts and occasionally generating new accounts. Many companies are diversifying their marketing efforts to include some direct mail and telephone sales. Increased use of computers will lessen the workload of agents by creating a database for tailor-made policies. Rising productivity among existing agents also will hold down new job openings. In addition, the life insurance industry has come under increasing competition from financial institutions that offer retirement investment plans such as mutual funds.

FOR MORE INFORMATION

The American College is the nation's oldest distance learning institution for financial service education. For information regarding the CLU and ChFC designations, contact:

The American College
270 South Bryn Mawr Avenue
Bryn Mawr, PA 19010-2196
Tel: 888-263-7265
Email: studentservices@amercoll.edu
http://www.amercoll.edu

The IIABA is the nation's oldest and largest independent agent and broker association and offers some job information.

Independent Insurance Agents and Brokers of America, Inc. (IIABA)
127 South Peyton Street
Alexandria, VA 22314
Tel: 800-221-7917
Email: info@iiaba.org
http://www.independentagent.com

For information on insurance aptitude tests, contact:
LIMRA International
300 Day Hill Road
Windsor, CT 06095
Tel: 800-235-4672
Email: online@limra.com
http://www.limra.com

For information on continuing education, contact:
National Association of Insurance and Financial Advisors
2901 Telestar Court
Falls Church, VA 22042-1205
Tel: 703-770-8100
http://www.naifa.org

This society is a professional organization consisting of graduates from The American College and other professionals in the insurance and finance fields.

Society of Financial Service Professionals
270 South Bryn Mawr Avenue
Bryn Mawr, PA 19010-2195
Tel: 610-526-2500
http://www.financialpro.org

MANAGEMENT ANALYSTS AND CONSULTANTS

QUICK FACTS

School Subjects
Business
Computer science
Speech

Personal Skills
Communication/ideas
Leadership/management

Work Environment
Primarily indoors
Primarily multiple locations

Minimum Education Level
Bachelor's degree

Salary Range
$35,020 to $57,970 to $250,000+

Certification or Licensing
Voluntary

Outlook
Faster than the average

DOT
161

GOE
05.01.06

NOC
1122

O*NET-SOC
13-1111.00

OVERVIEW

Management analysts and consultants analyze business or operating procedures to devise the most efficient methods of accomplishing work. They gather and organize information about operating problems and procedures and prepare recommendations for implementing new systems or changes. They may update manuals outlining established methods of performing work and train personnel in new applications. There are approximately 501,000 management analysts and consultants employed in the United States.

HISTORY

A number of people in business began experimenting with accepted management practices after the Industrial Revolution. For example, in the 1700s Josiah Wedgwood (1730–1795) applied new labor- and work-saving methods to his pottery business and was the first to formulate the concept of mass-producing articles of uniform quality. He believed the manufacturing process could be organized into a system that would use, and not abuse, the people harnessed to it. He organized the interrelationships between people, material, and events in his factory and took the time to reflect upon them. In short, he did in the 18th century what management analysts and consultants do today.

Frederick W. Taylor (1856–1915) was the creator of the "efficiency cult" in American business. Taylor invented the world-famous "differential piecework" plan, in which a productive worker could significantly increase take-home pay by stepping up the pace of work. Taylor's well-publicized study of the Midvale Steel plant in Pennsylvania was the first time-and-motion study. This study broke down elements of each part of each job and timed it; the study was therefore able to quantify maximum efficiency. Taylor earned many assignments and inspired James O. McKinsey, in 1910, to found a firm dealing with management and accounting problems.

Today, management analysts and consultants are thriving. As technological advances lead to the possibility of dramatic loss or gain in the business world, many executives feel more secure relying on all the specialized expertise they can find.

THE JOB

Management analysts and consultants are called in to solve any of a vast array of organizational problems. They are often needed when a rapidly growing small company needs a better system of control over inventories and expenses.

The role of the consultant is to come into a situation in which a client is unsure or inexpert and to recommend actions or provide assessments. There are many different types of management analysts and consultants, all of whom require knowledge of general management, operations, marketing, logistics, materials management and physical distribution, finance and accounting, human resources, electronic data processing and systems, and management science.

Management analysts and consultants may be called in when a major manufacturer must reorganize its corporate structure when acquiring a new division. For example, they assist when a company relocates to another state by coordinating the move, planning the new facility, and training new workers.

The work of management analysts and consultants is quite flexible and varies from job to job. In general, management analysts and consultants collect, review, and analyze data, make recommendations, and assist in the implementation of their proposals. Some projects require that several consultants work together, each specializing in a different area. Other jobs require the analysts to work independently.

Public and private organizations use management analysts for a variety of reasons. Some organizations lack the resources necessary to handle a project. Other organizations, before they pursue a particular course of action, will consult an analyst to determine what resources will be required or what problems will be encountered. Some companies seek outside advice on how to resolve organizational problems that have already been identified or to avoid troublesome problems that could arise.

Firms providing consulting practitioners range in size from solo practitioners to large international companies employing hundreds of people. The services are generally provided on a contract basis. A company will choose a consulting firm that specializes in the area that needs assistance, and then the two firms negotiate the conditions of the contract. Contract variables include the proposed cost of the project, staffing requirements, and the deadline.

After getting a contract, the analyst's first job is to define the nature and extent of the project. He or she analyzes statistics, such as annual revenues, employment, or expenditures. He or she may also interview employees and observe the operations of the organization on a day-to-day basis.

The next step for the analyst is to use his or her knowledge of management systems to develop solutions. While preparing recommendations, he or she must take into account the general nature of the business, the relationship of the firm to others in its industry, the firm's internal organization, and the information gained through data collection and analysis.

Once they have decided on a course of action, management analysts and consultants usually write reports of their findings and recommendations and present them to the client. They often make formal oral presentations about their findings as well. Some projects require only reports; others require assistance in implementing the suggestions.

REQUIREMENTS
High School
High school courses that will give you a general preparation for this field include business, mathematics, and computer science.

Management analysts and consultants must pass on their findings through written or oral presentations, so be sure to take English and speech classes, too.

Postsecondary Training

Employers generally prefer to hire management analysts and consultants with a master's degree in business or public administration, or at least a bachelor's degree and several years of appropriate work experience. Many fields of study provide a suitable formal educational background for this occupation because of the diversity of problem areas addressed by management analysts and consultants. These include many areas in the computer and information sciences, engineering, business and management, education, communications, marketing and distribution, and architecture and environmental design.

When hired directly from school, management analysts and consultants often participate in formal company training programs. These programs may include instruction on policies and procedures, computer systems and software, and management practices and principles. Regardless of their background, most management analysts and consultants routinely attend conferences to keep abreast of current developments in the field.

Certification and Licensing

The Institute of Management Consultants offers the Certified Management Consultant designation to those who pass an examination and meet minimum educational and experience criteria. Certification is voluntary but may provide an additional advantage to job seekers.

Other Requirements

Management analysts and consultants are often responsible for recommending layoffs of staff, so it is important that they learn to deal with people diplomatically. Their job requires a great deal of tact, enlisting cooperation while exerting leadership, debating their points, and pointing out errors. Consultants must be quick thinkers, able to refute objections with finality. They also must be able to make excellent presentations.

A management analyst must also be unbiased and analytical, with a disposition toward the intellectual side of business and a natural curiosity about the way things work best.

EXPLORING

The reference departments of most libraries include business areas that will have valuable research tools such as encyclopedias of business consultants and "who's who" of business consultants. These books should list management analysis and consulting firms across the country, describing their annual sales and area of specialization, like industrial, high tech, small business, and retail. After doing some research, you can call or write to these firms and ask for more information.

For more general business exploration, see if your school has a business or young leaders club. If there is nothing of the sort, you may want to explore Junior Achievement, a nationwide association that connects young business-minded students with professionals in the field for mentoring and career advice. Visit http://www.ja.org for more information.

EMPLOYERS

About a third of all management analysts and consultants are self-employed. Federal, state, and local governments employ many of the others. The Department of Defense employs the majority of those working for the federal government. The remainder work in the private sector for companies providing consulting services. Although management analysts and consultants are found throughout the country, the majority are concentrated in major metropolitan areas.

STARTING OUT

Most government agencies offer entry-level analyst and consultant positions to people with bachelor's degrees and no work experience. Many entrants are also career changers who were formerly mid- and upper-level managers. With one-third of the practicing management consultants self-employed, career changing is a common route into the field.

Anyone with some degree of business expertise or an expert field can begin to work as an independent consultant. The number of one- and two-person consulting firms in this country is well over 100,000. Establishing a wide range of appropriate personal contacts is by far the most effective way to get started in this field. Consultants have to sell themselves and their expertise, a task far tougher than selling a tangible product the customer can see and handle. Many consultants get their first clients by advertising in newspapers, magazines, and trade or professional periodicals. After some time in the field, word-of-mouth advertising is often the primary force.

ADVANCEMENT

A new consultant in a large firm may be referred to as an *associate* for the first couple of years. The next progression is to *senior associate,* a title that indicates three to five years' experience and the ability to supervise others and do more complex and independent work. After about five years, the analyst who is progressing well may become an *engagement manager* with the responsibility to lead a consulting team on a particular client project. The best managers become *senior engagement managers,* leading several study teams or a very large project team. After about seven years, those who excel will be considered for appointment as *junior partners* or *principals.* Partnership involves responsibility for marketing the firm and leading client projects. Some may be promoted to senior partnership or *director,* but few people successfully run this full course. Management analysts and consultants with entrepreneurial ambition may open their own firms.

EARNINGS

In 2001, management analysts and consultants had median annual earnings of $57,970, according to the Bureau of Labor Statistics. The lowest 10 percent earned less than $35,020, and the highest 10 percent earned more than $109,620.

Salaries and hourly rates for management analysts and consultants vary widely, according to experience, specialization, education, and employer. The *Occupational Outlook Handbook* reports that analysts and consultants working in the management and public relations industries earned median annual earnings of $61,290 in 2000, while those employed in the computer and data processing services industry earned $56,070. Management analysts and consultants employed by state government earned a median of $43,470.

Many consultants can demand between $400 and $1,000 per day. Their fees are often well over $40 per hour. Self-employed management consultants receive no fringe benefits and generally have to maintain their own office, but their pay is usually much higher than salaried consultants. They can make more than $2,000 per day or $250,000 in one year from consulting just two days per week.

Typical benefits for salaried analysts and consultants include health and life insurance, retirement plans, vacation and sick leave, profit sharing, and bonuses for outstanding work. All travel expenses are generally reimbursed by the employer.

WORK ENVIRONMENT

Management analysts and consultants generally divide their time between their own offices and the client's office or production facility. They can spend a great deal of time on the road.

Most management analysts and consultants work at least 40 hours per week plus overtime depending on the project. The nature of consulting projects—working on location with a single client toward a specific goal—allows these professionals to immerse themselves totally in their work. They sometimes work 14–16-hour days, and six- or seven-day workweeks can be fairly common.

While self-employed, consultants may enjoy the luxury of setting their own hours and doing a great deal of their work at home; the tradeoff is sacrificing the benefits provided by the large firms. Their livelihood depends on the additional responsibility of maintaining and expanding their clientele on their own.

Although those in this career usually avoid much of the potential tedium of working for one company all day, every day, they face many pressures resulting from deadlines and client expectations. Because the clients are generally paying generous fees, they want to see dramatic results, and the management analyst can feel the weight of this.

OUTLOOK

Employment of management analysts is expected to grow faster than the average for all occupations through the next decade, according to the U.S. Department of Labor. Industry and government agencies are expected to rely more and more on the expertise of these professionals to improve and streamline the performance of their organizations. Many job openings will result from the need to replace personnel who transfer to other fields or leave the labor force.

Competition for management consulting jobs will be strong. Employers can choose from a large pool of applicants who have a wide variety of educational backgrounds and experience. The challenging nature of this job, coupled with high salary potential, attracts many. A graduate degree, experience and expertise in the industry, as well as a knack for public relations, are needed to stay competitive.

Trends that have increased the growth of employment in this field include advancements in information technology and e-commerce, the growth of international business, and fluctuations in the economy that have forced businesses to streamline and downsize.

FOR MORE INFORMATION

For industry information, contact the following organizations:

American Institute of Certified Public Accountants
1211 Avenue of the Americas
New York, NY 10036
Tel: 212-596-6200
http://www.aicpa.org

American Management Association
1601 Broadway
New York, NY 10019
Tel: 800-262-9699
http://www.amanet.org

Association of Management Consulting Firms
380 Lexington Avenue, Suite 1700
New York, NY 10168
Tel: 212-551-7887
Email: info@amcf.org
http://www.amcf.org

For information on certification, contact:

Association of Internal Management Consultants, Inc.
19 Harrison Street
Framingham, MA 01702
Tel: 508-820-3434
Email: info@aimc.org
http://aimc.org

For information on certification, contact:

Institute of Management Consultants
2025 M Street, NW, Suite 800
Washington, DC 20036-3309
Tel: 800-221-2557
http://www.imcusa.org

MANUFACTURING SUPERVISORS

QUICK FACTS

School Subjects
Business
Mathematics
Technical/shop

Personal Skills
Communication/ideas
Leadership/management

Work Environment
Primarily indoors
Primarily one location

Minimum Education Level
Bachelor's degree

Salary Range
$37,420 to $64,510 to
$109,950+

Certification or Licensing
None available

Outlook
Little change or more
slowly than the average

DOT
183

GOE
05.02.03

NOC
0911

O*NET-SOC
11-3051.00

OVERVIEW

Manufacturing supervisors monitor employees and their working conditions and effectiveness in production plants and factories. They ensure that work is carried out correctly and on schedule by promoting high product quality and output levels. In addition to balancing the budget and other bookkeeping duties, supervisors are responsible for maintaining employee work schedules, training new workers, and issuing warnings to workers who violate established rules. Manufacturing managers in various industries hold nearly 255,000 jobs.

HISTORY

Manufacturing has been through many technological developments, from innovations in fuel-powered machinery to the assembly line.

As these processes became more complex, no single worker could be responsible for the production of particular items. Manufacturing became a long process involving many workers' contributions. If one worker caused a defect in the product, it was not always easy to track down the source of the problem. The role of the supervisor emerged as a means of keeping track of the work of numerous employees involved in the production process, allowing production to run smoothly.

THE JOB

The primary roles of manufacturing supervisors are to oversee their employees and ensure the effectiveness of the production process. They are responsible for the amount of work and the quality of work being done by the employees under their direction. Supervisors make work schedules, keep production and employee records, and plan on-the-job activities. Their work is highly interpersonal. They not only monitor employees, but also guide workers in their efforts and are responsible for disciplining and counseling poor performers as well as recommending valuable employees for raises and promotions. They also make sure that workers adhere to safety regulations and other rules.

In monitoring production and output levels, manufacturing supervisors must keep in mind the company's limitations, such as budgetary allowances, time constraints, and any workforce shortages. They must be realistic about the abilities of their employees and set production schedules accordingly. Supervisors may use mathematical calculations and test various production methods to reach high production levels while still maintaining the quality of the product.

Manufacturing supervisors may be employed by small companies, such as custom furniture shops, or large industrial factories, such as automotive plants. Supervisors answer to company managers, who direct them on production goals and set budgets. Another important part of the supervisor's job is to act as a liaison between factory workers and company managers who are in charge of production. Supervisors announce new company policies and plans to the workers in their charge and report to their managers about any problems they may be having or other important issues. Supervisors also may meet with other company supervisors to discuss progress toward company objectives, department operations, and employee performance. In companies where employees belong to labor unions, supervisors must know and follow all work-related guidelines outlined by labor-management contracts.

REQUIREMENTS
High School

If you are interested in becoming a manufacturing supervisor, take high school courses in business, math, and science to prepare for the demands of the job. In order to balance the budget and determine production schedules, supervisors often use mathematical computations. They also use computers to do much of their paperwork, so take any available classes to become familiar with word processing and spreadsheet programs.

Postsecondary Training

Because manufacturing areas differ, there is no single path to a supervisory position. However, most manufacturing supervisors hold a college degree in business administration or industrial management. College courses in business, industrial relations, math, and computer applications help to familiarize prospective supervisors with the many responsibilities they will have to handle. Interpersonal skills are also highly valuable, so classes in public relations and human resource management are also important.

Many supervisors obtain graduate degrees to become more marketable to employers or for a better chance of advancing within a company. As manufacturing processes have become more complex, advanced degrees in business administration, engineering, or industrial management are more and more common among those in higher-level positions.

Other Requirements

Manufacturing supervisors deal with many people on a highly personal level. They must direct, guide, and discipline others, so you should work on developing strong leadership qualities. You will also need good communication skills and the ability to motivate people and maintain morale.

EXPLORING

To better gauge your interest and expand your knowledge about manufacturing careers, ask your school's guidance counselor for advice on setting up a tour of a local production factory or plant. At the factory or plant, you might be able to talk to workers about their jobs or at least see the environment in which they work. Simply reading more about the field of manufacturing and its many different employment opportunities is also a good way to explore this career. Visit your local library or surf the Internet for recent articles and information.

A summer or part-time job in an office or retail setting can give you business experience and expose you to management practices. Depending on the job and industry, you might even be promoted to an assistant manager position.

EMPLOYERS

There are approximately 255,000 manufacturing supervisors working all over the United States, but the majority of jobs are located in highly industrial areas. Whether it be in a small production facility or a large factory or plant, supervisors are needed to oversee all manufacturing processes. The major employment areas are industrial machinery and equipment, transportation equipment, electronic and electrical equipment, metal instruments and related products, and food industries. A small number of these managers are self-employed.

STARTING OUT

Many supervisors enter their jobs by moving up from factory worker positions. They may also apply for supervisory positions from outside the company. Companies that hire manufacturing supervisors look for experience, knowledge of the job or industry, organizational skills, and leadership abilities. Supervisory positions may be found in classified ads, but for those just looking to get started, part-time or full-time jobs in a factory setting may help provide some experience and familiarity with the work of supervisors.

ADVANCEMENT

In most manufacturing companies, an advanced degree in business management or administration along with accumulated work experience is the best method for advancement into higher level supervisory positions. From the position of supervisor, one may advance to manager or head of an entire manufacturing plant or factory.

EARNINGS

Salaries for manufacturing supervisors vary depending on the factory or plant in which they work, the area of production that they supervise, and their years of experience in the position. The Bureau of Labor Statistics reports that the median annual salary for manufacturing supervisors was $64,510 in 2001. The lowest 10 percent earned less than $37,420, and the highest 10 percent earned more than $109,950.

WORK ENVIRONMENT

Most supervisors work on the manufacturing or factory floor. They may be on their feet most of the time, which can be tiring, and work near loud and hazardous machines. Supervisors may begin their day early so that they arrive before their workers, and they may stay later than their workers. Some may work for plants that operate around the clock and may work overnight shifts, weekends, and holidays. Sometimes the best hours go to those who have been with the company the longest. Plant downsizing and restructuring often leads to fewer supervisors. As a result, manufacturing supervisors may face larger departments to oversee and other increased demands.

OUTLOOK

To some extent, the future of the manufacturing supervisor job depends on the individual industry, whether it be automobiles or food products. In manufacturing as a whole, employment of supervisors is expected to grow more slowly than the average as supervisors have begun to oversee more workers. Corporate downsizing and the use of computers for tasks such as producing production schedules and budget plans also require fewer supervisors than before. However, there will be a need to replace job-changing or retiring managers. Job candidates with higher levels of education and related work experience will fare the best in landing a supervisory position.

FOR MORE INFORMATION

For information on workplace trends and management and leadership training, contact:

American Management Association
1601 Broadway
New York, NY 10019
Tel: 800-262-9699
http://www.amanet.org

For general information on manufacturing careers, industry news, and training tools, contact:

National Association of Manufacturers
1331 Pennsylvania Avenue, NW
Washington, DC 20004-1790
Tel: 202-637-3000
Email: manufacturing@nam.org
http://www.nam.org

MARKETING RESEARCH ANALYSTS

QUICK FACTS

School Subjects Business Mathematics	**Certification or Licensing** None available
	Outlook Faster than the average
Personal Skills Following instructions Technical/scientific	
	DOT 050
Work Environment Primarily indoors Primarily one location	**GOE** 11.06.03
Minimum Education Level Bachelor's degree	**NOC** N/A
Salary Range $28,500 to $53,450 to $96,980+	**O*NET-SOC** 19-3021.00

OVERVIEW

Marketing research analysts collect, analyze, and interpret data in order to determine potential demand for a product or service. By examining the buying habits, wants, needs, and preferences of consumers, research analysts are able to recommend ways to improve products, increase sales, and expand customer bases.

HISTORY

Knowing what customers want and what prices they are willing to pay have always been concerns of manufacturers and producers of goods and services. As industries have grown and competition for consumers of manufactured goods has increased, businesses have turned to marketing research as a way to measure public opinion and assess customer preferences.

Marketing research formally emerged in Germany in the 1920s and in Sweden and France in the 1930s. In the United States, emphasis on marketing research began after World War II. With a desire to study potential markets and gain new customers, U.S. firms hired marketing research specialists, professionals who were able to use statistics and refine research techniques to help companies reach their marketing goals. By the 1980s, research analysts could be found even in a variety of Communist countries, where the quantity of consumer goods being produced was rapidly increasing.

Today, the marketing research analyst is a vital part of the marketing team. By conducting studies and analyzing data, research professionals help companies address specific marketing issues and concerns.

THE JOB

Marketing researchers collect and analyze all kinds of information in order to help companies improve their products, establish or modify sales and distribution policies, and make decisions regarding future plans and directions. In addition, research analysts are responsible for monitoring both in-house studies and off-site research, interpreting results, providing explanations of compiled data, and developing research tools.

One area of marketing research focuses on company products and services. In order to determine consumer likes and dislikes, research analysts collect data on brand names, trademarks, product design, and packaging for existing products, items being test-marketed, and those in experimental stages. Analysts also study competing products and services that are already on the market to help managers and strategic planners develop new products and create appropriate advertising campaigns.

In the sales methods and policy area of marketing research, analysts examine firms' sales records and conduct a variety of sales-related studies. For example, information on sales in various geographical areas is analyzed and compared to previous sales figures, changes in population, and total and seasonal sales volume. By analyzing this data, marketing researchers can identify peak sales periods and recommend ways to target new customers. Such information helps marketers plan future sales campaigns and establish sales quotas and commissions.

Advertising research is closely related to sales research. Studies on the effectiveness of advertising in different parts of the country are conducted and compared to sales records. This research is helpful in planning future advertising campaigns and in selecting the appropriate media to use.

Marketing research that focuses on consumer demand and preferences solicits opinions of the people who use the products or services being considered. In addition to actually conducting opinion studies, marketing researchers often design the ways to obtain the information. They write scripts for telephone interviews, develop direct-mail questionnaires and field surveys, and design focus group programs.

Through one or a combination of these studies, market researchers are able to gather information on consumer reaction to the need for

Top 25 Graduate Business Schools of 2002

1. Northwestern (Kellogg) (IL)
   http://www.kellogg.northwestern.edu

2. University of Chicago (IL)
   http://gsb.uchicago.edu

3. Harvard University (MA)
   http://www.hbs.edu

4. Stanford University (CA)
   http://www.gsb.stanford.edu

5. University of Pennsylvania (Wharton)
   http://www.wharton.upenn.edu

6. Massachusetts Institute of Technology (Sloan)
   http://mitsloan.mit.edu

7. Columbia University (NY)
   http://www.columbia.edu/cu/business

8. University of Michigan
   http://www.bus.umich.edu

9. Duke University (Fuqua) (NC)
   http://www.fuqua.duke.edu

10. Dartmouth (Tuck) (NH)
    http://www.tuck.dartmouth.edu

11. Cornell University (Johnson) (NY)
    http://www.cornellbusinessl.edu/

12. University of Virginia (Darden) (VA)
    http://www.darden.edu

13. University of California at Berkeley (Haas)
    http://www.haas.berkeley.edu

14. Yale University (CT)
    http://mba.yale.edu

15. New York University (Stern)
    http://www.stern.nyu.edu

16. University of California at Los Angeles
    (Anderson)
    http://www.anderson.ucla.edu

17. University of South Carolina (Moore)
    http://mooreschool.sc.edu

18. University of North Carolina at Chapel Hill
    (Kenan-Flagler)
    http://www.bschool.unc.edu

19. Carnegie Mellon University (PA)
    http://web.gsia.cmu.edu

20. Indiana University (Kelley)
    http://www.bus.indiana.edu

21. University of Texas (McCombs)
    http://www.bus.utexas.edu

22. Emory University (Goizueta) (GA)
    http://www.goizueta.emory.edu

23. Michigan State University (Broad)
    http://www.bus.msu.edu

24. Washington University (Olin) (MO)
    http://www.olin.wustl.edu

25. University of Maryland (Smith)
    http://www.rhsmith.umd.edu

Source: *Business Week*

and style, design, price, and use of a product. The studies attempt to reveal who uses various products or services, identify potential customers, or get suggestions for product or service improvement. This information is helpful for forecasting sales, planning design modifications, and determining changes in features.

Once information has been gathered, marketing researchers analyze the findings. They then detail their findings and recommendations in a written report and often orally present them to management.

A number of professionals compose the marketing research team. The *project supervisor* is responsible for overseeing a study from beginning to end. The *statistician* determines the sample size—the number of people to be surveyed—and compares the number of responses. The project supervisor or statistician, in conjunction with other specialists (such as *demographers* and *psychologists*), often determines the number of interviews to be conducted as well as their locations. *Field interviewers* survey people in various public places, such as shopping malls, office complexes, and popular attractions. *Telemarketers* gather information by placing calls to current or potential customers, to people listed in telephone books, or to those who appear on specialized lists obtained from list houses. Once questionnaires come in from the field, *tabulators* and *coders* examine the data, count the answers, code non-categorical answers, and tally the primary counts. The marketing research analyst then analyzes the returns, writes up the final report, and makes recommendations to the client or to management.

Marketing research analysts must be thoroughly familiar with research techniques and procedures. Sometimes the research problem is clearly defined, and information can be gathered readily. Other times, company executives may know only that a problem exists as evidenced by a decline in sales. In these cases, the market research analyst is expected to collect the facts that will aid in revealing and resolving the problem.

REQUIREMENTS
High School
Most employers require their marketing research analysts to hold at least a bachelor's degree, so a college preparatory program is advised. Classes in English, marketing, mathematics, psychology, and sociology are particularly important. Courses in computing are especially useful, since a great deal of tabulation and statistical analysis is required in the marketing research field.

Postsecondary Training
A bachelor's degree is essential for careers in marketing research. Majors in marketing, business administration, statistics, computer science, or economics provide a good background for most types of research positions. In addition, course work in sociology and psychology is helpful for those who are leaning toward consumer demand and opinion research. Since quantitative skills are important in various types of industrial or analytic research, students

interested in these areas should take statistics, econometrics, survey design, sampling theory, and other mathematics courses.

Many employers prefer that a marketing research analyst hold a master's degree as well as a bachelor's degree. A master's of business administration, for example, is frequently required on projects calling for complex statistical and business analysis. Graduate work at the doctorate level is not necessary for most positions, but it is highly desirable for those who plan to become involved in advanced research studies.

Other Requirements

To work in this career, you should be intelligent, detail oriented, and accurate; have the ability to work easily with words and numbers; and be particularly interested in solving problems through data collection and analysis. In addition, you must be patient and persistent, since long hours are often required when working on complex studies.

As part of the market research team, you must be able to work well with others and have an interest in people. The ability to communicate, both orally and in writing, is also important, since you will be responsible for writing up detailed reports on the findings in various studies and presenting recommendations to management.

EXPLORING

You can also seek part-time employment as a survey interviewer at local marketing research firms. Gathering field data for consumer surveys offers valuable experience through actual contact with both the public and marketing research supervisors. In addition, many companies seek a variety of other employees to code, tabulate, and edit surveys; monitor telephone interviews; and validate the information entered on written questionnaires. You can search for job listings in local newspapers and on the Web or apply directly to research organizations.

EMPLOYERS

Marketing research analysts are employed by large corporations, industrial firms, advertising agencies, data collection businesses, and private research organizations that handle local surveys for companies on a contract basis. While many marketing research organizations offer a broad range of services, some firms subcontract parts of an overall project out to specialized companies. For example, one research firm may concentrate on product interviews, while another might focus on measuring the effectiveness of product advertising. Similarly, some marketing analysts specialize in one industry or area. For example, agricultural marketing specialists prepare sales forecasts for food businesses, which use the information in their advertising and sales programs.

Although many smaller firms located all across the country outsource studies to marketing research firms, these research firms, along with most large corporations that employ marketing research analysts, are located in such big cities as New York or Chicago. Private industry employs about 90 percent of salaried marketing research analysts, but opportunities also exist in government and academia, as well as at hospitals, public libraries, and a variety of other types of organizations.

STARTING OUT

Students with a graduate degree in marketing research and experience in quantitative techniques have the best chances of landing jobs as marketing research analysts. Since a bachelor's degree in marketing or business is usually not sufficient to obtain such a position, many employees without postgraduate degrees start out as research assistants, trainees, interviewers, or questionnaire editors.

Use your college placement office, the Web, and help wanted sections of local newspapers to look for job leads. Another way to get into the marketing research field is through personal and professional contacts. Names and telephone numbers of potential employers may come from professors, friends, or relatives. Finally, students who have participated in internships or have held marketing research-related jobs on a part-time basis while in school or during the summer may be able to obtain employment at these firms or at similar organizations.

ADVANCEMENT

Most marketing research professionals begin as junior analysts or research assistants. In these positions, they help in preparing questionnaires and related materials, training survey interviewers, and tabulating and coding survey results. After gaining sufficient experience in these and other aspects of research project development, employees are often assigned their own research projects, which usually involve supervisory and planning responsibilities. A typical promotion path for those climbing the company ladder might be from assistant researcher to marketing research analyst to assistant manager and then to manager of a branch office for a large private research firm. From there, some professionals become market research executives or research directors for industrial or business firms.

Since marketing research analysts learn about all aspects of marketing on the job, some advance by moving to positions in other departments, such as advertising or sales. Depending on the interests and experience of marketing professionals, other areas of employment to which they can advance include data processing, teaching at the university level, statistics, economics, and industrial research and development.

In general, few employees go from starting positions to executive jobs at one company. Advancement often requires changing employers. Therefore, marketing research analysts who want to move up the ranks frequently go from one company to another, sometimes many times during their careers.

EARNINGS

Beginning salaries in marketing research depend on the qualifications of the employee, the nature of the position, and the size of the firm. Interviewers, coders, tabulators, editors, and a variety of other employees usually get paid by the hour and may start at $6 or more per hour. The Bureau of Labor Statistics reported that in 2001, median annual earnings of market research analysts were $53,450. The middle 50 percent earned between $38,280 and $74,460. Salaries ranged from less than $28,500 to more than $96,980. Experienced analysts working in supervisory positions at large firms can have even higher earnings. Market research directors earn up to $200,000.

Because most marketing research workers are employed by business or industrial firms, they receive fringe benefit packages that include health and life insurance, pension plans, and paid vacation and sick leave.

WORK ENVIRONMENT

Marketing research analysts usually work a 40-hour week. Occasionally, overtime is necessary in order to meet project deadlines. Although they frequently interact with a variety of marketing research team members, analysts also do a lot of independent work, analyzing data, writing reports, and preparing statistical charts.

While most marketing research analysts work in offices located at the firm's main headquarters, those who supervise interviewers may go into the field to oversee work. In order to attend conferences, meet with clients, or check on the progress of various research studies, regular travel is required of many market research analysts.

OUTLOOK

The U.S. Department of Labor predicts that employment for marketing research analysts will grow faster than the average through the next decade. Increasing competition among producers of consumer goods and services and industrial products, combined with a growing awareness of the value of marketing research data, will contribute to opportunities in the field. Opportunities will be best for those with graduate degrees who seek employment in marketing research firms, financial services organizations, health care institutions, advertising firms, manufacturing firms producing consumer goods, and insurance companies.

While many new graduates are attracted to the field, creating a competitive situation, the best jobs and the highest pay will go to those individuals who hold a master's degree or doctorate in marketing research, statistics, economics, or computer science.

FOR MORE INFORMATION

For information on college chapters, internship opportunities, and financial aid opportunities, contact:

American Advertising Federation
1101 Vermont Avenue, NW, Suite 500
Washington, DC 20005-6306
Tel: 202-898-0089
Email: aaf@aaf.org
http://www.aaf.org

For information on agencies, contact:

American Association of Advertising Agencies
405 Lexington Avenue, 18th Floor
New York, NY 10174-1801
Tel: 212-682-2500
http://www.aaaa.org

For career resources and job listings, contact or check out the following website:

American Marketing Association
311 South Wacker Drive, Suite 5800
Chicago, IL 60606
Tel: 800-262-1150
Email: info@ama.org
http://www.marketingpower.com

MEDIA PLANNERS AND BUYERS

QUICK FACTS

School Subjects
Business
English
Speech

Personal Skills
Artistic
Communication/ideas

Work Environment
Primarily indoors
One location with
some travel

Minimum Education Level
Bachelor's degree

Salary Range
$18,000 to $35,850 to
$120,000+

Certification or Licensing
None available

Outlook
Much faster than the
average

DOT
162

GOE
11.09.01

NOC
1225

O*NET-SOC
N/A

OVERVIEW

Media specialists are responsible for placing advertisements that will reach targeted customers and get the best response from the market for the least amount of money. Within the media department, *media planners* gather information about the sizes and types of audiences that can be reached through each of the various media and about the cost of advertising in each medium. *Media buyers* purchase space in printed publications, as well as time on radio or television stations. A *media director*, who is accountable for the overall media plan, supervises advertising media workers. In addition to advertising agencies, media planners and buyers work for large companies that purchase space or broadcast time. There are approximately 155,000 advertising sales agents employed in the United States.

HISTORY

The first formal media that allowed advertisers to deliver messages about their products or services to the public were newspapers and magazines, which began selling space to advertisers in the late 19th century. This system of placing ads gave rise to the first media planners and buyers, who were in charge of deciding what kind of advertising to put in which publications and then actually purchasing the space.

In the broadcast realm, radio stations started offering program time to advertisers in the early 1900s. Although television advertising began just before the end of World War II, producers were quick to realize that they could reach huge audiences by placing ads on TV. Television advertising proved to be beneficial to the TV stations as well, since they relied on sponsors for financial assistance in order to bring programs into people's homes. In the past, programs were sometimes named not for the host or star of the program, but for the sponsoring company that was paying for the broadcast of that particular show.

During the early years of radio and television, one sponsor could pay for an entire 30-minute program. However, the cost of producing shows on radio and television increased dramatically, thereby requiring many sponsors to support a single radio or television program. Media planners and buyers learned to get more for their money by buying smaller amounts of time—60, 30, and even 10 second spots—on a greater number of programs.

Today's media planners and buyers have a wide array of media from which to choose. The newest of these, the World Wide Web, allows advertisers not only to target customers precisely, but to interact with them as well. In addition to Web banner ads, producers can also advertise via sponsorships, their own websites, CD catalogs, voicemail telephone shopping, and more. With so many choices, media planners and buyers must carefully determine target markets and select the ideal media mix in order to reach these markets at the least cost.

THE JOB

While many employees may work in the media department, the primary specialists are the media planner and the media buyer. They work with professionals from a wide range of media—from billboards, direct mail, and magazines to television, radio, and the Internet. Both types of media specialists must be familiar with the markets that each medium reaches, as well as the advantages and disadvantages of advertising in each.

Media planners determine target markets based on their clients' advertising approaches. Considering their clients' products and services, budget, and image, media planners gather information about the public's viewing, reading, and buying habits by administering questionnaires and conducting other forms of market research. Through this research, planners are able to identify target markets by sorting data according to people's ages, incomes, marital status, interests, and leisure activities.

By knowing which groups of people watch certain shows, listen to specific radio stations, or read particular magazines or newspapers, media planners can help clients select air time or print space to reach the consumers most likely to buy their products. For example, Saturday morning television shows attract children, while prime-time programs often draw family audiences. For shows broadcast at these times, media planners will recommend air time to their clients who manufacture products of interest to these viewers, such as toys and automobiles, respectively.

Media planners who work directly for companies selling air time or print space must be sensitive to their clients' budgets and resources. When tailoring their sales pitch to a particular client's needs, planners often go to great lengths to persuade the client to buy air time or advertising space. They produce brochures and reports that detail the characteristics of their viewing or reading market, including the average income of those individuals, the number of people who see the ads, and any other information that may be likely to encourage potential advertisers to promote their products.

Media planners try to land contracts by inviting clients to meetings and presentations and educating them about various marketing strategies. They must not only pursue new clients but also attend to current ones, making sure that they are happy with their existing advertising packages. For both new and existing clients, the media planner's main objective is to sell as much air time or ad space as possible.

Media buyers do the actual purchasing of the time on radio or television or the space in a newspaper or magazine in which an advertisement will run. In addition to tracking the time and space available for purchase, media buyers ensure that ads appear when and where they should, negotiate costs for ad placement, and calculate rates, usage, and budgets. They are also responsible for maintaining contact with clients, keeping them informed of all advertising-related developments and resolving any conflicts that arise. Large companies that generate a lot of advertising or those that place only print ads or only broadcast ads sometimes differentiate between the two main media groups by employing *space buyers* and/or *time buyers.*

Workers who actually sell the print space or air time to advertisers are called *print sales workers* or *broadcast time salespeople.* Like media planners, these professionals are well versed about the target markets served by their organizations and can often provide useful information about editorial content or broadcast programs.

In contrast to print and broadcast planners and buyers, *interactive media specialists* are responsible for managing all critical aspects of their clients' online advertising campaigns. While interactive media planners may have responsibilities similar to those of print or broadcast planners, they also act as new technology specialists, placing and tracking all online ads and maintaining relationships with clients and webmasters alike.

The typical online media planning process begins with an agency spreadsheet that details the criteria about the media buy. These criteria often include target demographics, start and end dates for the ad campaign, and online objectives. After sending all relevant information to a variety of websites, the media specialist receives cost, market, and other data from the sites. Finally, the media specialist places the order and sends all creative information needed to the selected websites. Once the order has been placed, the media specialist receives tracking and performance data and then compiles and analyzes the information in preparation for future ad campaigns.

Media planners and buyers may have a wide variety of clients. Restaurants, hotel chains, beverage companies, food product manufacturers, and automobile dealers all need to advertise to attract potential customers. While huge companies, such as soft drink manufacturers, major airlines, and vacation resorts, pay a lot of money to have their products or services advertised nationally, many smaller firms need to advertise only in their immediate area. Local advertising may come from a health club that wants to announce a special membership rate or from a retail store promoting a sale. Media planners and buyers must be aware of their various clients' advertising needs and create campaigns that will accomplish their promotional objectives.

REQUIREMENTS
High School
Although most media positions, including those at the entry level, require a bachelor's degree, you can prepare for a future job as media planner and/or buyer by taking specific courses offered at the high school level. These include business, marketing, advertising, cinematography, radio and television, and film and video. General liberal arts classes, such as economics, English, communication, and journalism, are also important, since media planners and buyers must be able to communicate clearly with both clients and co-workers. Mathematics classes will give you the skills to work accurately with budget figures and placement costs.

Postsecondary Training
Increasingly media planners and buyers have college degrees, often with majors in marketing or advertising. Even if you have prior work experience or training in media, you should select college classes that provide a good balance of business coursework, broadcast and print experience, and liberal arts studies.

Business classes may include economics, marketing, sales, and advertising. In addition, courses that focus on specific media, such as cinematography, film and video, radio and television, and new technologies (like the Internet), are important. Additional classes in journalism, English, and speech will also prove helpful. Media directors often need to have a master's degree, as well as extensive experience working with the various media.

Other Requirements
Media planners and buyers in broadcasting should have a keen understanding of programming and consumer buying trends, as well as a knowledge of each potential client's business. Print media specialists must be familiar with the process involved in creating print ads and the markets reached by various publications. In addition, all media workers need to be capable of maintaining good relationships with current clients, as well as pursuing new clients on a continual basis.

Communication and problem solving skills are important, as are creativity, common sense, patience, and persistence. Media planners and buyers must also have excellent oral, written, and analytical skills, knowledge of interactive media planning trends and tools, and the ability to handle multiple assignments in a fast-paced work environment. Strategic thinking skills, industry interest, and computer experience with both database and word processing programs are also vital.

EXPLORING
Many high schools and two-year colleges and most four-year colleges have media departments that may include radio stations and public access or cable television channels. In order to gain worthwhile experience in media, you can work for these departments as aides, production assistants, programmers, or writers. In addition, high school and college newspapers and yearbooks often need students to sell advertising to local merchants. Theater departments also frequently look for people to sell ads for performance programs.

In the local community, newspapers and other publications often hire high school students to work part-time and/or in the summer in sales and clerical positions for the classified advertising department. Some towns have cable television stations that regularly look for volunteers to operate cameras, sell advertising, and coordinate various programs. In addition, a variety of church- and synagogue-sponsored activities, such as craft fairs, holiday boutiques, and rummage sales, can provide you with opportunities to create and place ads and work with the local media to get exposure for the events.

EMPLOYERS
Media planners and buyers often work for advertising agencies in large cities, such as Chicago, New York, and Los Angeles. These agencies represent various clients who are trying to sell everything from financial services to dishwasher soap. Other media specialists work directly for radio and television networks, newspapers, magazines, and websites selling air time and print space. While many of these media organizations are located in large urban areas, particularly radio and television stations, most small towns put out newspapers and therefore need specialists to sell ad space and coordinate accounts. Approximately 155,000 advertising sales agents work in the United States.

STARTING OUT
More than half of the jobs in print and broadcast media do not remain open long enough for companies to advertise available positions in the classified sections of newspapers. As a result, many media organizations, such as radio and television stations, do not

usually advertise job openings in the want ads. Media planners and buyers often hear about available positions through friends, acquaintances, or family members and frequently enter the field as entry-level broadcasting or sales associates. Both broadcasting and sales can provide employees just starting out with experience in approaching and working for clients, as well as knowledge about the specifics of programming and its relationship with air-time sales.

Advertising agencies sometimes do advertise job openings, both in local and national papers and on the Web. Competition is quite fierce for entry-level jobs, however, particularly at large agencies in big cities.

Print media employees often start working on smaller publications as in-house sales staff members, answering telephones and taking orders from customers. Other duties may include handling classified ads or coordinating the production and placement of small print ads created by in-house artists and typesetters. While publications often advertise for entry-level positions, the best way to find work in advertising is to send resumes to as many agencies, publications, and broadcasting offices as possible.

While you are enrolled in a college program, you should investigate opportunities for internships or on-campus employment in related areas. Your school's career planning center or placement office should have information on such positions. Previous experience often provides a competitive edge for all job seekers, but it is crucial to aspiring media planners and buyers.

ADVANCEMENT

Large agencies and networks often hire only experienced people, so it is common for media planners and buyers to learn the business at smaller companies. These opportunities allow media specialists to gain the experience and confidence they need to move up to more advanced positions. Jobs at smaller agencies and television and radio stations also provide possibilities for more rapid promotion than those at larger organizations.

Media planners and buyers climbing the company ladder can advance to the position of media director or may earn promotions to executive-level positions. For those already at the management level, advancement can come in the form of larger clients and more responsibility. In addition, many media planners and buyers who have experience with traditional media are investigating the opportunities and challenges that come with the job of interactive media planner/buyer or Web media specialist.

EARNINGS

Because media planners and buyers work for a variety of organizations all across the country and abroad, earnings can vary greatly. In general, however, those just entering the field as marketing assistants make an average of $25,750 to $30,500 per year, according to OfficeTeam's *2002 Salary Guide*. A *media desk coordinator* makes $27,500 to $32,500 annually, according to *Advertising Age*.

Media directors can earn between $46,000 and $118,400, depending on the type of employer and the director's experience level. For example, directors at small agencies make an average of $42,100, while those at large agencies can earn more than $120,000, according to a 2002 *Advertising Age* salary survey.

Media planners and buyers in television typically earn higher salaries than those in radio. In general, however, beginning broadcasting salespeople usually earn between $18,000 and $35,000 per year and can advance to as much as $46,000 after a few years of experience.

Starting salaries for print advertising salespeople range from $24,500 to $30,500 a year. Experienced workers may earn salaries up to $44,200 a year, on average. Some salespeople draw straight salaries, some receive bonuses that reflect their level of sales, and still others earn their entire wage based on commissions. These commissions are usually calculated as a percentage of sales that the employee brings into the company.

According to the U.S. Bureau of Labor Statistics, advertising sales agents had median annual earnings of $35,850 in 2000. Salaries ranged from $18,570 to more than $87,240.

Most employers of media planners and buyers offer a variety of benefits, including health and life insurance, a retirement plan, and paid vacation and sick days.

WORK ENVIRONMENT

Although media planners and buyers often work a 40-hour week, their hours are not strictly nine to five. Service calls, presentations, and meetings with ad space reps and clients are important parts of the job that usually have a profound effect on work schedules. In addition, media planners and buyers must invest considerable time investigating and reading about trends in programming, buying, and advertising.

The variety of opportunities for media planners and buyers results in a wide diversity of working conditions. Larger advertising agencies, publications, and networks may have modern and comfortable working facilities. Smaller markets may have more modest working environments.

Whatever the size of the organization, many planners seldom go into the office and must call in to keep in touch with the home organization. Travel is a big part of media planners' responsibilities to their clients, and they may have clients in many different types of businesses and services, as well as in different areas of the country.

While much of the media planner and buyer's job requires interaction with a variety of people, including co-workers, sales reps, supervisors, and clients, most media specialists also perform many tasks that require independent work, such as researching and writing reports. In any case, the media planner and buyer must be able to handle many tasks at the same time in a fast-paced, continually changing environment.

OUTLOOK

The employment outlook for media planners and buyers, like the outlook for the advertising industry itself, depends on the general health of the economy. When the economy thrives, companies produce an increasing number of goods and seek to promote them via newspapers, magazines, television, radio, the Internet, and various other media. The U.S. Department of Labor anticipates that employment in the advertising industry is projected to grow 32 percent over the 2000–10 period, much faster than the average for all occupations.

More and more people are relying on radio and television for their entertainment and information. With cable and local television channels offering a wide variety of programs, advertisers are increasingly turning to TV in order to get exposure for their products and services. Although newspaper sales are in decline, there is growth in special-interest periodicals and other print publications. Interactive media, such as the Internet, CD catalogs, and voicemail shopping, are providing a flurry of advertising activity all around the world. The Web alone promises advertising exposure in 65 million American households. All of this activity will increase market opportunities for media planners and buyers.

Employment possibilities for media specialists are far greater in large cities, such as New York, Los Angeles, and Chicago, where most magazines and many broadcast networks have their headquarters. However, smaller publications are often located in outlying areas, and large national organizations usually have sales offices in several cities across the country.

Competition for all advertising positions, including entry-level jobs, is expected to be intense. Media planners and buyers who have considerable experience will have the best chances of finding employment.

FOR MORE INFORMATION

The AAF is the professional advertising association that binds the mutual interests of corporate advertisers, agencies, media companies, suppliers, and academia. Student membership is available at the college level.

American Advertising Federation (AAF)
1101 Vermont Avenue, NW, Suite 500
Washington, DC 20005-6306
Tel: 202-898-0089
Email: aaf@aaf.org
http://www.aaf.org

The AAAA is the management-oriented national trade organization representing the advertising agency business.

American Association of Advertising Agencies (AAAA)
405 Lexington, 18th Floor
New York, NY 10174-1801
Tel: 212-682-2500
http://www.aaaa.org

OFFICE ADMINISTRATORS

QUICK FACTS

School Subjects
Business
Mathematics
Speech

Personal Skills
Communication/ideas
Leadership/management

Work Environment
Primarily indoors
Primarily one location

Minimum Education Level
Associate's degree

Salary Range
$23,000 to $35,000 to
$63,000+

Certification or Licensing
None available

Outlook
Little change or more
slowly than the average

DOT
169

GOE
07.01.02

NOC
1221

O*NET-SOC
11-3011.00,
43-1011.02

OVERVIEW

Office administrators direct and coordinate the work activities of office workers within an office. They supervise office clerks and other workers in their tasks and plan department activities with other supervisory personnel. Administrators often define job duties and develop training programs for new workers. They evaluate the progress of their clerks and work with upper management officials to ensure that the office staff meets productivity and quality goals. Office administrators often meet with office personnel to discuss job-related issues or problems, and they are responsible for maintaining a positive office environment. There are approximately 1.4 million office administrators employed in the United States.

HISTORY

The growth of business since the Industrial Revolution has been accompanied by a corresponding growth in the amount of work done in offices. Records, bills, receipts, contracts, and other paper-work have proliferated. Phone calls, emails, and other communications have multiplied. Accounting and bookkeeping practices have become more complicated.

The role of the office administrator has also grown over time. In the past, such supervisors were responsible mainly for ensuring productivity and good work from their clerks and for reporting information to management. Today, office administrators play a more active part in the operations of busy offices. They are responsible for coordinating the activities of many departments, informing management of departmental performance, and making sure the highly specialized sectors of an office run smoothly and efficiently every day.

THE JOB

As modern technology and an increased volume of business communications become a normal part of daily business, offices are becoming complicated workplaces. By directing and coordinating the activities of clerks and other office workers, office administrators are an integral part of an effective organization.

The day-to-day work of office administrators, also known as *office managers,* involves organizing and overseeing many different activities. Although specific duties vary with the type and size of the particular office, all supervisors and managers have several basic job responsibilities. The primary responsibility of the office administrator is to run the office; that is, whatever the nature of the office's business, the office administrator must see to it that all workers have what they need to do their work.

Office administrators are usually responsible for interviewing prospective employees and making recommendations on hiring. They train new workers, explain office policies, and explain performance criteria. Office administrators are also responsible for delegating work responsibilities. This requires a keen understanding of the strengths and weaknesses of each worker, as well as the ability to determine what needs to be done and when it must be completed. For example, if a supervisor knows that one worker is especially good at filing business correspondence, that person will probably be assigned filing tasks. Office administrators often know how to do many of the tasks done by their subordinates and assist or relieve them whenever necessary.

Office administrators not only train clerical workers and assign them job duties but also recommend increases in salaries, promote workers when approved, and occasionally fire them. Therefore, they must carefully observe clerical workers performing their jobs (whether answering the telephones, opening and sorting mail, or inputting computer data) and make positive suggestions for any necessary improvements. Managers who can communicate effectively, both verbally and in writing, will be better able to carry out this kind of work. Motivating employees to do their best work is another important component of an office administrator's responsibilities.

Office administrators must be very good at human relations. Differences of opinion and personality clashes among employees are inevitable in almost any office, and the administrator must be able to deal with grievances and restore good feelings among the staff. Office administrators meet regularly with their staff, alone and in groups, to discuss and solve any problems that might affect people's job performance.

Planning is a vital and time-consuming portion of the job responsibilities of office administrators. Not only do they plan the work of subordinates, they also assist in planning current and future office space needs, work schedules, and the types of office equipment and supplies that need to be purchased.

Office administrators must always keep their superiors informed as to the overall situation in the clerical area. If there is a delay on an important project, for example, upper management must know the cause and the steps being taken to expedite the matter.

REQUIREMENTS
High School

A high school diploma is essential for this position, and a college degree is highly recommended. You should take courses in English, speech and communications, mathematics, sociology, history, and as many business-related courses, such as typing and bookkeeping, as possible. Knowledge of a wide variety of computer software programs is also very important.

Postsecondary Training

In college, pursue a degree in business administration or at least take several courses in business management and operations. In some cases, an associate's degree is considered sufficient for a supervisory position, but a bachelor's degree will make you more attractive to employers and help in advancement.

Many community colleges and vocational schools offer business education courses that help train office administrators. The American Management Association has a Self-Study Certificate Program in several areas, including customer service management, human resources management, general management, strategic leadership, and others. (See contact information at the end of this article.)

Colleges and universities nationwide offer bachelor's degrees in business administration; a few may offer programs targeted to specific industries, such as medical administration or hotel management.

Other Requirements

Offices can be hectic places. Deadlines on major projects can create tension, especially if some workers are sick or overburdened. Office administrators must constantly juggle the demands of their superiors with the capabilities of their subordinates. Thus, they need an even temperament and the ability to work well with others. Additional important attributes include organizational ability, attention to detail, dependability, and trustworthiness. Since many offices promote administrators from clerical work positions within their organization, relevant work experience is also helpful.

EXPLORING

You can get general business experience by taking on clerical or bookkeeping responsibilities with a school club or other organization. Volunteering in your school office is an ideal introduction to office work. This will allow you to become more familiar with computer programs often used in offices and practice business skills such as opening and sorting mail, answering telephones, and filing documents.

Community colleges and other institutions may offer basic or advanced computer training courses for students of all ages. After high school, you may want to explore work-study programs where you can work part time and gain on-the-job training with local businesses while earning your degree.

EMPLOYERS

Approximately 1.4 million office administrators are employed in the United States. Administrators are needed in all types of offices that have staffs large enough to warrant a manager. The federal government is a major employer of office administrators. Other job opportunities are found in private companies with large clerical staffs, such as hospitals, banks, and telecommunications companies.

STARTING OUT

To break into this career, you should contact the personnel offices of individual firms directly. This is especially appropriate if you have previous clerical experience. College placement offices or other job placement offices may also know of openings. You can also locate jobs through help wanted advertisements. Another option is to sign up with a temporary employment service. Working as a "temp" provides the advantage of getting a firsthand look at a variety of office settings and making many contacts.

Often, a firm will recruit office administrators from its own clerical staff. A clerk with potential supervisory abilities may be given periodic supervisory responsibilities. Later, when an opening occurs for an administrator, that person may be promoted to a full-time position.

ADVANCEMENT

Skilled administrators may be promoted to group manager positions. Promotions, however, often depend on the individual's level of education and other appropriate training, such as training in the company's computer system. Firms usually encourage their employees to pursue further education and may even pay for some tuition costs. Supervisory and management skills can be obtained through company training or community colleges and local vocational schools.

Some companies will prepare office clerks for advancement to administrative positions by having them work in several company departments. This broad experience allows the administrator to better coordinate numerous activities and make more knowledgeable decisions.

EARNINGS

According to OfficeTeam, an administrative staffing company, office managers earned between $27,500 and $35,000 a year in 2002. Senior office managers earned between $33,500 and $44,000.

In 2001, the Bureau of Labor Statistics reported that office administrators earned an average of about $37,990 a year. Fifty percent earned between $29,210 and $49,570 a year. The lowest-paid 10 percent earned less than $23,000, and the top 10 percent earned over $63,340.

The size and geographic location of the company and the person's individual skills can be key determinants of earnings. Higher wages will be paid to those who work for larger private companies located in and around major metropolitan areas. Full-time workers also receive paid vacations and health and life insurance. Some companies offer year-end bonuses and stock options.

WORK ENVIRONMENT

As is the case with most office workers, office administrators work an average of 35 to 40 hours a week, although overtime is not unusual. Depending on the company, night, weekend, holiday, or shift work may be expected. Most offices are pleasant places to work. The environment is usually well ventilated and well lighted, and the work is not physically strenuous. The administrator's job can be stressful, however, as it entails supervising a variety of employees with different personalities, temperaments, and work habits.

OUTLOOK

According to the U.S. Department of Labor, the employment rate of office administrators is projected to change little or grow at a rate more slowly than the average for all occupations through the next decade. The increased use of data processing and other automated equipment as well as corporate downsizing may reduce the number of administrators in the next decade. However, this profession will still offer good employment prospects because of its sheer size. A large number of job openings will occur as administrators transfer to other industries or leave the workforce for other reasons. Since some clerical occupations will be affected by increased automation, some office administrators may have smaller staffs and be asked to perform more professional tasks.

The federal government should continue to be a good source for job opportunities. Private companies, particularly those with large clerical staffs, such as hospitals, banks, and telecommunications companies, should also have numerous openings. Employment opportunities will be especially good for those trained to operate computers and other types of modern office machinery.

FOR MORE INFORMATION

For information on seminars, conferences, and news on the industry, contact:

American Management Association International
1601 Broadway
New York, NY 10019-7420
Tel: 212-586-8100
Email: customerservice@amanet.org
http://www.amanet.org

**National Association of Executive Secretaries and
    Administrative Assistants**
900 South Washington Street, Suite G-13
Falls Church, VA 22046
Tel: 703-237-8616
http://www.naesaa.com

For a career brochure, contact:
National Management Association
2210 Arbor Boulevard
Dayton, OH 45439-1580
Tel: 937-294-0421
Email: nma@nma1.org
http://www.nma1.org

For information on careers and related education, contact:
Canadian Management Centre of AMA International
150 York Street, 5th Floor
Toronto, ON M5H 3S5 Canada
Tel: 800-262-9699
Email: cmcinfo@amanet.org
http://www.cmcamai.org

PERSONNEL AND LABOR RELATIONS SPECIALISTS

QUICK FACTS

School Subjects
Business
Psychology

Personal Skills
Communication/ideas
Leadership/management

Work Environment
Primarily indoors
One location with
some travel

Minimum Education Level
Bachelor's degree

Salary Range
$31,963 to $59,000 to
$104,020+

Certification or Licensing
Recommended

Outlook
About as fast as the
average

DOT
166

GOE
11.05.02

NOC
1223

O*NET-SOC
11-3040.00, 11-3041.00,
13-1071.00, 13-1071.01,
13-1071.02, 13-1072.00,
13-1073.00, 43-4111.00,
43-4161.00

OVERVIEW

Personnel specialists, also known as *human resources professionals,* formulate policy and organize and conduct programs relating to all phases of personnel activity. *Labor relations specialists* serve as mediators between employees and the employer. They represent management during the collective-bargaining process, when contracts with employees are negotiated. They also represent the company at grievance hearings, which are required when a worker feels management has not fulfilled its end of an employment contract. There are approximately 709,000 personnel specialists employed in the United States.

HISTORY

The concept of personnel work developed as businesses grew in size from small owner-operated affairs to large corporate structures with many employees. As these small businesses became larger, it became increasingly difficult for owners and managers to stay connected and in touch with all their employees and still run the day-to-day operations of the business. Smart business owners and managers, however, were aware that the success of their companies depended upon attracting good employees, matching them to jobs they were suited for, and motivating them to do their best. To meet these needs, the personnel department was established, headed by a specialist or staff of specialists whose job was to oversee all aspects of employee relations.

The field of personnel, or human resources, grew as business owners and managers became more aware of the importance of human psychology in managing employees. The development of more sophisticated business methods, the rise of labor unions, and the enactment of government laws and regulations concerned with the welfare and rights of employees have all created an even greater need for personnel specialists who can balance the needs of both employees and employers for the benefit of all.

The development and growth of labor unions in the late 1700s and early 1800s created the need for a particular kind of personnel specialist—one who could work as a liaison between a company's management and its unionized employees. Labor relations specialists often try to arbitrate, or settle, employer–employee disagreements. One of the earliest formal examples of this sort of arbitration in the United States was the first arbitral tribunal created by the New York Chamber of Commerce in 1768. Although arbitration resolutions were often ignored by the courts in preindustrial United States, by the end of World War I the court system was overwhelmed by litigation. In 1925 the Federal Arbitration Act was passed, which enforced arbitration agreements reached independent of the courts. Today, personnel and labor relations workers are an integral part of the corporate structure, promoting and communicating the needs of workers to management.

THE JOB

Personnel and labor relations specialists are the liaison between the management of an organization and its employees. They see that management makes effective use of employees' skills, while at the same time improving working conditions for employees and help-ing them find fulfillment in their jobs. Most positions in this field involve heavy contact with people, at both management and non-management levels.

Both personnel specialists and labor relations specialists are experts in employer–employee relations, although the labor rela-tions specialists concentrate on matters pertaining to union mem-bers. Personnel specialists interview job applicants and select or recommend those who seem best suited to the company's needs. Their choices for hiring and advancement must follow the federal guidelines for equal employment opportunity (EEO) and affirma-tive action. Personnel specialists also plan and maintain programs for wages and salaries, employee benefits, and training and career development.

In small companies, one person often handles all the personnel work. This is the case for Susan Eckerle, human resources manager for Crane Federal Credit Union. She is responsible for all aspects of personnel management for 50 employees who work at three differ-ent locations. "I handle all hiring, employee relations counseling, corrective action, administration of benefits, and termination," she says. When Eckerle started working for the credit union, there was no specific human resources department. Therefore, much of her time is spent establishing policies and procedures to ensure that personnel matters run smoothly and consistently. "I've had to write job descrip-tions, set up interview procedures, and write the employee hand-book," she says. "In addition, we don't have a long-term disability plan, and I think we need one. So I've been researching that."

Although Eckerle handles all phases of the human resources process, this is not always the case. The personnel department of a large organization may be staffed by many specialists, including recruiters, interviewers, job analysts, and specialists in charge of benefits, training, and labor relations. In addition, a large personnel department might include *personnel clerks* and assistants who issue forms, maintain files, compile statistics, answer inquiries, and do other routine tasks.

Personnel managers and *employment managers* are concerned with the overall functioning of the personnel department and may be involved with hiring, employee orientation, record-keeping, insur-ance reports, wage surveys, budgets, grievances, and analyzing sta-tistical data and reports. *Industrial relations directors* formulate the policies to be carried out by the various department managers.

Of all the personnel specialists, the one who first meets new employees is often the recruiter. Companies depend on *personnel recruiters* to find the best employees available. To do this, recruiters develop sources through contacts within the community. In some cases, they travel extensively to other cities or to college campuses to meet with college placement directors, attend campus job fairs, and conduct preliminary interviews with potential candidates.

Employment interviewers interview applicants to fill job vacancies, evaluate their qualifications, and recommend hiring the most promising candidates. They sometimes administer tests, check references and backgrounds, and arrange for indoctrination and training. They must also be familiar with current guidelines for EEO and affirmative action.

In very large organizations, the complex and sensitive area of EEO is handled by specialists who may be called *EEO representatives, affirmative-action coordinators,* or *job development specialists.* These specialists develop employment opportunities and on-the-job training programs for minority or disadvantaged applicants; devise systems or set up representative committees through which grievances can be investigated and resolved as they come up; and monitor corporate practices to prevent possible EEO violations. Preparing and submitting EEO statistical reports is also an important part of their work.

Job analysts are sometimes also called *compensation analysts.* They study all of the jobs within an organization to determine job and worker requirements. Through observation and interviews with employees, they gather and analyze detailed information about job duties and the training and skills required. They write summaries describing each job, its specifications, and the possible route to advancement. Job analysts classify new positions as they are introduced and review existing jobs periodically. These job descriptions, or position classifications, form a structure for hiring, training, evaluating, and promoting employees, as well as for establishing an equitable pay system.

Occupational analysts conduct technical research on job relationships, functions, and content; worker characteristics; and occupational trends. The results of their studies enable business, industry, and government to utilize the general workforce more effectively.

Developing and administering the pay system is the primary responsibility of the *compensation manager.* With the assistance of other specialists on the staff, compensation managers establish a wage scale designed to attract, retain, and motivate employees. A realistic and fair compensation program takes into consideration company policies, government regulations concerning minimum wages and overtime pay, rates currently being paid by similar firms and industries, and agreements with labor unions. The compensation manager is familiar with all these factors and uses them to determine the compensation package.

Training specialists prepare and conduct a wide variety of education and training activities for both new and existing employees. Training specialists may work under the direction of an *education and training manager*. Training programs may cover such special areas as apprenticeship programs, sales techniques, health and safety practices, and retraining displaced workers. The methods for maximum effectiveness that training specialists choose may include individual training, group instruction, lectures, demonstrations, meetings, or workshops, all of which use such teaching aids as handbooks, demonstration models, multimedia programs, and reference works. These specialists also confer with management and supervisors to determine the needs for new training programs or revision of existing ones, maintain records of all training activities, and evaluate the success of the various programs and methods. Training instructors may work under the direction of an education and training manager. *Coordinators of auxiliary personnel* specialize in training nonprofessional nursing personnel in medical facilities.

Training specialists may help individuals establish career-development goals and set up a timetable in which to strengthen job-related skills and learn new ones. Sometimes this involves outside study paid for by the company or rotation to jobs in different departments of the organization. The extent of the training program and the responsibilities of the training specialists vary considerably, depending on the size of the firm and its organizational objectives.

Benefits managers or *employee-welfare managers* handle employee benefits programs.Insurance and pension plans are generally the major parts of such programs. Since the enactment of the Employee Retirement Income Security Act (ERISA), reporting requirements has become a primary responsibility for personnel departments in large companies. *Retirement officers* handle the retirement program for state and local government employees. In addition to regular health insurance and pension coverage, employee benefit packages have grown to include such things as dental insurance, accidental death and disability insurance, automobile insurance, homeowner's insurance, profit sharing and thrift/savings plans, and stock options. The expertise of benefits analysts and administrators is extremely important in designing and carrying out these complex programs. These specialists also develop and coordinate additional services related to employee welfare, such as car pools, child care, cafeterias and lunchrooms, newsletters, annual physical exams, recreation and physical fitness programs, and counseling. Personal and financial counseling for employees close to retirement age is becoming especially important.

In some cases—especially in smaller companies—the personnel department is responsible for administering the occupational safety and health programs. But the establishing a separate safety department under the direction of a safety engineer, industrial hygienist, or other safety and health professionals is the current trend.

Personnel departments may have access to resources outside the organization. For example, *employer relations representatives* promote the use of public employment services and programs among local employers. *Employee-health maintenance program specialists* help set up local government-funded programs among area employers to provide assistance in treating employees with alcoholism or behavioral medical problems.

In companies where employees are covered by union contracts, labor relations specialists form the link between union and management. Prior to negotiation of a collective-bargaining agreement, *labor relations managers* counsel management on their negotiating position and provide background information on the provisions of the current contract and the significance of the proposed changes. They also provide reference materials and statistics pertaining to labor legislation, labor market conditions, prevailing union and management practices, wage and salary surveys, and employee benefit programs. This work requires labor relations managers to be familiar with sources of economic and wage data and to have an extensive knowledge of labor law and collective-bargaining trends. In the actual negotiation, the director of labor relations or another top-level official usually represents the employer, but the members of the company's labor relations staff play an important role throughout the negotiations.

Specialists in labor relations, or union-management relations, usually work for unionized organizations, helping company officials prepare for collective-bargaining sessions, participating in contract negotiations, and handling day-to-day labor relations matters. A large part of the work of labor relations specialists is analyzing and interpreting the contract for management and monitoring company practices to ensure their adherence to the terms. Of particular importance is the handling of grievance procedures. To investigate and settle grievances, these specialists arrange meetings for workers who raise a complaint, managers and supervisors, and a union representative. A grievance, for example, may concern seniority rights during a layoff. Labor relations disputes are sometimes investigated and resolved by *professional conciliators* or *mediators*. Labor relations work requires keeping up to date on developments in labor law, including arbitration decisions, and maintaining close contact with union officials.

Government personnel specialists do essentially the same work as their counterparts in business, except that they deal with public employees whose jobs are subject to civil service regulations. Much of government personnel work concentrates on job analysis, because civil service jobs are strictly classified as to entry requirements, duties, and wages. In response to the growing importance of training and career development in the public sector, however, an entire industry of educational and training consultants has sprung up to provide similar services for public agencies. The increased union strength among government workers has resulted in a need for more highly trained labor relations specialists to handle negotiations, grievances, and arbitration cases on behalf of federal, state, and local agencies.

REQUIREMENTS
High School

To prepare for a career as a personnel or labor relations specialist, you should take high school classes that will help prepare you for college. A solid background in the basics—math, science, and English—should be helpful in college-level work. You should especially focus on classes that will help you understand and communicate easily with people. Psychology, English, and speech classes are all good choices. Business classes can help you understand the fundamental workings of the business world, which is also important. Finally, foreign language skills could prove very helpful, especially in areas where there are large numbers of people who speak a language other than English.

Postsecondary Training

High school graduates may start out as personnel clerks and advance to a professional position through experience, but such situations are becoming rare. Most employers require personnel specialists and labor relations specialists to have a college degree. After high school, Susan Eckerle attended a four-year college and received a bachelor's degree in retail management, with a minor in psychology. She says that if she were starting over now, however, she would get a degree in human resources instead.

There is little agreement as to what type of undergraduate training is preferable for personnel and labor relations work. Some employers favor college graduates who have majored in personnel administration or industrial and labor relations, while others prefer individuals with a general business background. Another opinion is that personnel specialists should have a well-rounded liberal arts education, with a degree in psychology, sociology, counseling, or education. A master's degree in business administration is also considered suitable preparation. Students interested in personnel work with a government agency may find it an asset to have a degree in personnel administration, political science, or public administration.

Individuals preparing for a career as a personnel specialist will benefit from a wide range of courses. Classes might include business administration, public administration, psychology, sociology, political science, and statistics. For prospective labor relations specialists, valuable courses include labor law, collective bargaining, labor economics, labor history, and industrial psychology.

Work in labor relations may require graduate study in industrial or labor relations. While not required for entry-level jobs, a law degree is a must for those who conduct contract negotiations, and a combination of industrial relations courses and a law degree is especially desirable. A career as a professional arbitrator requires a degree in industrial and labor relations, law, or personnel management.

Certification or Licensing

Some organizations for human resources professionals offer certification programs, which usually consist of a series of classes and a test. For example, the International Foundation of Employee Benefits Plans offers the Certified Employee Benefits Specialist designation to candidates who complete a series of college-level courses and pass exams on employee benefits plans. Though voluntary, certification is highly recommended and can improve chances for advancement.

Other Requirements

Personnel and labor relations specialists must be able to communicate effectively and clearly both in speech and in writing and deal comfortably and easily with people of different levels of education and experience. "You must be people oriented," says Eckerle. "You have to love people and like working with them. "

Objectivity and fair-mindedness are also necessary in this job, where you often need to consider matters from both the employee's and the employer's point of view. "Being the liaison between management and employees can put you in a tough spot sometimes," Eckerle says. "You're directly between the two poles, and you have to be able to work with both sides."

These workers cooperate as part of a team; at the same time, they must be able to handle individual responsibility. Eckerle says organization skills are important because you are often responsible for tracking many different things regarding many different people. "You can't be sloppy in your work habits, because you're dealing with a lot of important information and it all has to be processed correctly," she says.

EXPLORING

If you enjoy working with others, you can find helpful experience in managing school teams, planning banquets or picnics, working in your dean's or counselor's office, or reading books about personnel practices in businesses. You might also contact and interview the personnel director of a local business to find out more about the day-to-day responsibilities of this job. Part-time and summer employment in firms that have a personnel department are very good ways to explore the personnel field. Large department stores usually have personnel departments and should not be overlooked as a source of temporary work.

EMPLOYERS

Personnel specialists hold approximately 709,000 jobs, with close to 90 percent working in the private sector. Of those specialists who work in the private sector, 46 percent work in the service industries, including health, business, social services, management, and educational services. Thirteen percent work in manufacturing, and 11 percent work in the fields of finance, insurance, and real estate. The companies that are most likely to hire personnel specialists are the larger ones, which have more employees to manage.

STARTING OUT

Colleges and universities have placement counselors who can help graduates find employment. Also, large companies often send recruiters to campuses looking for promising job applicants. Otherwise, interested individuals may apply directly to local companies.

While still in high school, you may apply for entry-level jobs as personnel clerks and assistants. Private employment agencies and local offices of the state employment service are other possible sources for work. In addition, newspaper and online want ads often contain listings of many personnel jobs.

Beginners in personnel work are trained on the job or in formal training programs, where they learn how to classify jobs, interview applicants, or administer employee benefits. Then they are assigned to specialized areas in the personnel department. Some people enter the labor relations field after first gaining experience in general personnel work, but it is becoming more common for qualified individuals to enter that field directly.

ADVANCEMENT

After trainees have mastered basic personnel tasks, they are assigned to specific areas in the department to gain specialized experience. In time, they may advance to supervisory positions or to manager of a major part of the personnel program, such as training, compensation, or EEO/affirmative action. Advancement may also be achieved by moving into a higher position in a smaller organization. A few experienced employees with exceptional ability ultimately become top executives with titles such as director of personnel or director of labor relations. As in most fields, employees with advanced education and a proven track record are the most likely to advance in human resources positions.

EARNINGS

Jobs for personnel and labor relations specialists pay salaries that vary widely depending on the nature of the business and the size and location of the firm, as well as on the individual's qualifications and experience.

According to a survey conducted by the National Association of Colleges and Employers, an entry-level human resources specialist with a bachelor's degree earned $31,963 annually in 2001.

The *Occupational Outlook Handbook* (*OOH*) reports that median annual earnings of human resources managers were $59,000 in 2000. Salaries ranged from less than $33,360 to more than $104,020. The average salary for personnel managers in the federal government was $64,411 in 2001. The *OOH* also reports the following 2000 median annual earnings for the following workers by specialty: training specialists, $40,830; job and benefits managers, $41,660; and personnel recruiters, $36,480.

WORK ENVIRONMENT

Personnel employees work under pleasant conditions in modern offices. Personnel specialists are seldom required to work more than 35 or 40 hours per week, although they may do so if they are developing a program or special project. The hours you work as a personnel specialist may depend upon which company you work for. "I work Monday through Friday," says Susan Eckerle, "but if you work for a company that has weekend hours, you'll probably have to work some weekends too. If you never work weekends, you won't know your employees."

Labor relations specialists often work longer hours, especially when contract agreements are being prepared and negotiated. The difficult aspects of the work may involve firing people, taking disciplinary actions, or handling employee disputes.

OUTLOOK

The U.S. Department of Labor predicts that there will be average growth for personnel, training, and labor relations specialists. Competition for jobs will continue to be strong, however, as there will be an abundance of qualified applicants. Opportunities will be best in the private sector as businesses continue to increase their staffs and devote more resources to increasing employee productivity, retraining, safety, and benefits. Employment should also be strong with consulting firms who offer personnel services to business that cannot afford to have their own extensive staffs. As jobs change with new technology, more employers will need training specialists to teach new skills. Personnel specialist jobs may be affected by the trend in corporate downsizing and restructuring.

FOR MORE INFORMATION

For information on standards and procedures in arbitration, contact:
American Arbitration Association
335 Madison Avenue, 10th Floor
New York, NY 10017
Tel: 212-716-5800
http://www.adr.org

For news and information on compensation and benefits administration, contact:
American Compensation Association
14040 North Northsight Boulevard
Scottsdale, AZ 85260
Tel: 877-951-9191
http://www.worldatwork.org

For information about the Certified Employee Benefit Specialist Program, contact:
International Foundation of Employee Benefits Plans
18700 West Bluemound Road
PO Box 69
Brookfield, WI 53008-0069
Tel: 262-786-8670
http://www.ifebp.org

For a list of U.S. and Canadian schools offering degrees in industrial relations and human resource degree programs, contact:
Industrial Relations Research Association
121 Labor and Industrial Relations
University of Illinois—Urbana-Champaign
504 East Armory, MC-504
Champaign, IL 61820
Email: irra@uiuc.edu
http://www.irra.uiuc.edu

For information on training, job opportunities, human resources publications, or online discussions, contact:
International Personnel Management Association
1617 Duke Street
Alexandria, VA 22314
Tel: 703-549-7100
http://www.ipma-hr.org

PROPERTY AND CASUALTY INSURANCE AGENTS AND BROKERS

QUICK FACTS

School Subjects Business Mathematics Speech	**Certification or Licensing** Required by all states
	Outlook Little change or more slowly than the average
Personal Skills Communication/ideas Leadership/management	**DOT** 250
Work Environment Primarily indoors Primarily one location	**GOE** 08.01.02
Minimum Education Level Some postsecondary training	**NOC** 6231
Salary Range $20,630 to $46,320 to $94,040+	**O*NET-SOC** 41-3021.00

OVERVIEW

Property and casualty insurance agents and brokers sell policies that help individuals and companies cover expenses and losses from disasters such as fires, burglaries, traffic accidents, and other emergencies. These salespeople also may be known as *fire, casualty, and marine insurance agents or brokers*. There are approximately 30,240 property and casualty insurance agents and brokers employed in the United States.

HISTORY

The development of the property and casualty insurance industry parallels the history of human economic development. This type of insurance was first established in the maritime field. A single shipwreck could put a ship owner out of business, so it became essential for trade financiers to share this risk. Organized maritime insurance began in the late 17th century at Lloyd's coffeehouse in London, where descriptions of individual ships, their cargoes, and their destinations were posted. Persons willing to share the possible loss, in return for a fee, signed their names below these descriptions indicating what percentage of the financial responsibility they were willing to assume. Those who signed were known as "underwriters," a term still used in the insurance business.

As people became more experienced in this procedure, predictions of loss became more accurate and rates were standardized. To provide protection for larger risks, individuals organized companies. The first marine insurance company in the United States—the Insurance Company of North America—was founded in Philadelphia in 1792 and still does business today.

Other types of insurance developed in response to people's need for protection. Insurance against loss by fire became available after the disastrous lesson of the London Fire of 1666. The first accident insurance policy in the United States was sold in 1863. Burglary insurance—protection against property taken by forced entry—was offered soon thereafter. Theft insurance, which covers any form of stealing, was first written in 1899.

Around the turn of the century, the development of the "horseless carriage" led to the automobile insurance industry. The first automobile policy was sold in 1898. This area of the insurance field grew rapidly. In the mid-1990s premiums written for automobile insurance (including liability and collision and comprehensive policies) totaled more than $102 billion.

Growth of business and industrial organizations required companies to offer protection for employees injured on the job. The first workers' compensation insurance was sold in 1910.

Insurance companies have always been alert to new marketing possibilities. In the past few decades, increasing emphasis has been placed upon "package" policies offering comprehensive coverage. A typical package policy is the homeowner's policy, which, in addition to fire protection for the insured's home and property, also covers losses for liability, medical payments, and additional living expenses. In the mid-1950s, a group of private firms provided the first insurance on the multimillion-dollar reactors used in atomic energy plants.

Over the course of the past decade, costs associated with the property and casualty insurance industry (including underwriting losses) have outstripped the annual rate of inflation. This has generally led to an increase in the premium rates charged to customers. The largest increases have occurred in the automobile insurance sector of the industry. The overall trend reflects some basic changes in American society, including a substantial rise in crime and litigation and the development of expensive new medical technologies. The main challenge of the property and casualty insurance industry in the coming years is to stabilize premium rates to remain competitive with alternative forms of risk financing.

THE JOB

Property and casualty insurance salespeople work as either agents or brokers. An agent serves as an authorized representative of an insurance company. A broker, on the other hand, serves as the representative for the client and has no contracts with insurance companies.

Agents can be *independent agents*, *exclusive agents*, or *direct writers*. Independent agents may represent one or more insurance companies, are paid by commission, are responsible for their own expenses, and own the rights to the policies they sell. Exclusive agents represent only one insurance company, are generally paid by commission, are generally responsible for all of their own expenses, and usually own the rights to the policies that they sell. Direct writers represent only one insurance company, are employees of that company (and therefore are often paid a salary and are not responsible for their own expenses), and do not own the rights to the policies that are owned by the company.

Regardless of the system that is used, salespeople operate in a similar fashion. Each one orders or issues policies, collects premiums, renews and changes existing coverage, and assists clients with reports of losses and claims settlement. Backed by the resources of the companies that they represent, individual agents may issue policies insuring against loss or damage for everything from furs and automobiles to ocean liners and factories.

Agents are authorized to issue a "binder" to provide temporary protection for customers between the time the policy application is signed and when the insurance company issues the policy. The agent must be selective in the risks accepted under a binder. Sometimes a risk will be refused by a company, which might cause the agent to lose goodwill with the customer. Because brokers do not directly represent or have contracts with insurance companies, they cannot issue binders.

Some agents or brokers specialize in one type of insurance, such as automobile insurance. All agents or brokers, however, must be aware of the kind of protection required by their clients and the exact coverage offered by each company that they represent.

One of the most significant aspects of the property and casualty agent's work is the variety encountered on the job. An agent's day may begin with an important conference with a group of executives seeking protection for a new industrial plant and its related business activities. Following this meeting, the agent may proceed to the office and spend several hours studying the needs of the customer and drafting an insurance plan. This proposal must be thorough and competitively priced because several other local agents will likely be competing for the account. While working at the office, the agent usually receives several calls and visits from prospective or current clients asking questions about protection, policy conditions, changes, or new developments.

At noon, the agent may attend a meeting of a service club or have lunch with a policyholder. After lunch, the agent may visit a garage with a customer to discuss the car repairs needed as the result of the client's automobile accident. Back at the office, the agent may talk on the telephone with an adjuster from the insurance company involved.

In the late afternoon, the agent may call on the superintendent of schools to discuss insurance protection for participants and spectators at athletic events and other public meetings. If the school has no protection, the agent may evaluate its insurance needs and draft a proposed policy.

Upon returning to the office, the agent may telephone several customers, dictate responses to the day's mail, and handle other matters that have developed during the day. In the evening, the agent may call on a family to discuss insurance protection for a new home.

REQUIREMENTS
High School

Insurance companies typically insist that their agents have at least a high school degree, and they strongly prefer their agents to have a college education. There are a number of classes you can take in high school to prepare yourself both for college and for working in the insurance industry. If your high school offers business, economics, or finance classes, be sure to take advantage of these courses.

Mathematics classes will also give you the opportunity to develop your skills working with numbers, which is an important aspect of insurance work. Computer courses will allow you to become familiar with this technology, which you will use throughout your career. Take English and speech classes to develop the communication skills that are essential for any salesperson. Finally, consider taking classes that will give you insight into people's actions, which is another important skill for a salesperson. Psychology and sociology classes are courses that may offer this opportunity.

Postsecondary Training

Although college training is not a prerequisite for insurance work, those who have a college degree in economics or business will probably have an advantage starting out in this field. Many colleges and universities offer courses in insurance, and a number of schools offer a bachelor's degree in insurance. Classes you are likely to take in college include finance, accounting, and economics. Business law and business administration classes will give you an understanding of legal issues and insurance needs. Also, psychology courses may help you to increase your understanding of people. Finally, keep up with your computer work. Courses that teach you to use software, such as spreadsheet programs, will keep your skills up-to-date and make you more marketable. For some specialized areas of property insurance, such as fire protection for commercial establishments, an engineering background may prove helpful.

Certification or Licensing

All agents and brokers must obtain licenses from the states in which they sell insurance. Most states require that the agent pass a written examination dealing with state insurance laws and the fundamentals of property and casualty insurance. Often, candidates for licenses must show evidence of some formal study in the field of insurance.

Those agents who wish to seek the highest professional status may pursue the designation of Chartered Property Casualty Underwriter (CPCU). The CPCU requires the agent to complete at least three years in the field successfully, demonstrate high ethical practices in all work, and pass a series of examinations offered by the American Institute for Chartered Property and Casualty Underwriters (AICPCU). Agents and brokers may prepare for these examinations through home study or by taking courses offered by colleges, insurance associations, or individual companies. In 2003,

AICPCU introduced a new eight-exam CPCU program that allows agents to specialize in either personal or commercial insurance.

The Insurance Educational Association (together with the AICPCU and the Insurance Institute of America) offers the designation Accredited Adviser in Insurance (AAI). To earn the AAI designation, an agent must pass three national exams. The AAI designation fulfills certain requirements toward the CPCU designation.

Other Requirements

An agent or broker must thoroughly understand insurance fundamentals and recognize the differences between the many options provided by various policies. This knowledge is essential to gain the respect and confidence of clients. To provide greater service to customers and increase sales volume, beginning agents must study many areas of insurance protection. This requires an analytical mind and the capacity for hard work.

Successful agents and brokers are able to interact with strangers easily and talk readily with a wide range of people. For example, an agent or broker may need to talk with teenagers about their first cars, with business executives faced with heavy responsibilities, or with widows confronted for the first time with financial management of a home. Agents and brokers must be resourceful, self-confident, conscientious, and cheerful. As in other types of sales occupations, a strong belief in the service being sold helps agents to be more successful in their presentations.

Because they spend so much of their time with others, agents and brokers must have a genuine liking for people. Equally important is the desire to serve others by providing financial security. To be successful, they must be able to present insurance information in a clear, nontechnical fashion. They must be able to develop a logical sales sequence and presentation style that is comfortable for prospects and clients.

Successful agents and brokers may participate in community and service activities to stay visible within their communities and to maintain or increase their volume of business. Agents and brokers often have an unusual facility for recalling people's names and past conversations they've had with them.

EXPLORING

Because of state licensing requirements, it is difficult for young people to obtain part-time experience in this field. Summer employment of any sort in an insurance office may give you helpful insights into the field. Because many offices are small and must have someone on premises during business hours, you may find summer positions with individual agencies or brokerage firms. Colleges with work–study programs may offer opportunities for practical experience in an insurance agency.

EMPLOYERS

According to the Department of Labor, there are approximately 378,000 insurance agents and brokers employed in the United States. Approximately 8 percent or 30,240 workers work specifically for property and casualty insurance carriers. Insurance companies are the principal employers; however, some agents and brokers (approximately a third of all insurance salespeople) are self-employed.

STARTING OUT

College graduates are frequently hired through campus interviews for salaried sales positions with major companies. Other graduates secure positions directly with local agencies or brokerages through placement services, employment offices, or classified advertisements in newspapers. Many high school and college graduates apply directly to insurance companies. Sometimes individuals employed in other fields take evening or home-study courses in insurance to prepare for employment in this field.

Once hired, the new agent or broker uses training materials prepared by the company or by industry trade groups. In smaller agencies, newcomers may be expected to assume most of the responsibility for their own training by using the agency's written resources and working directly with experienced agents. In larger organizations, initial training may include formal classroom instruction and enrollment in education programs such as those offered by the American Institute for Chartered Property and Casualty Underwriters. Sometimes insurance societies sponsor courses designed to help the beginning agent. Almost all agents receive directed, on-the-job sales supervision.

ADVANCEMENT

Sales agents may advance in one of several ways. They may decide to establish their own agency or brokerage firm, join or buy out an established agency, or advance into branch or home office management with an insurance company.

Self-employed agents or brokers often remain with the organization that they have developed for the length of their careers. They may grow professionally by expanding the scope of their insurance activities. Many agents expand their responsibilities and their office's sales volume by hiring additional salespeople. Occasionally an established agent may enter related areas of activity. Many property insurance agents, for example, branch out into real estate sales. Many agents and brokers devote an increasing amount of their time to worthwhile community projects, which helps to build goodwill and probable future clients.

EARNINGS

Recently hired sales agents are usually paid a moderate salary while learning the business. After becoming established, however, most agents are paid on the basis of a commission on sales. Agents who work directly for an insurance company often receive a base salary in addition to some commission on sales production. Unlike life insurance agents, who receive a high first-year commission, the property and casualty agent usually receives the same percentage each time the premium is paid.

In 2001, all insurance sales agents (including property and casualty) earned a median salary of $38,890 a year, according to the Bureau of Labor Statistics. The lowest 10 percent earned $20,630, and the highest 10 percent earned over $94,040.

In 2000, the Department of Labor reported that property and casualty insurance agents had median annual earnings of $46,320.

Salespeople employed by companies often receive fringe benefits such as retirement income, sick leave, and paid vacations, whereas self-employed agents or brokers receive no such benefits.

WORK ENVIRONMENT

Property and casualty insurance agents must be in constant contact with people: clients, prospective clients, and the workers in the home office of the insurance companies. This can be very time-consuming and occasionally frustrating, but it is an essential element of the work.

Two of the biggest drawbacks to this type of work are the long hours and the irregular schedule. Agents often are required to work their schedules around their clients' availability. Especially in their first years in the business, agents may find that they have to work three or four nights a week and one or two days on the weekend.

Most agents work 40 hours a week, but some agents, particularly those just beginning in the field and those with a large clientele, may work 60 hours a week or more.

OUTLOOK

The employment rate of all insurance agents and brokers is expected to grow more slowly than the average for all occupations, according to the U.S. Department of Labor. Nevertheless, individuals with determination and the right skills (including fluency in a foreign language, especially Spanish) should have numerous job opportunities for several reasons. The overall demand for insurance should be strong as the general population grows and the amount of personal and corporate possessions increases. Most homeowners and business executives budget insurance as a necessary expense. In addition, laws that require businesses to provide workers' compensation insurance and car owners to obtain automobile liability protection help to maintain an insurance market.

However, a number of factors are responsible for restraining job growth of insurance agents and brokers. Computers enable agents to perform routine clerical tasks more efficiently, and more policies are being sold by mail and phone. Also, as insurance becomes more and more crucial to their financial health, many large businesses are hiring their own risk managers, who analyze their insurance needs and select the policies that are best for them.

There is a high rate of turnover in this field. Many beginning agents and brokers find it hard to establish a large, profitable client base, and they eventually move on to other areas in the insurance industry. Most openings will occur as a result of this turnover and as workers retire or leave their positions for other reasons.

FOR MORE INFORMATION

For information regarding the CPCU designation, continuing education courses, and industry news, contact:

American Institute for Chartered Property and Casualty Underwriters/Insurance Institute of America
720 Providence Road
PO Box 3016
Malvern, PA 19355-0716
Tel: 800-644-2101
Email: cserv@cpcuiia.org
http://www.aicpcu.org

For information on scholarships and women in the insurance industry, contact:

Association of Professional Insurance Women
c/o The Beaumont Group, Inc.
551 Fifth Avenue, Suite 1625
New York, NY 10175
Tel: 212-867-0228
Email: info@apiw.org
http://www.apiw.org

For information on the industry and education programs, contact:

Independent Insurance Agents and Brokers
of America
127 South Peyton Street
Alexandria, VA 22314
Tel: 800-221-7917
Email: info@iiaba.org
http://www.independentagent.com

For information on the AAI designation and other educational programs, contact:

Insurance Educational Association
100 California Street, Suite 650
San Francisco, CA 94111
Tel: 800-655-4432
Email: info@ieatraining.com
http://www.ieatraining.com

PUBLIC RELATIONS SPECIALISTS

QUICK FACTS

School Subjects Business English Journalism **Personal Skills** Communication/ideas Leadership/management **Work Environment** Primarily indoors One location with some travel **Minimum Education Level** Bachelor's degree **Salary Range** $23,930 to $41,010 to $72,910+	**Certification or Licensing** Voluntary **Outlook** Much faster than the average **DOT** 165 **GOE** 11.09.03 **NOC** 5124 **O*NET-SOC** 11-2031.00, 27-3031.00

OVERVIEW

Public relations (PR) specialists develop and maintain programs that present a favorable public image for an individual or organization. They provide information to the target audience (generally, the public at large) about the client, its goals and accomplishments, and any further plans or projects that may be of public interest.

PR specialists may be employed by corporations, government agencies, nonprofit organizations—almost any type of organization. Many PR specialists hold positions in public relations consulting firms or work for advertising agencies. There are approximately 137,000 public relations specialists in the United States.

HISTORY

The first public relations counsel was a reporter named Ivy Ledbetter Lee, who in 1906 was named press representative for coalmine operators. Labor disputes were becoming a large concern of the operators, and they had run into problems because of their continual refusal to talk to the press and the hired miners. Lee convinced the mine operators to start responding to press questions and supply the press with information on the mine activities.

During and after World War II, the rapid advancement of communications techniques prompted firms to realize they needed professional help to ensure their messages were given proper public attention. Manufacturing firms that had turned their production facilities over to the war effort returned to the manufacture of peacetime products and enlisted the aid of public relations professionals to forcefully bring products and the company name before the buying public.

Large business firms, labor unions, and service organizations, such as the American Red Cross, Boy Scouts of America, and the YMCA, began to recognize the value of establishing positive, healthy relationships with the public that they served and depended on for support. The need for effective public relations was often emphasized when circumstances beyond a company's or institution's control created unfavorable reaction from the public.

Public relations specialists must be experts at representing their clients before the media. The rapid growth of the public relations field since 1945 is a testament to an increased awareness by all industries of the power of professional media usage and PR campaigns to maintain good relationships with many different publics: customers, employees, stockholders, contributors, and competitors.

THE JOB

Public relations specialists do a wide variety of tasks. Some work primarily as writers, creating reports, news releases, and booklet texts. Others write speeches or create copy for radio, TV, or film sequences. These workers spend much of their time contacting the press, radio, TV, and magazines on behalf of their employers. Some PR specialists work more as editors than writers, fact-checking and rewriting employee publications, newsletters, shareholder reports, and other management communications.

Specialists may choose to concentrate in graphic design, using their background knowledge of art and layout for developing brochures, booklets, and photographic communications. Other PR workers handle special events, such as press parties, convention exhibits, open houses, or anniversary celebrations.

PR specialists must be alert to any and all company or institutional events that are newsworthy. They prepare news releases and

Best Cities for Women in Business in 2002

1. Burlington, VT	14. San Bernardino, CA
2. Portland, ME	15. Glendale, CA
3. Vallejo, CA	16. Ontario, CA
4. Providence, RI	17. Fresno, CA
5. Eugene, OR	18. Paterson, NJ
6. Riverside, CA	19. New Haven, CT
7. Huntington Beach, CA	20. Reno, NV
8. Springfield, MA	21. Billings, MT
9. Moreno Valley, CA	22. Fullerton, CA
10. Sioux Falls, SD	23. Abilene, TX
11. Thousand Oaks, CA	24. Tucson, AZ
12. Rancho Cucamonga, CA	25. Stockton, CA
13. Escondido, CA	

Source: *Ladies' Home Journal*

direct them toward the proper media. Specialists working for manufacturers and retailers are concerned with efforts that will promote sales and create goodwill for the firm's products. They work closely with the marketing and sales departments to announce new products, prepare displays, and attend occasional dealers' conventions.

A large firm may have a *director of public relations,* who is a vice president of the company and in charge of a staff that includes writers, artists, researchers, and other specialists. Publicity for an individual or a small organization may involve many of the same areas of expertise but may be carried out by a few people or possibly even one person.

Many PR workers act as consultants (rather than staff) of a corporation, institution, or organization. These workers have the advantage of being able to operate independently, state opinions objectively, and work with more than one type of business or association.

PR specialists are called upon to work with the public-opinion aspects of almost every corporate or institutional problem. These can range from the opening of a new manufacturing plant to a college's dormitory dedication to a merger or sale of a company.

Public relations professionals can also specialize. *Lobbyists* try to persuade legislators and other office holders to pass laws favoring the interests of the firms or people they represent. *Fund-raising directors* develop and direct programs designed to raise funds for social welfare agencies and other nonprofit organizations.

Early in their careers, public relations specialists become accustomed to having others receive credit for their behind-the-scenes work. The speeches they draft will be delivered by company officers, the magazine articles they prepare may be credited to the president of the company, and they may be consulted to prepare the message to stockholders from the chairman of the board that appears in the annual report.

REQUIREMENTS
High School
While in high school, take courses in English, journalism, public speaking, humanities, and languages, because public relations is based on effective communication with others. Courses such as these will develop your skills in written and oral communication as well as provide a better understanding of different fields and industries to be publicized.

Postsecondary Training
Most people employed in public relations service have a college degree. Major fields of study most beneficial to developing the proper skills are public relations, English, and journalism. Some employers feel that majoring in the area in which the public relations person will eventually work is the best training. A knowledge of business administration is most helpful, as is a native talent for selling. A graduate degree may be required for managerial positions. People with a bachelor's degree in public relations can find staff positions with either an organization or a public relations firm.

More than 200 colleges and about 100 graduate schools offer degree programs or special courses in public relations. In addition, many other colleges offer at least courses in the field. The journalism or communication departments of schools sometimes offer PR programs. In addition to courses in theory and techniques of public relations, PR students may study organization, management and administration, and practical applications; they often specialize in areas such as business, government, and nonprofit organizations. Other preparation includes courses in creative writing, psychology, communications, advertising, and journalism.

Certification or Licensing

The Public Relations Society of America, the International Association of Business Communicators, and the Canadian Public Relations Society, Inc., accredit public relations workers who have passed a comprehensive examination. Such accreditation is a sign of competence in this field, although it is not a requirement for employment.

Other Requirements

Today's public relations specialist must be a businessperson first, both to understand how to perform successfully in business and to comprehend the needs and goals of the organization or client. Additionally, the public relations specialist needs to be a strong writer and speaker with good interpersonal, leadership, and organizational skills.

EXPLORING

Almost any experience in working with other people will help you to develop strong interpersonal skills, which are crucial in public relations. The possibilities are almost endless. Summer work on a newspaper or trade paper or with a radio or television station may give insight into communications media. Working as a volunteer on a political campaign can help you to understand the ways in which people can be persuaded. Being selected as a page for the U.S. Congress or a state legislature will help you grasp the fundamentals of government processes. A job in retail will help you to understand some of the principles of product presentation. A teaching job will develop your organization and presentation skills.

EMPLOYERS

Public relations specialists hold about 137,000 jobs. Workers may be paid employees of the organization they represent or they may be part of a public relations firm that works for organizations on a contract basis. Others are involved in fund-raising or political campaigning. Public relations may be done for a corporation, retail business, service company, utility, association, nonprofit organization, or educational institution.

Most PR firms are located in large cities that are centers of communications. New York, Chicago, Los Angeles, and Washington, DC are good places to search for a public relations job. Nevertheless, there are many good opportunities in cities across the United States.

STARTING OUT

There is no clear-cut formula for getting a job in public relations. Individuals often enter the field after gaining preliminary experience in another occupation closely allied to the field, usually some segment of communications, frequently journalism. Coming into public relations from newspaper work is still a recommended route. Another good method is to gain initial employment as a public relations trainee or intern, or as a clerk, secretary, or research assistant in a public relations department or a counseling firm.

ADVANCEMENT

In some large companies, an entry-level public relations specialist may start as a trainee in a formal training program for new employees. In others, new employees may expect to receive work that has a minimum of responsibility. They may assemble clippings or do rewrites on material that has already been accepted. They may make posters or assist in conducting polls or surveys, or compile reports from data submitted by others.

As workers acquire experience, they are given more responsibility. They write news releases, direct polls or surveys, or advance to writing speeches for company officials. Progress may seem to be slow, because some skills take a long time to master.

Some lower level PR workers advance in responsibility and salary in the same firm in which they started. Others find that the path to advancement is to accept a more attractive position in another firm. The goal of many public relations specialists is to open an independent office or to join an established consulting firm. To start an independent office requires a large outlay of capital and an established reputation in the field. However, those who are successful in operating their own consulting firms probably attain the greatest financial success in the public relations field.

EARNINGS

The Bureau of Labor Statistics reports that public relations specialists had median annual earnings of $41,010 in 2001. Salaries ranged from less than $23,930 to more than $72,910.

The U.S. Department of Labor reports the following 2000 median salaries for public relations specialists by type of employer: management and public relations, $43,690; state government, $39,560; local government, $40,760; and colleges and universities, $35,080.

Many PR workers receive a range of fringe benefits from corporations and agencies employing them, including bonus/incentive compensation, stock options, profit sharing/pension plans/401-K programs, medical benefits, life insurance, financial planning, maternity/paternity leave, paid vacations, and family college tuition. Bonuses can range from 5 to 100 percent of base compensation and often are based on individual and/or company performance.

WORK ENVIRONMENT

Public relations specialists generally work in offices with adequate secretarial help, regular salary increases, and expense accounts. They are expected to make a good appearance in tasteful, conservative clothing. They must have social poise, and their conduct in their personal life is important to their firms or their clients. The public relations specialist may have to entertain business associates.

The PR specialist seldom works the conventional office hours for many weeks at a time; although the workweek may consist of 35 to 40 hours, these hours may be supplemented by evenings and even weekends when meetings must be attended and other special events covered. Time behind the desk may represent only a small part of the total working schedule. Travel is often an important and necessary part of the job.

The life of the PR worker is so greatly determined by the job that many consider this a disadvantage. Because the work is concerned with public opinion, it is often difficult to measure the results of performance and to sell the worth of a public relations program to an employer or client. Competition in the consulting field is keen, and if a firm loses an account, some of its personnel may be affected. The demands it makes for anonymity will be considered by some as one of the profession's less inviting aspects. Public relations involves much more hard work and a great deal less glamour than is popularly supposed.

OUTLOOK

Employment of public relations professionals is expected to grow much faster than average for all other occupations, according to the U.S. Department of Labor. Competition will be keen for beginning jobs in public relations because so many job seekers are enticed by the perceived glamour and appeal of the field; those with both education and experience will have an advantage.

Most large companies have some sort of public relations resource, either through their own staff or through the use of a firm of consultants. They are expected to expand their public relations activities and create many new jobs. More of the smaller companies are hiring public relations specialists, adding to the demand for these workers.

FOR MORE INFORMATION

To read Communication World Online and other information for professionals in public relations, employee communications, marketing communications, and public affairs, contact:

International Association of Business Communicators
One Hallidie Plaza, Suite 600
San Francisco, CA 94102-2818
Tel: 415-544-4700
http://www.iabc.com

For statistics, salary surveys, and other information about the profession, contact:

Public Relations Society of America
33 Irving Place
New York, NY 10003-2376
Tel: 212-995-2230
Email: hq@prsa.org
http://www.prsa.org

This professional association for public relations professionals offers an accreditation program and opportunities for professional development.

Canadian Public Relations Society, Inc.
4195 Dundas Street West, Suite 346
Toronto, ON M8X 1Y4 Canada
Tel: 416-239-7034
http://www.cprs.ca

PURCHASING AGENTS

QUICK FACTS

School Subjects Business Economics Mathematics	**Certification or Licensing** Voluntary
	Outlook About as fast as the average
Personal Skills Helping/teaching Technical/scientific	**DOT** 162
Work Environment Primarily indoors Primarily one location	**GOE** 11.05.04
Minimum Education Level High school diploma	**NOC** 1225
Salary Range $26,780 to $43,230 to $70,430+	**O*NET-SOC** 11-3061.00, 13-1021.00, 13-1023.00

OVERVIEW

Purchasing agents work for businesses and other large organizations, such as hospitals, universities, and government agencies. They buy raw materials, machinery, supplies, and services required for the organization. They must consider cost, quality, quantity, and time of delivery. Purchasing managers and agents hold approximately 536,000 jobs in the United States.

HISTORY

Careers in the field of purchasing are relatively new and came into real importance only in the last half of the 20th century. The first purchasing jobs emerged during the Industrial Revolution, when manufacturing plants and businesses became bigger. This led to the division of management jobs into various specialties, one of which was buying.

By the late 1800s, buying was considered a separate job in large businesses. Purchasing jobs were especially important in the railroad, automobile, and steel industries. The trend toward creating specialized buying jobs was reflected in the founding of professional organizations, such as the National Association of Purchasing Agents (now the National Association of Purchasing Management) and the American Purchasing Society. It was not until after World War II, however, with the expansion of the U.S. government and the increased complexity of business practices, that the job of purchasing agent became firmly established.

THE JOB

Purchasing agents generally work for organizations that buy at least $100,000 worth of goods a year. Their primary goal is to purchase the best quality materials for the best price. To do this, the agent must consider the exact specifications for the required items, cost, quantity discounts, freight handling or other transportation costs, and delivery time. In the past, much of this information was obtained by comparing listings in catalogs and trade journals, interviewing suppliers' representatives, keeping up with current market trends, examining sample goods, and observing demonstrations of equipment. Increasingly, information can be found through computer databases. Sometimes agents visit plants of company suppliers. The agent is responsible for following up on orders and ensuring that goods meet the order specifications.

Most purchasing agents work in firms that have fewer than five employees in the purchasing department. In some small organizations, there is only one person responsible for making purchases. Very large firms, however, may employ as many as 100 purchasing agents, each responsible for specific types of goods. In such organizations there is usually a *purchasing director* or *purchasing manager.*

Some purchasing agents seek the advice of *purchase-price analysts*, who compile and analyze statistical data about the manufacture and cost of products. Based on this information, they can make recommendations to purchasing personnel regarding the feasibility of producing or buying certain products and suggest ways to reduce costs.

Purchasing agents often specialize in a particular product or field. For example, *procurement engineers* specialize in aircraft equipment. They establish specifications and requirements for construction, performance, and testing of equipment.

Field contractors negotiate with farmers to grow or purchase fruits, vegetables, or other crops. These agents may advise growers on methods, acreage, and supplies, and arrange for financing, transportation, or labor recruitment.

Head tobacco buyers are engaged in the purchase of tobacco on the auction warehouse floor. They advise other buyers about grades and quantities of tobacco and suggest prices.

Grain buyers manage grain elevators. They are responsible for evaluating and buying grain for resale and milling. They are concerned with the quality, market value, shipping, and storing of grain.

Grain broker-and-market operators buy and sell grain for investors through the commodities exchange. Like other brokers, they work on a commission basis.

REQUIREMENTS
High School

Most purchasing and buying positions require at least a bachelor's degree. Therefore, in high school take a college preparatory curriculum. Helpful subjects include English, business, mathematics, social science, and economics.

Postsecondary Training

Although it is possible to obtain an entry-level purchasing job with only a high school diploma, many employers prefer or require college graduates for the job. College work should include courses in general economics, purchasing, accounting, statistics, and business management. A familiarity with computers also is desirable. Some colleges and universities offer majors in purchasing, but other business-related majors are appropriate as well.

Purchasing agents with a master's degree in business administration, engineering, technology, or finance tend to have the best jobs and highest salaries. Companies that manufacture machinery or chemicals may require a degree in engineering or a related field. A civil service examination is required for employment in government purchasing positions.

Certification or Licensing

There are no specific licenses or certification requirements imposed by law for purchasing agents. There are, however, several professional organizations to which many purchasing agents belong, including the Institute for Supply Management, the National Institute of Government Purchasing, and the American Purchasing Society. These organizations offer certification to applicants who meet their educational and other requirements and who pass the necessary examinations.

The Institute for Supply Management offers the Accredited Purchasing Practitioner and Certified Purchasing Manager designations. The National Institute of Government Purchasing and the Universal Public Purchasing Certification Council offer the Certified Public Purchasing Officer and the Certified Professional Public Buyer designations. The American Purchasing Society offers the Certified Purchasing Professional designation. Although certification is not essential, it is a recognized mark of professional competence that enhances a purchasing agent's opportunities for promotion to top management positions.

Other Requirements

Purchasing agents should have calm temperaments and confidence in their decision-making abilities. Because they work with other people, they need to be diplomatic, tactful, and cooperative. A thorough knowledge of business practices and an understanding of the needs and activities of the employer are essential. It also is helpful to be familiar with social and economic changes in order to predict the amounts or types of products to buy.

EXPLORING

If you are interested in becoming a purchasing agent, you can learn more about the field through a summer job in the purchasing department of a business. Even working as a stock clerk can offer some insight into the job of purchasing agent or buyer. You may also learn about the job by talking with an experienced purchasing agent or reading publications on the field such as *Purchasing Magazine* (http://www.purchasing.com). Keeping abreast of economic trends, fashion styles, or other indicators may help you to predict the market for particular products. Making educated and informed predictions is a basic part of any buying job.

EMPLOYERS

There are approximately 536,000 purchasing managers and agents (wholesale, retail, farm products, and other) currently working in the United States. They work for a wide variety of businesses, both wholesale and retail, as well as for government agencies. Employers range from small stores, where buying may be only one function of a manager's job, to multinational corporations, where a buyer may specialize in one type of item and buy in enormous quantity. Nearly every business that sells products requires someone to purchase the goods to be sold, and such businesses can be found in almost every city and town. Of course, the larger the town is, the more businesses and thus more buying positions there will be. Larger cities provide the best opportunities for higher salaries and advancement.

STARTING OUT

Students without a college degree may be able to enter the field as clerical workers and then receive on-the-job training in purchasing. A college degree is required for most higher level positions. College and university placement services offer assistance to graduating students who are looking for jobs.

Entry into the purchasing department of a private business can be made by direct application to the company. Some purchasing agents start in another department, such as accounting, shipping, or receiving, and transfer to purchasing when an opportunity arises. Many large companies send newly hired agents through orientation programs, where they learn about goods and services, suppliers, and purchasing methods.

Another means of entering the field is through the military. Service in the Quartermaster Corps of the Army or the procurement divisions of the Navy or Air Force can provide excellent preparation either for a civilian job or a career position in the service.

ADVANCEMENT

In general, purchasing agents begin by becoming familiar with departmental procedures, such as keeping inventory records, filling out forms to initiate new purchases, checking purchase orders, and dealing with vendors. With more experience, they gain responsibility for selecting vendors and purchasing products. Agents may become *junior buyers* of standard catalog items, *assistant buyers*, or managers, perhaps with overall responsibility for purchasing, warehousing, traffic, and related functions. The top positions are *head of purchasing*, *purchasing director*, *materials manager*, and *vice-president of purchasing*. These positions include responsibilities concerning production, planning, and marketing.

Many agents advance by changing employers. Frequently an assistant purchasing agent for one firm will be hired as a purchasing agent or head of the purchasing department by another company.

EARNINGS

How much a buyer earns depends on various factors, including the employer's sales volume. Mass merchandisers, such as discount or chain department stores, pay some of the highest salaries. According to 2001 Bureau of Labor Statistics data, earnings for purchasing agents ranged from about $26,780 for the lowest 10 percent to more than $70,430 for the top 10 percent. Median salaries were $43,230.

In addition to their salaries, buyers often receive cash bonuses based on performance and may be offered incentive plans, such as profit sharing and stock options. Most buyers receive the usual company benefits, such as vacation, sick leave, life and health insurance, and pension plans. They generally receive an employee's discount of 10 to 20 percent on merchandise purchased for personal use, as well.

WORK ENVIRONMENT

Working conditions for a purchasing agent are similar to those of other office employees. They usually work in rooms that are pleasant, well lighted, and clean. Work is year-round and generally steady because it is not particularly influenced by seasonal factors. Most have 40-hour workweeks, although overtime is not uncommon. In addition to regular hours, agents may have to attend meetings, read, prepare reports, visit suppliers' plants, or travel. While most work is done indoors, some agents occasionally need to inspect goods outdoors or in warehouses.

It is important for purchasing agents to have good working relations with others. They must interact closely with suppliers as well as with personnel in other departments of the company. Because of the importance of their decisions, purchasing agents sometimes work under great pressure.

OUTLOOK

The number of purchasing agents is likely to grow about as fast as the average rate for all occupations, according to the U.S. Department of Labor. Computerized purchasing methods and the increased reliance on a select number of suppliers boost the productivity of purchasing personnel and have somewhat reduced the number of new job openings. But as more and more hospitals, schools, state and local governments, and other service-related organizations turn to professional purchasing agents to help reduce costs, they will become good sources of employment. Nevertheless, most job openings will replace workers who retire or otherwise leave their jobs.

Demand will be strongest for those with a master's degree in business administration or an undergraduate degree in purchasing. Among firms that manufacture complex machinery, chemicals, and other technical products, the demand will be for graduates with a master's degree in engineering, another field of science, or business administration. Graduates of two-year programs in purchasing or materials management should continue to find good opportunities, especially in smaller companies.

FOR MORE INFORMATION

For career and certification information, contact:
American Purchasing Society, Inc.
North Island Center
8 East Galena Boulevard, Suite 203
Aurora Place, IL 60506
Tel: 630-859-0250
http://www.american-purchasing.com

For career and certification information and lists of colleges with purchasing programs, contact:
Institute for Supply Management
PO Box 22160
Tempe, AZ 85285-2160
Tel: 800-888-6276
http://www.ism.ws

For an information packet on purchasing careers in government, contact:
National Institute of Government Purchasing
151 Spring Street
Herndon, VA 20170-5223
Tel: 800-367-6447
http://www.nigp.org

For materials on educational programs in the retail industry, contact:
National Retail Federation
325 7th Street, NW, Suite 1100
Washington, DC 20004
Tel: 800-673-4692
http://www.nrf.com

REAL ESTATE DEVELOPERS

QUICK FACTS

School Subjects
Business
Mathematics

Personal Skills
Communication/ideas
Leadership/management

Work Environment
Indoors and outdoors
Primarily multiple locations

Minimum Education Level
High school diploma

Salary Range
$20,000 to $82,100 to
$1,000,000

Certification or Licensing
None available

Outlook
Little change or more
slowly than the average

DOT
N/A

GOE
N/A

NOC
0121

O*NET-SOC
N/A

OVERVIEW

Real estate developers envision, organize, and execute construction or renovation projects for commercial or private use. This process involves negotiation with property owners, real estate agents, investors, lending institutions such as banks and insurance companies, architects, lawyers, general contractors, government officials, and other interested parties. Developers may work independently as consultants or in partnership with other professionals involved in real estate development.

HISTORY

The United States is a relatively young country (compared to many European countries) without a long history of densely populated cities. In Europe, however, there is evidence of city-dwelling patterns from as far back as 3,000 years ago. In areas of early Roman settlement, archaeologists have discovered the remnants of street grids, sewage lines, and uniform construction, indicating some level of formal planning. Since the Middle Ages, Paris has had municipal regulations governing the placement and use of buildings.

Such planning and regulations emerge when many people try to live harmoniously in a limited space. In these situations, land has value and, therefore, it is expensive. Construction of homes, roads for travel, or public buildings for commerce and government requires a substantial investment of money. The developer is the entrepreneur who sees an opportunity to make money by providing services, in the form of buildings or infrastructure, to the community. The developer's role throughout history has been to envision development, organize investors to fund land purchase and construction, and oversee the project.

This role has existed in much the same way for as long as people have lived in settled communities. What has changed, and what continues to change, are the zoning laws and building codes regulating development and the tax laws affecting the organization of the development entity.

THE JOB

A developer may be involved in purchasing 500 suburban acres and developing 1,000 condominiums, a couple of parks, a golf course, and a small shopping center with a grocery store, full-service dry cleaner, video rental store, and health club. Or a developer may renovate and remodel an existing structure, such as a warehouse, for use as a restaurant and office space. The developer's actual day-to-day activities vary depending on the type and size of the project.

Whether a group of investors approaches the developer or the developer searches out investors, the first step is to structure the *development entity,* a group made up of the *project owner* (the person or group who will receive the profits or suffer the losses from the proposed development), the *investors* who put up the initial equity funds, and the developer. In many cases, the developer is the owner. These individuals may establish a development entity with only one owner, a partnership with a lead owner, a limited partnership, or a corporation that sells stock to stockholders.

The legal definitions of each type of entity vary according to locale, and the benefits and risks of each are quite different. The developer, who facilitates the process of structuring the contract, is concerned with three main issues: managing risk, gathering equity to facilitate borrowing money, and creating a functioning structure with a limited number of people involved in decision-making.

The developer's job at the beginning of a project has been compared to pitching a tent in high wind: The toughest thing is getting the first corner nailed down. In negotiating with potential investors, the developer brings all interested parties to the table to secure an initial commitment of equity funds. Without equity, the developer is unable to approach banks or insurance companies for loans to complete the project.

The developer may come to the table with $100,000 of personal money to invest—or none. With an excellent track record and a solid proposal, the developer's involvement in the project may be enough to secure the confidence of potential investors. But the developer must show a willingness to protect these investors by creating a development entity that exposes them only to reasonable risk.

Most investors want to risk only the equity money they contribute. In other words, if the project fails, they do not want to be held liable for all the money lost. The contract needs to protect their other assets, such as their homes, savings accounts, and other investments, in case of a default on the loans. So the contract must be written in such a way that the investors are willing to accept the risk involved.

After securing the equity necessary to convince financial institutions to participate in the project, the developer approaches these institutions (primarily banks and insurance companies) to secure financing.

Most development projects require both short-term and long-term financing. Banks often provide the money to buy land and complete construction. However, to receive this short-term financing, sometimes called a *construction loan,* the developer must already have equity funds from the investors. The equity money might equal from 10 to 40 percent of the total amount of the loan.

Insurance companies are the most common providers of long-term financing, which is used to pay off the construction loan. Long-term financing commitments are based on the economic projections of the completed development and usually must be obtained before securing short-term financing. Occasionally one institution will provide both the short-term and long-term financing, but this is less likely to happen with larger projects.

Another participant in real estate financing is the government. Sometimes a municipal government will issue a bond to raise money from taxes. These funds may provide long-term financing to a private developer for the construction of a stadium, for example, or for some infrastructure improvement, such as widening the streets. Municipal governments frequently participate in projects to develop run-down areas of the city. In exchange for shouldering some of the financial risk, the city can benefit from the increased productivity of the renovated neighborhood.

Before receiving a building permit, the real estate developer may have to complete impact studies to assess how the proposed project will affect the community and the environment. He or she may also have to meet with the zoning board if there are regulations that the new building will be unable to meet.

At this stage, the project needs an *architect*. The architect's first job usually is to hire a *structural engineer* and a *mechanical engineer*. Together they create the building plans, which the developer submits to the building department.

This process of creating the plans involves economic factors, aesthetic architectural concerns, building codes, and other legal constraints imposed by the community. This is one of the most exciting and important times in the development process. Through the competition of the interests of all the involved parties, the best use for the site evolves, and the project is born.

While waiting for the building permit to be issued, the developer also puts the building plans out for bids from *general contractors*. The general contractor selected for the job hires subcontractors, such as carpenters, plumbers, roofers, and drywallers.

In applying for the building permit and preparing to break ground on the construction site, developers spend a lot of time dealing with government regulations. They must make sure that they understand and meet building codes designed to ensure the safety of future occupants. Windows in a residential building, for example, must have a certain number of square feet for light and a certain number for ventilation.

Developers must be aware not only of building codes but also of laws affecting construction. New buildings, for example, must meet handicap access codes to comply with the Americans with Disabilities Act.

On large projects, such as the development of a skyscraper in an urban center, the developer will contract out much of the work, such as public relations and advertising, the completion of impact studies, and the general contractor's job. On smaller projects, however, the developer may perform some or all of these functions.

As general contractor, the developer is involved on a daily basis with work at the construction site. If someone else is hired as general contractor, the developer may only be involved only at weekly construction meetings, where the architect, engineers, and various subcontractors discuss progress and changes necessary in the plans.

In either case, the developer, who is ultimately responsible for the success or failure of the project, must be knowledgeable about all aspects of the development process and capable of hiring a group of people who can work successfully as a team. Though the developer may or may not be an investor who stands to lose money, the developer's career is on the line with every project.

If a developer secures city approval and necessary funds to construct a new office building in a highly visible spot, the whole city may be watching. The local government officials may have used their influence to change zoning laws in favor of the project. Therefore, their reputations also may be riding on the building's success. If, for example, the construction costs exceed the initial estimates, and the developer is unable to raise the additional money to cover the costs, construction on the building may be halted at any stage, and the empty shell may stand for years as an eyesore in the community.

Failure to successfully complete such projects inhibits the developer's ability to secure investors and government cooperation in the future. Depending on the terms of the developer's contract, it may also mean that the developer is never compensated for the time and work spent on the project.

Once the project is complete, the developer's role depends on the specifications set forth by the development entity. With a high-rise residential building, for example, the developer may be involved in selling or renting the apartments. As an owner in the project, the developer may be involved in the management of rental property for many years.

REQUIREMENTS
High School

There are no specific educational requirements or certifications for becoming a real estate developer, but many developers have college degrees, and some have advanced degrees. While you are in high school, you can prepare for a career in real estate development by pursuing a broad-based liberal arts curriculum that will prepare you for a college education. In addition, courses in business, economics, finance, mathematics, speech communications, drafting, and shop will be helpful.

Postsecondary Training

Schools generally do not offer a specific curriculum that leads to a career as a real estate developer. Because the position requires a broad base of knowledge as well as some experience in the business community, most people become real estate developers after leaving an earlier career.

There are a few schools that offer undergraduate degrees in real estate, usually as a concentration within a general business degree program. Ohio State University, for example, offers a bachelor's degree in Real Estate and Urban Analysis. There are even fewer graduate degree programs in real estate, such as the University of South Carolina's master's degree in real estate development and Massachusetts Institute of Technology's master's program in real estate development. Some schools offer master of business administration programs with a concentration in real estate.

Graduate degrees in law, business, and architecture are among the most beneficial to the real estate developer. If you are interested in pursuing an advanced degree in one of these areas, you should complete the necessary preparatory work as an undergraduate.

To pursue a law degree, you need a strong background in the liberal arts, including English, philosophy, history, and government. Good preparation for a master's degree in business includes course work in finance, marketing, accounting, business communications, and higher level mathematics. An advanced degree in architecture requires an emphasis on drafting, mathematics, engineering, and physics.

Other Requirements

Real estate development is regarded as one of the most challenging careers in the real estate industry. You must have the ability to speculate about the economy and envision profitable ventures as well as have a broad knowledge of the legal, financial, political, and construction issues related to development. Consequently, a background in law, architecture, or general contracting can be highly beneficial.

A working knowledge of both zoning laws and building codes is also useful. Although it is the architect's primary responsibility to ensure that the plans ultimately submitted to the building department will be approved, the knowledgeable developer may decide it is appropriate to seek a variance in zoning or code. This is most common in nonsafety areas, such as the number of parking spaces required. A municipality might grant a variance if a developer presents a convincing case, such as highlighting how the project will create a significant number of jobs for the community.

You also must understand the marketplace. For this reason, experience in appraising, leasing, or selling real estate can prove very helpful. Real estate brokers who lease office space often have excellent contacts and knowledge for entering the development business. They know where the potential tenants are, and they understand the issues involved in developing large buildings for commercial use. You also must grasp the basics of finance to structure the development entity effectively.

EXPLORING

Read the real estate section of the local newspaper and follow the building and development activities in the community to gain exposure to this industry. A local librarian should also be able to refer you to books and magazines about real estate development. Sometimes a teacher will be able to arrange for a developer or other real estate professional to visit and talk about his or her work.

You can also prepare for your careers by working in the offices of the following professionals: real estate developers, lawyers practicing within the real estate industry, architects, and general contractors. Spending time in any of these offices will introduce you to the general milieu of the real estate developer's world. The early exposure can also help you decide in which of these areas you most want to develop expertise.

You can gain good experience in certain aspects of real estate development by doing public relations, publicity, or advertising work and participating in fund-raising campaigns for school and community organizations. Volunteering with a housing advocacy organization, such as Habitat for Humanity, may provide opportunities to learn about home construction, bank financing, and legal contracts. To gain confidence and develop a business sense, take on leadership roles at school and in extracurricular activities, such as the student council or the business club.

EMPLOYERS

Real estate developers often work independently or open offices in communities that have property with the potential for development.

The activity of the real estate marketplace will dictate the number of opportunities in a given community.

STARTING OUT

There is no specific way to become a real estate developer. Successful real estate developers are always the heart of the project, facilitating communication among the various participants. This often requires finely tuned diplomatic skills. Their proven track record, professional manner, and influence in the real estate world are their biggest assets. They have the ability to sell ideas and secure large sums of money from investors and lending institutions.

Most developers do not begin their careers in this field. They frequently have backgrounds as lawyers, architects, real estate brokers, or general contractors, positions that allow them to gain the expertise and contacts necessary for success in real estate development.

Many real estate developers secure work because they have an established reputation. Their contacts and knowledge in a particular community or type of real estate allow them to work more effectively than others. But developers also are successful because of their abilities in analyzing the marketplace, structuring solid investment proposals, facilitating the creation of the development entity, and overseeing projects.

ADVANCEMENT

The real estate developer is really at the top of the profession. Advancement involves larger, more prestigious projects and earning more money. Such achievement may take several years. It is important to keep in mind that even the most successful developers suffer setbacks when projects fail. For those not-so-successful developers, such setbacks can end a career.

EARNINGS

There is no set pay scale for real estate developers. Developers' earnings depend on their skill and experience, the size of the projects they work on, the structure established for their payment in the development entity contract, and the successful completion of the project.

Sometimes, developers are contracted by a group of individual investors or a company to manage a project. In this case they may work out a consulting agreement with a certain secured fee up front, preset fees paid throughout the duration of the project, and some percentage of the profits once the project is complete. Or the agreement may contain some combination of these payment options.

A less experienced developer will often shoulder more risk on a project to gain expertise and complete work that will improve the developer's reputation. In these instances, developers may be undercompensated or not paid at all for their time and effort if the project fails.

According to the Ford Career Center of the University of Texas, graduates with a bachelor's degree in business administration with a concentration in insurance and real estate earned an average salary of $36,583 in 2001. The average base starting salary for M.B.A.'s in real estate was $82,100.

WORK ENVIRONMENT

Real estate developers are often highly visible individuals in the community. It is important that they have excellent communication skills, be able to work with all kinds of people, and enjoy the speculative nature of the business.

Developers spend a great deal of time negotiating with executives in banks and insurance companies, government officials, and private or corporate business investors. A certain professionalism and comfort in executive situations is necessary for success.

However, some developers report to the job site every day, don a hard hat, and oversee the work of roofers, plumbers, and electricians. The developer must be flexible enough to adjust to the job's varying demands.

In addition to staying in touch with investors and overseeing the project, developers sometimes may need to respond to the public and the media. Controversial, high-profile projects often put the developer under a spotlight, requiring excellent public relations skills.

Real estate developers, because of the complexity of their jobs and the often large sums of money at stake, work under a great deal of pressure and stress. While the level of risk and the potential profit depend on the developer's role in the development entity, those who like a steady schedule with a dependable paycheck may not be suited for this career.

Hours can be long and frequently vary with the type of project and stage of development. Developers may have to attend city council meetings or neighborhood meetings in the evening if they are seeking changes in zoning laws before applying for a building permit. In addition to having the potential to earn a large sum of money, developers enjoy the satisfaction of seeing a project evolve from idea inception through various stages of planning and finally into a finished usable structure.

Though their work depends on the cooperation of other individuals and organizations, developers also enjoy a certain level of independence and flexibility in their lifestyles. As entrepreneurs, they shoulder a lot of personal risk for their businesses, but this brings with it great opportunities to do creative work and positively influence their communities while potentially earning a handsome profit.

OUTLOOK

The outlook for real estate developers is subject to the fluctuations of the general economy. In the late 1990s, economic conditions were excellent for real estate developers. Record-low interest rates roused many formerly depressed areas of the country to renewed economic vigor. In the beginning of the 21st century there was slow growth in the real estate industry, and that is expected to continue through the near future. But economic conditions are never fixed. In addition, the real estate market can be quite strong in some parts of the country and weak in others.

FOR MORE INFORMATION

For information on the real estate industry and career opportunities, contact:

National Association of Realtors
430 North Michigan Avenue
Chicago, IL 60611
Tel: 312-329-8292
http://www.realtor.com

For information on real estate lenders and other related topics, contact:

The Real Estate Library
http://www.relibrary.com

RETAIL BUSINESS OWNERS

QUICK FACTS

School Subjects
Business
Mathematics

Personal Skills
Communication/ideas
Leadership/management

Work Environment
Primarily indoors
Primarily one location

Minimum Education Level
High school diploma

Salary Range
$15,000 to $35,000 to
$100,000+

Certification or Licensing
Required by certain states

Outlook
About as fast as the
average

DOT
N/A

GOE
N/A

NOC
0621

O*NET-SOC
N/A

OVERVIEW

Retail business owners are entrepreneurs who start or buy their own businesses or franchise operations. They are responsible for all aspects of a business operation, from planning and ordering merchandise to overseeing day-to-day operations. Retail business owners sell such items as clothing, household appliances, groceries, jewelry, and furniture.

HISTORY

Retailing is a vital commercial activity, providing customers with an opportunity to purchase goods and services from various types of merchants. The first retail outlets in America were trading posts and general stores. At trading posts, goods obtained from Native Americans were exchanged for items imported from Europe or manufactured in other parts of the country. As villages and towns grew, trading posts developed into general stores and began to sell food, farm necessities, and clothing. Typically run by a single person,

335

these stores sometimes served as the post office and became the social and economic center of their communities.

Since World War II, giant supermarkets, discount houses, chain stores, and shopping malls have grown in popularity. Even so, individually owned businesses still thrive, often giving customers more personal and better informed service. Moreover, despite the large growth in retail outlets and the increased competition that has accompanied it, retailing still provides the same basic, important function it did in the early years of the United States.

THE JOB

Although retail business owners sell a wide variety of products, from apples to automobiles, the basic job responsibilities remain the same. Simply stated, the retail business owner must do everything necessary to ensure the successful operation of a business.

There are five major categories of job responsibilities within a retail establishment: merchandising and buying, store operations, sales promotion and advertising, bookkeeping and accounting, and personnel supervision. Merchandising and buying determine the type and amount of actual goods to be sold. Store operations involve maintaining the building or retail space and providing for the movement of goods and personnel within the space. Sales promotion and advertising are the marketing methods used to inform customers and potential customers about the goods and services that are available. In bookkeeping and accounting, records kept include payroll, taxes, and money spent and received. Personnel involves staffing the store with people who are trained and qualified to handle all the work that needs to be done.

The owner must be aware of all aspects of the business operation so that he or she can make informed decisions. Specific duties of an individual owner depend on the size of the store and the number of employees. In a store with more than 10 employees, many of the operational, promotional, and personnel activities may be supervised by a manager. The owner may plan the overall purpose and function of the store and hire a manager to oversee the day-to-day operations. In a smaller store, the owner may also do much of the operational activities, including sweeping the floor, greeting customers, and balancing the accounting books.

In both large and small operations, an owner must keep up to date on product information, as well as on economic and technological conditions that may have an impact on business. This entails reading catalogs about product availability, checking current inventories and prices, and researching and implementing any technological advances that may make the operation more efficient. For example, an owner may decide to purchase data processing equipment to help with accounting functions, as well as to generate a mailing list to inform customers of special sales.

Because of the risks involved in opening a business and the many economic and managerial demands put on individual owners, a desire to open a retail business should be combined with proper management skills, sufficient economic backing, and a good sense of what the public wants. The large majority of retail businesses fail because of a lack of managerial experience on the part of owners.

Franchise ownership, whereby an individual owner obtains a license to sell an existing company's goods or services, grew phenomenally during the 1980s. In a franchise agreement, the prospective business owner receives expert advice from the sponsoring company about location, hiring and training of employees, arrangement of merchandise, display of goods, and record keeping. However, some entrepreneurs do not want to be limited to the product lines and other restrictions that accompany running a franchise store. Franchise operations also may fail, but their likelihood of success is greater than that of a totally independent retail store.

REQUIREMENTS
High School

A high school diploma is important in order to understand the basics of business ownership, though there are no specific educational or experiential requirements for this position. Course work in business administration is helpful, as is previous experience in the retail trade. Hard work, constant analysis and evaluation, and sufficient capital are important elements of a successful business venture.

If you are interested in owning a business, you should take courses in mathematics, business management, and business-related subjects such as accounting, typing, and computer science. In addition, pursue English and other courses that enhance your communications skills. You should also develop the specific skill areas that will complement your retail business. For example, if you want to open an electronics repair shop, learn as much about electronics as possible.

Owners of small retail businesses often manage the store and work behind the counter. For example, the owner of a meat market is sometimes the butcher, as well.

Postsecondary Training

As the business environment gets more and more competitive, many people are opting for an academic degree as a way of getting more training. A bachelor's program emphasizing business communications, marketing, business law, business management, and accounting should be pursued. Some people choose to get a master's in business administration or other related graduate degree. There are also special business schools that offer a one- or two-year program in business management. Some correspondence schools also offer courses on how to plan and run a business.

Certification or Licensing

A business license may be a requirement in some states. Individual states or communities may have zoning codes or other regulations specifying what type of business can be located in a particular area. Check with your state's chamber of commerce or department of revenue for more information on obtaining a license, or visit http://www.sba.gov/hotlist/license.html.

Other Requirements

Whatever your experience and training, a retail business owner needs a lot of energy, patience, and fortitude to overcome the slow times and other difficulties involved in running a business. Other important personal characteristics include maturity, creativity, and good business judgment. Retail business owners also should be able to motivate employees and delegate authority.

EXPLORING

Working full- or part-time as a sales clerk or in some other capacity within a retail business is a good way to learn about the responsibilities of operating a business. Talking with owners of small shops is also helpful, as is reading periodicals that publish articles on self-employment, such as *Entrepreneur* magazine (http://www.entrepreneurmag.com).

Most communities have a chamber of commerce whose members usually will be glad to share their insights into the career of a retail business owner. The Small Business Administration, an agency of the U.S. government, is another possible source of information.

STARTING OUT

Few people start their career as an owner. Many start as a manager or in some other position within a retail business. While developing managerial skills or while pursuing a college degree or other relevant training, you should decide what type of business you would like to own. Many people decide to buy an existing business because it already has a proven track record and because banks and other lending institutions often are more likely to loan money to an existing facility. A retail business owner should anticipate having at least 50 percent of the money needed to start or buy a business. Some people find it helpful to have one or more partners in a business venture.

Owning a franchise is another way of starting a business without a large capital investment, as franchise agreements often require some assistance in planning and start-up costs. Franchise operations, however, are not necessarily less expensive to run than a totally independent business.

ADVANCEMENT

Because an owner is by definition the boss, there are limited opportunities for advancement. Advancement often takes the form of expansion of an existing business, leading to increased earnings and prestige. Expanding a business also can entail added risk, as it involves increasing operational costs. A successful franchise owner may be offered an additional franchise location or an executive position at the corporate headquarters.

A small number of successful independent business owners choose to franchise their business operations in different areas. Some owners become part-time consultants, while others teach a course at a college or university or in an adult education program. This teaching often is done not only for the financial rewards but as a way of helping others investigate the option of retail ownership.

EARNINGS

Earnings vary widely and are greatly influenced by the ability of the individual owner, the type of product or service being sold, and existing economic conditions. Some retail business owners may earn less than $15,000 a year, while the most successful owners earn $100,000 or more.

WORK ENVIRONMENT

Retail business owners generally work in pleasant surroundings. Even so, ownership is a demanding occupation, with owners often working six or seven days a week. Working more than 60 hours a week is not unusual, especially during the Christmas season and other busy times. An owner of a large establishment may be able to leave a manager in charge of many parts of the business, but the owner still must be available to solve any pressing concerns. Owners of small businesses often stay in the store throughout the day, spending much of the time on their feet.

A retail business owner may occasionally travel out of town to attend conferences or to solicit new customers and product information. An owner of a small business, especially, should develop a close relationship with steady customers.

OUTLOOK

The retail field is extremely competitive, and many businesses fail each year. The most common reason for failure is poor management. Thus people with some managerial experience or training will likely have the best chance at running a successful business.

Retail is reported to be the second-largest industry in the United States, employing more than 22 million Americans and generating more than $3 trillion in retail sales annually. Over 95 percent of all U.S. retailers are single-store businesses, but they generate less than 50 percent of all retail store sales, according to Retail Industry (http://retailindustry.about.com).

Increasing unemployment, the weakening of consumer confidence, increased competition from other retailers and direct marketers, and the growth of Internet businesses are just some of the issues retail businesses will face in the next decade.

FOR MORE INFORMATION

The following foundation conducts research and analysis of women-owned businesses.

Center for Women's Business Research (founded as The National Foundation for Women Business Owners)
1411 K Street, NW, Suite 1350
Washington, DC 20005-3407
Tel: 202-638-3060
Email: info@womensbusinessresearch.org
http://www.nfwbo.org

For materials on educational programs in the retail industry, contact:
National Retail Federation
325 7th Street, NW, Suite 1100
Washington, DC 20004
Tel: 202-783-7971
http://www.nrf.com

For a business starter packet with information about their loan program and services, and basic facts about starting a business, contact:

U.S. Small Business Administration
6302 Fairview Road, Suite 300
Charlotte, NC 28210
Tel: 800-827-5722
Email: answerdesk@sba.gov
http://www.sbaonline.sba.gov

RETAIL MANAGERS

QUICK FACTS

School Subjects Business Mathematics	**Certification or Licensing** None available
Personal Skills Helping/teaching Leadership/management	**Outlook** Little change or more slowly than the average
Work Environment Primarily indoors Primarily one location	**DOT** 185 **GOE** 11.11.05
Minimum Education Level High school diploma	**NOC** 0621, 6211
Salary Range $17,700 to $28,590 to $100,000+	**O*NET-SOC** 41-1011.00

OVERVIEW

Retail managers are responsible for the profitable operation of retail trade establishments. They oversee the selling of food, clothing, furniture, sporting goods, novelties, and many other items. Their duties include hiring, training, and supervising other employees, maintaining the physical facilities, managing inventory, monitoring expenditures and receipts, and maintaining good public relations. Retail managers hold about 2.5 million jobs in the United States.

HISTORY

In the United States, small, family owned stores have been around for centuries. The first large chain store began to operate in the late 19th century. One of the aims of early chain stores was to provide staples for the pioneers of the newly settled West. Because chain store corporations were able to buy goods in large quantities and store them in warehouses, they were able to undersell private merchants.

The number of retail stores, especially supermarkets, began to grow rapidly during the 1930s. Stores often were owned and operated by chain corporations, which were able to benefit from bulk buying and more sophisticated storage practices. Cheaper transportation also contributed to the growth of retail stores because goods could be shipped and sold more economically.

Unlike the early family owned stores, giant retail outlets employed large numbers of people, requiring various levels of management to oversee the business. Retail managers were hired to oversee particular areas within department stores, for example, but higher level managers also were needed to make more general decisions about a company's goals and policies. Today, retailing is one of the nation's largest industries, employing more than 5 million people.

THE JOB

Retail managers are responsible for every phase of a store's operation. They often are one of the first employees to arrive in the morning and the last to leave at night. Their duties include hiring, training, and supervising other employees, maintaining the physical facilities, managing inventory, monitoring expenditures and receipts, and maintaining good public relations.

Perhaps the most important responsibility of retail managers is hiring and training qualified employees. Managers then assign duties to employees, monitor their progress, promote employees, and increase salaries when appropriate. When an employee's performance is not satisfactory, a manager must find a way to improve the performance or, if necessary, fire him or her.

Managers should be good at working with all different kinds of people. Differences of opinion and personality clashes among employees are inevitable, therefore the manager must be able to restore good feelings among the staff. Managers often have to deal with upset customers and must attempt to restore goodwill toward the store when customers are dissatisfied.

Retail managers keep accurate and up-to-date records of store inventory. When new merchandise arrives, the manager ensures items are recorded, priced, and displayed or shelved. They must know when stock is getting low and order new items in a timely manner.

Some managers are responsible for merchandise promotions and advertising. The manager may confer with an advertising agency representative to determine appropriate advertising methods for the store. The manager also may decide what products to put on sale for advertising purposes.

The duties of store managers vary according to the type of merchandise sold, the size of the store, and the number of employees. In small, owner-operated stores, managers often are involved in accounting, data processing, marketing, research, sales, and shipping. In large retail corporations, however, managers may be involved in only one or two activities.

REQUIREMENTS
High School

You will need at least a high school education in order to become a retail manager. Helpful courses include business, mathematics, marketing, and economics. English and speech classes are also important. These courses will teach you to communicate effectively with all types of people, including employees and customers.

Postsecondary Training

Most retail stores prefer applicants with a college degree and many hire only college graduates. Liberal arts, social sciences, and business are the most common degrees held by retail managers.

To prepare for a career as a retail store manager, take courses in accounting, business, marketing, English, advertising, and computer science. If you are unable to attend college as a full-time student, consider getting a job in a store to gain experience and attend college part-time. All managers, regardless of their education, must have good marketing, analytical, communication, and people skills.

Many large retail stores and national chains have established formal training programs, including classroom instruction, for their new employees. The training period may last a week or as long as one year. Training for a department store manager, for example, may include working as a salesperson in several departments in order to learn about the store's operations.

Other Requirements

To be a successful retail manager, you should have good communication skills, enjoy working with and supervising people, and be willing to put in very long hours. Diplomacy often is necessary when creating schedules for workers and in disciplinary matters. There is a great deal of responsibility in retail management, and such positions often are stressful. A calm disposition and ability to handle stress will serve you well.

EXPLORING

If you are interested in becoming a retail manager, you may be able to find part-time, weekend, or summer jobs in a clothing store, supermarket, or other retail trade establishment. You can gain valuable work experience through such jobs and will have the opportunity to observe the retail industry to determine whether you are interested in pursuing a career in it. It also is useful to read periodicals that publish articles on the retail field, such as *Stores Online* (http://www.stores.org), published by the National Retail Federation.

EMPLOYERS

There are about 2.5 million retail managers in the United States, and about one-third are self-employed (many are store owners). Nearly every type of retail business requires management, though owners of small businesses may their own stores. Wherever retail sales are made there is an opportunity for a management position, though most people have to begin in a lower level job. The food industry employs more workers than nearly any other, and retail food businesses always need managers, though smaller businesses may not pay very well. In general, the larger the business and the bigger the city, the more a retail manager can earn. Most other retail managers work in grocery and department stores, motor vehicle dealerships, and clothing and accessory stores.

STARTING OUT

Many new college graduates are able to find managerial positions through their schools' placement service. Some of the large retail chains recruit on college campuses.

Not all store managers, however, are college graduates. Many store managers are promoted to their positions from jobs of less responsibility within their organization. Some may be in the retail industry for more than a dozen years before being promoted. Those with more education often receive promotions faster.

Regardless of educational background, people who are interested in the retail industry should consider working in a retail store at least part-time or during the summer. Although there may not be an opening when the application is made, there often is a high turnover of employees in retail management, and vacancies occur from time to time.

ADVANCEMENT

Advancement opportunities in retailing vary according to the size of the store, where the store is located, and the type of merchandise sold. Advancement also depends on the individual's work experience and educational background.

A store manager who works for a large retail chain, for example, may be given responsibility for a number of stores in a given area or region or transferred to a larger store in another city. Willingness to relocate to a new city may increase an employee's promotional opportunities.

Some managers decide to open their own stores after they have acquired enough experience in the retail industry. After working as a retail manager for a large chain of clothing stores, for example, a person may decide to open a small boutique.

Sometimes becoming a retail manager involves a series of promotions. A person who works in a supermarket, for example, may advance from clerk, checker, or bagger to a regular assignment in one of several departments in the store. After a period of time, he or she may become an assistant manager and eventually a manager.

EARNINGS

Salaries depend on the size of the store, the responsibilities of the job, and the number of customers served. According to the U.S. Department of Labor's 2001 *National Occupational Employment and Wage Estimates,* median annual earnings of supervisors of retail sales workers, including commission, were $28,590. Salaries ranged from less than $17,700 to more than $53,830 per year. Median annual earnings of grocery store managers in 2000 were $27,380, and managers of drugstores and proprietary stores earned $27,250. Those who managed miscellaneous shopping goods stores had median annual earnings of $25,750, and department store managers earned $23,530. Managers who oversee an entire region for a retail chain can earn more than $100,000.

In addition to a salary, some stores offer their managers special bonuses, or commissions, which are typically connected to the store's performance. Many stores also offer employee discounts on store merchandise.

WORK ENVIRONMENT

Most retail stores are pleasant places to work, and managers often are given comfortable offices. Many, however, work long hours.

Managers often work six days a week and as many as 60 hours a week, especially during busy times of the year such as the Christmas season. Because holiday seasons are peak shopping periods, it is extremely rare that managers can take holidays off or schedule vacations around a holiday, even if the store is not open on that day.

Although managers usually can get away from the store during slow times, they must often be present if the store is open at night. It is important that the manager be available to handle the store's daily receipts, which usually are put in a safe or taken to a bank's night depository at the close of the business day.

OUTLOOK

Employment of retail managers is expected to grow more slowly than the average for all occupations, according to the U.S. Department of Labor. Although retailers have reduced their management staff to cut costs and make operations more efficient, there still are good opportunities in retailing. However, competition for jobs will probably continue to increase, and computerized systems for inventory control may reduce the need for some managers. Applicants with the best educational backgrounds and work experience will have the best chances of finding jobs.

FOR MORE INFORMATION

For information on jobs in retail, contact:
International Mass Retail Association
1700 North Moore Street, Suite 2250
Arlington, VA 22209
Tel: 703-841-2300
http://www.imra.org

For materials on educational programs in the retail industry, contact:
National Retail Federation
325 7th Street, NW, Suite 1100
Washington, DC 20004
Tel: 800-673-4692
http://www.nrf.com

SPORTS EXECUTIVES

QUICK FACTS

School Subjects Business Physical education	**Certification or Licensing** None available
Personal Skills Communication/ideas Leadership/management	**Outlook** Little change or more slowly than the average
Work Environment Primarily indoors Primarily one location	**DOT** 153
Minimum Education Level Bachelor's degree	**GOE** 11.12.03
Salary Range $20,000 to $50,000 to $1,000,000+	**NOC** 0513
	O*NET-SOC N/A

OVERVIEW

Sports executives, sometimes known as *team presidents, CEOs,* and *general managers,* manage professional, collegiate, and minor league sports teams. They are responsible for the teams' finances, as well as overseeing the other departments within the organization, such as marketing, public relations, accounting, ticket sales, advertising, sponsorship, and community relations. Sports executives also work on establishing long-term contacts and support within the communities where the teams play.

HISTORY

The sports industry has matured into one of the largest industries in the United States. Professional teams are the most widely recognized industry segment in sports. Professional teams include all of the various sports teams, leagues, and governing bodies for which individuals get paid for their performance. Some of the most notable areas include the National Football League, National Basketball Association,

National Hockey League, and Major League Baseball. These are commonly known as the four majors. During recent decades, more professional leagues have started, such as the Women's National Basketball League, Arena Football, and Major League Soccer. There are also many minor league and collegiate organizations.

THE JOB
The two top positions in most sports organizations are team president and general manager. Depending on the size of the franchise, these two positions might be blended together and held by one person.

Team presidents are the chief executive officers of the club. They are responsible for the overall financial success of the team. Presidents oversee several departments within the organization, including marketing, public relations, broadcasting, sales, advertising, ticket sales, community relations, and accounting. Since team presidents must develop strategies to encourage fans to attend games, it is good if they have some experience in public relations or marketing. Along with the public relations manager, team presidents create give-away programs, such as cap days or poster nights.

Another one of the team president's responsibilities is encouraging community relations by courting season ticket-holders, as well as those who purchase luxury box seats, known as skyboxes. Usually, this involves selling these seats to corporations.

General managers handle the daily business activities of the teams, such as hiring and firing, promotions, supervising scouting, making trades, and negotiating player contracts. All sports teams have general managers, and usually the main functions of the job are the same regardless of the professional level of the team. However, some general managers that work with minor league teams might also deal with additional job duties, including managing the souvenir booths or organizing the ticket offices. The most important asset the general manager brings to an organization is knowledge of business practices. The sport can be learned later.

REQUIREMENTS
High School
High school courses that will help you to become a sports executive include business, mathematics, and computer science. English, speech, and physical education courses will also be beneficial. Managing a school club or other organization will give you a general idea of the responsibilities and demands that this career involves.

Postsecondary Training

To become a sports executive, you will need at least a bachelor's degree. Remember, even though this is a sport-related position, presidents and general managers are expected to have the same backgrounds as corporate executives. Undergraduate classes in business administration, marketing, accounting, and finance will serve you well. A few schools also offer undergraduate programs in sports administration. Most sports executives have master's degrees in sports administration, and some have master's in business administration.

Other Requirements

Sports executives must create a positive image for their teams. In this age of extensive media coverage (including frequent public speaking engagements, which are required of sports executives), excellent communications skills are a must. Sports executives need to be dynamic public speakers. They also need a keen business sense and an intimate knowledge of how to forge a good relationship with their communities. They also should have excellent organizational skills, be detail oriented, and be sound decision makers.

EXPLORING

One way to start exploring this field is to volunteer to do something for your school's sports teams, for example, by charting statistics or taking on the duties of equipment manager. These are good ways to learn how athletic departments work. Talk to the general manager of your local minor league baseball club, and try to get a part-time job with the team during the summer. When you are in college, try to get an internship within the athletic department to supplement your course of study. Any way you can gain experience in any area of sports administration will be valuable to you in your career as a sports executive. You may also find it helpful to read publications such as *Sports Business Journal* (http://www.sportsbusinessjournal.com).

EMPLOYERS

Employers include professional, collegiate, and minor league football, hockey, baseball, basketball, soccer, and other sports teams. They are located across the United States and the world. About 11 percent of all athletes, coaches, and sports officials and related workers are employed in the commercial sports industry.

Learn from Students

Be sure to check out the MBA Journals page on the *Business Week* website (http://www.businessweek.com/bschools/mbajournal/index.htm). Here you can read first-hand accounts of students' experiences in business school. You can also choose the journal from the student names and schools attended and learn why they choose to attend, how their admissions process went, and their current progress in the program. The section includes journals from both part-time and full-time students and stories from alumni.

STARTING OUT

A majority of all sports executives begin their careers as interns. Interning offers the opportunity to gain recognition in an otherwise extremely competitive industry. Internships vary in length and generally include college credits. They are available in hundreds of sports categories and are offered by more than 90 percent of existing sports organizations. If you are serious about working in the sports industry, an internship is the most effective method of achieving your goals.

Entry-level positions in the sports industry are generally reserved for individuals with intern or volunteer experience. One you have obtained this experience, you are eligible for thousands of entry-level positions in hundreds of fields. Qualified employees are hard to find in any industry, so the experience you have gained through internships will prove invaluable at this stage of your career.

ADVANCEMENT

The experience prerequisite to qualify for a management-level position is generally three to five years in a specific field within the sports industry. At this level, an applicant should have experience managing a small- to medium-sized staff and possess specific skills, including marketing, public relations, broadcasting, sales, advertising, publications, sports medicine, licensing, and specific sport player development.

The minimum experience to qualify for an executive position is generally seven years. Executives with proven track records in the minors can be promoted to positions in the majors. Major league executives might receive promotions in the form of job offers from more prestigious teams.

EARNINGS

General managers, team presidents, and other sports executives earn salaries that range from $20,000 to $50,000 per year in the minor leagues to more than $1 million in the majors. Most sports executives are eligible for typical fringe benefits, including medical and dental insurance, paid sick and vacation time, and access to retirement savings plans.

WORK ENVIRONMENT

Sports team management is a fickle industry. When a team is winning, everyone loves the general manager or team president. When the team is losing, fans and the media often take out their frustrations on the team's executives. Sports executives must be able to handle that pressure. This industry is extremely competitive, and executives might find themselves without a job several times in their careers. Sports executives sleep, eat, and breathe their jobs, and definitely love the sports they manage.

OUTLOOK

The U.S. Department of Labor predicts that employment in amusement and recreation services (a category that includes sports-related careers) will grow by about 35 percent through 2010.

Although there are more sports executive positions available due to league expansion and the creation of new leagues, such as the Women's National Basketball Association, there still remain only a finite number of positions, and the competition for these jobs is very fierce.

FOR MORE INFORMATION

For information on educational programs, contact:

Sports Administration Specialization Coordinator
The University of North Carolina
Department of Exercise and Sport Science
209 Fetzer Gymnasium, CB#8700
Chapel Hill, NC 27599-8700
Tel: 919-962-0017
http://www.unc.edu/depts/exercise

To learn more about sports executives, contact:
   Teamwork Online LLC
   3645 Warrensville Center Road, Suite 246
   Shaker Heights, OH 44122
   Tel: 216-767-1790
   Email: info@teamworkonline.com
   http://www.teamworkonline.com

accounts payable: amounts owed by a company that must be paid off.

accounts receivable: amounts due to a company for products or services bought on credit by customers.

antitrust laws: policies that encourage industry competition by eliminating monopolistic or unfair business practices.

appreciation: an increase in the value of property.

asset: cash and products or services that can be turned into cash. *Fixed assets*, such as land and equipment, are items that cannot be turned into cash without disturbing the operation of a business.

bankruptcy: when an individual or business chooses or is forced by the court to turn all assets into cash to pay money that is owed to other individuals or business.

bear market: a period of slow economic growth when the majority of stocks lose value.

blue chip stock: a stock that has a known record of being profitable.

bull market: a period of economic growth when the majority of stocks gain value.

capital: money, property, or equipment used in a business. A *capital gain* occurs when an asset is sold for an amount higher than the amount at which it was purchased. A *capital loss* occurs when an asset is sold for less than the price at which it was bought.

commodities: products of mining or agriculture that are traded on the open market.

conglomerate: a company that operates many different types of business, usually by buying smaller companies in different industries.

deflation: an overall decrease in prices caused by lower rates of consumer and business spending.

depreciation: a decrease in the value of property.

durable goods: products, such as appliances, that are generally used for a long period of time.

equity: value of property minus its original cost. *Stockholder's equity* is the value of an individual's stocks. *Homeowners' equity* is the value of a house minus any amount still owed (unpaid mortgage).

fiscal year: a 12-month period that a business considers its year in book-keeping. It does not have to start January 1st.

futures: agreements to pay a set price for particular goods (usually commodities) delivered on a set date.

gross profit: amount of money earned from a product or service sold, minus all expenses incurred behind it (such as costs of labor, storing, and equipment maintenance).

hedging: protects a dealer from falling prices between the time he or she buys a good and the time he or she processes and resells it.

inflation: an overall increase in prices. *Cost-push inflation* is caused by higher costs of production. *Demand-pull inflation* is caused by a lack of goods available for purchase.

liabilities: money and other claims owed by a corporation; includes accounts payable, wages, bank loans, taxes payable, and more.

liquidation: turning assets into cash.

maturity: date on which a bond or other bank note expires and is paid out to the owner.

NASDAQ: acronym for the National Association of Securities Dealers Automated Quotations system, a computerized trading network.

net profit: amount of money earned by a company after taxes have been taken out.

protective tariff: a tax on foreign products and services that encourages people to buy from domestic manufacturers.

recession: a slow period of economic growth that is either temporary or could proceed into a longer period of economic depression.

revenue: amount of money earned by a company. Includes sales amounts, interest earned, royalties, and services provided.

sales: all money received for the goods or services provided by a company.

stock dividend: money paid out to common stockholders that reflects earnings from shares.

trademark: used by a manufacturer to label its product, such as the registered trademark, Kleenex® tissues. These names are protected by law against infringement by competitors.

Wall Street: refers to a financial district in New York City.

The following books provide additional information on business careers, college admissions, M.B.A. programs, resumes, and job interviews.

Alsop, Ron. *The Wall Street Journal Guide to the Top Business Schools.* New York: Fireside, 2002.

Field, Shelly. *Career Opportunities in Advertising and Public Relations.* New York: Facts On File, 2002.

Fitch, Thomas. *Career Opportunities in Banking, Finance, and Insurance.* New York: Facts On File, 2002.

Fry, Ronald. *101 Great Answers to the Toughest Interview Questions.* Franklin Lakes, N.J.: Career Press, 2000.

Guide to College Majors: Everything You Need to Know to Choose the Right Major. New York: Princeton Review, 2002.

Halloran, Edward Joseph. *Careers in International Business.* 2nd ed. New York: McGraw Hill/Contemporary Books, 2003.

Johnston, Susan M. *The Career Adventure: Your Guide to Personal Assessment, Career Exploration, and Decision Making.* 3rd ed. Upper Saddle Rive, N.J.: Prentice Hall, 2001.

Liu, Ying, ed. *The Harvard Business School Guide to Careers in Finance.* Cambridge, Mass.: Harvard Business School Press, 2002.

Marino, Kim. *Best Resumes for Accountants and Financial Professionals.* Hoboken, N.J.: Wiley, 1994.

Rubinstein, Ellen. *Scoring a Great Internship (Students Helping Students).* New York: Natavi Guides, 2002.

Symonds, Matt, and Alan Mendonca. *ABC of Getting the MBA Admissions Edge.* The MBA Site Ltd., 2001.

Tullier, L. Michelle. *Networking for Everyone.* Indianapolis, Ind.: Jist Works, 1998.

Wendleton, Kate, and Wendy Alfus Rothman. *Targeting the Job You Want.* 3rd ed. Franklin Lakes, N.J.: Career Press, 2000.